2985

Critical Theory
and
Frankfurt Theorists

CRITICAL THEORY
and
FRANKFURT THEORISTS

Lectures—Correspondence—Conversations

Communication in Society, Volume 4

Leo Lowenthal

Transaction Publishers
New Brunswick (U.S.A.) and Oxford (U.K.)

Copyright © 1989 by Transaction Publishers
New Brunswick, New Jersey 08903

Library of Congress Catalog Number: 88-18865
ISBN: 0-88738-224-X
Printed in the United States of America

Library of Congress Cataloging in Publication Data

Lowenthal, Leo.
    [Selections. English. 1988]
    Critical theory and frankfurt theorists : lectures,
correspondence, conversations / Leo Lowenthal.
        p.   cm. — (Communication in society ; v. 4)
    ISBN 0-88738-224-X
    1. Jews—Germany—Intellectual life. 2. Germany—
Intellectual life.   3. Germany—Civilization—Jewish
influences. 4. Germany—Ethnic relations. I. Title.
    II. Series: Lowenthal, Leo.
    Communication in society ; v. 4.
DS135.G33L632513 1988
943′.004924—dc 19   88-18865
                                                CIP

Contents

Acknowledgments

Donald Reneau translated from German into English, especially for this volume, Part I, Part III, and in Part IV the conversation with Mathias Greffrath. Ted R. Weeks translated "Sociology of Literature in Retrospect," (originally published in *Critical Inquiry*, vol. 14, No. 1, Autumn 1987), Sabine Wilke, "Recollections of Theodor W. Adorno," David J. Ward, "Walter Benjamin," Steven Stoltenberg, "Goethe and False Subjectivity," Carol Hamilton, "Caliban's Legacy," (originally published in *Cultural Critique*, No. 8, Winter 1987/8), and David J. Parent, "Scholarly Biography."

Again, I acknowledge with profound gratitude the overall editorial supervision of the American edition by Susanne Hoppmann Lowenthal. The corresponding German language edition was expertly edited by Helmut Dubiel whose afterword appears at the end of this volume.

PART I

German Jewish Intellectual Culture:
Essays from the 1920s

Introduction

The following essays introduce a number of Jewish figures of the last 150 years who have been chosen because their respective contributions correspond decisively with the main events of German intellectual history. Such an undertaking might at first seem questionable. It could arouse the suspicion that it is meant to assert, as apologia, that the Jews "have always been there too." It is easy to see that an apology is not out of the question. But the point of view from which this contribution to the history of Jewish biography is to be pursued is a social scientific one: the rise of bourgeois society, and the appearance of the contradictions for which bourgeois society is responsible, are reflected in the biographies of the leading Jewish personalities of our epoch. It is precisely there, where life circumstances are altogether and repeatedly stripped of illusion, where conditions are unsatisfying and subject to sudden transformation, that the bourgeois revolution, the class struggle of the proletariat, and the disillusioning force of modern scientific secularization find receptive carriers in exceptional degree.

Such a treatment of Jewish figures, as both creators and creatures of bourgeois society, necessarily proceeds somewhat generally. It is of no fundamental significance whether or not these persons were members of their religious communities or congregations. Nor is it decisive whether or not the topics to which these Jews devoted themselves were substantively Jewish. The great Jewish names of our epoch—Maimon and Heine, Börne and Moses Hess, Marx and Lassalle, Einstein and Freud, Landauer and Trotsky—are essentially not associated with specifically Jewish topics. It is for this reason that questions of biography take over the place of the evolution of questions within Judaism, so that this very substitution becomes one of the important problems of Jewish history.

In the first half of the period selected for treatment here, the problem of emancipation—that is, of integration into a bourgeois society itself in the process of early consolidation—stands in the forefront. For the trajectory of personal emancipation, whether a specific figure is of eastern or western Jewish heritage is, in every case, an essential distinguishing characteristic. The Jew who immigrated to Germany in the first half of the nineteenth century moved suddenly from one historical period into another; such was

3

the experience of Maimon and, in a certain sense, Lassalle. The Rheinlanders Heine and Marx, on the other hand, were born into the new world. In terms of character, the eastern Jew faced an endlessly more difficult task than the western Jew. The story of his personal life is, therefore, of far greater import than that of the westerner, in regard to whom the evolution of intellectual concerns becomes more interesting. Thus, it might be said that the lives of Heine and Marx can be elucidated through their work, and the work of Maimon and Lassalle through their lives.

1

Moses Mendelssohn

Moses Mendelssohn has yet to receive an exhaustive treatment, a fate he shares with the entire epoch to which he belongs. That the scholarly treatment of the modern bourgeoisie still has not made use of the most important sources of its social constitution is a special problem and one, to be sure, which explains why Mendelssohn above all has not yet found his biographer. In and of itself, the Enlightenment is neither geographically nor temporally accessible as a unified movement. Its single universal characteristic is that it is everywhere the reflection of the rise of the bourgeois class. It is a rise which already bears mature fruit in England as it is being achieved in bloody turmoil in France and is transforming itself in Germany into an almost century-long defeat.

Far beyond any specifically Jewish interest, Moses Mendelssohn deserves intellectual historical attention because all of the specifically German tendencies of the Enlightenment can be found in his work. But it is precisely for this reason that it is so difficult to treat him. The complex of concerns reflected in his work yields no unified, uncontradictory picture. To the polarities between which Mendelssohn moved in his life as a Jew (son of a Torah scribe, father of baptized children) correspond intellectual historical oppositions. In one significant philosophical point he falls back behind Immanuel Kant (who wished to have him as a disciple); he encourages Gottfried Ephraim Lessing in his aesthetic theories, while simultaneously misunderstanding their ultimate philosophical consequences; and with F. G. Jacobi, he carries on a polemic, presumably in defense of his friend, Lessing, that draws him once again nearer to Kant, from whom he has just expressly distanced himself.

In the customary historical treatments, Mendelssohn is depicted as a member of the Leibniz–Wolff school. Karl Lamprecht alone has drawn attention to Mendelssohn's significance in having achieved a new and particular stage in the philosophy of the German Enlightenment. He points correctly to a statement in which Mendelssohn attacks the thoughtlessness with which, "in all polite society," the "most profound truths" of Wolff's philosophy become "vogue expressions." "The truth itself became prejudice, through the fashion in which it was accepted." In fact, Mendelssohn was very much an adherent of Wolffian scholasticism. But if it supplied the music for the political and scientific institutions of the tone-setting court, newly ennobled and early *hautebourgeois* circles in the epoch of absolutism, then Mendelssohn and others appropriate its central themes for the broader bourgeois strata of the eighteenth century. Mendelssohn took over those tendencies in the philosophical movement of the sixteenth and seventeenth centuries that revolutionized science, to fashion, in the phrase he himself contributed to the literature, a philosophy of "healthy human understanding." It now has no more explicit task to perform than to satisfy the people's need for happiness. Here the character of the German Enlightenment, in contrast to the French, becomes clear to us for the first time. The goal of western philosophy was to dethrone all ruling powers, both theoretical and practical, that could be dethroned through the instruments of reason and experience. The agreeable mood in Mendelssohn's thought is merely a sign of the disagreeable narrowness of the German bourgeoisie, which was not in a position to accomplish any world-historical tasks.

Schopenhauer called Mendelssohn one of the "last sleepers" in philosophy before Kant. It seems necessary to interpret this statement from two sides to establish Mendelssohn's position in the intellectual history of the eighteenth and nineteenth centuries. First of all, we ask what the expression means in the context in which it appears. For Schopenhauer the phenomenal world, that is, the world perceptible to our senses, is merely appearance, a dream, a product of the imagination; nor are concepts which seek to comprehend this world of phenomena anything more than empty vapors, "phantasmagorias." True being is not to be comprehended by way of the understanding and its tools. Comprehension necessitates a special method of introspection. Here arises the opposition to Wolff's philosophy, and particularly to Mendelssohn's. Both are "rational metaphysicians" in that (a cardinal sin for Schopenhauer!) they teach not only that the highest truths are recognizable to the tools of understanding, but also that rational cognition takes no note of whether understanding's tools thereby apprehend the objects of our perceptions or whether they are at work in the realm to which such ideas as God and immortality belong. In opposition to Schopenhauer and, incidentally, in opposition to very influential currents in the most modern philosophy, there exists for Mendelssohn no boundary between the highest world of being and the simplest objects in our surroundings. According to his conception of immortality, for example, the soul simply continues to exist as it did before, beyond the decay of the body. The span of earthly life is merely a bounded piece of eternity for Mendelssohn, while for Kant this life and eternity stand utterly opposed. Kant, contrary to the speculations of Mendelssohn and others like him, seeks to apply all concepts of the understanding only to the world of mere appearance; in so doing, he destroys the possibility of a rational metaphysics which would be mediated through the understanding.

Schopenhauer's view of the relation of Mendelssohn to Kant tellingly locates Mendelssohn within an irrational philosophy, but it is one-sided and must be supplemented. It never even occurred to Kant to regard the rational methods for knowing the absolute as inaccessible in principle. On the contrary, he believed in the possibility of a rational metaphysics and, in a letter of January 1763 to Mendelssohn himself, urgently drew attention to its importance for the "true and lasting good of the human race." What in reality differentiates him from Wolff, and thereby from Mendelssohn, is the radical distinction between perception and understanding. For Mendelssohn this distinction does not exist in principle. Whatever sensuous perception, sentiment, or memory determines is proved for him once again by the understanding in its own specific way; the propositions found in experience become definitively correct only once the understanding has proven them to be logically necessary. Thus Mendelssohn lowers experience to the level of a source of knowledge, while he expands the competency of simple understanding to such an extent that the logically necessary also becomes the truly existing. Mendelssohn's concept of God emerges in this context: because it is possible to think the most complete being, it must also exist. It is significant of Mendelssohn's transitional position in intellectual history that, for the proof of the existence of God, he admits this old scholastic method of arguing from mere concepts to the existence of facts, while he maintains explicitly that such proof in the exact sciences, for example in mathematics, is completely impossible.

The correspondence of Kant and Mendelssohn is not without its tragic features. Again and again, with the warmest of words, Kant attempted to win Mendelssohn over to his philosophy. Indeed Kant saw in him a genius who could lead thinking out of the path of an obsolete metaphysics and into the light of critical science. But according to Mendelssohn's own confession (which is to be found, in addition to his correspondence, in the Foreword to "Morgenstunden") he not only had not read Kant's main work, but felt himself to be wholly of the spirit of the middle of the century in opposition to its last quarter. And in reality, as metaphysician and epistemologist, Mendelssohn does remain a thorough-going member of the mercantilist, prerevolutionary epoch. The Berlin Academy of Sciences, in giving precedence to a prize essay by Mendelssohn over one by Kant, might have erred as a forum of systematic philosophy, but in historical terms its judgment was wholly legitimate. Mendelssohn's essay affirms that one can enjoy the same confidence in matters of spiritual knowledge as in those of science based in experience. For one for whom such is the case, the world is completely in order just as it is in the moment. The world is excellent and just, and everything, including God and philosophy, have the single meaning of increasing human happiness. These views corresponded fully to the situation of the possessors of absolute power, even if Mendelssohn did not hold them for the sake of the powerful. In opposition to these views stands Kant's philosophy: the world is in no way finished, in no way in order; it is an eternal problem to be solved by means of scientific experience.

But thus far only one side of Mendelssohn's intellectual historical position has been treated. Insofar as Mendelssohn, a member of a class destined for emancipation, accepts a philosophy hostile to it, he is a reflex of the lack of independence of his social stratum. But he also represents its progressive tendencies. They are probably most apparent in his philosophical relation to Lessing; for the theory of art (and it is naturally no accident that it was precisely the theory of art) is the essential contribution by which the thought of the German Enlightenment of the mid-eighteenth century was further developed. To Mendelssohn is due the honor of a decisive share in the discovery that art is served by a particular type of human consciousness. Alongside the conventional division of consciousness into thinking and willing, there appears for Mendelssohn as a third capacity of mind the capacity of "approval" or of liking out of which, for him and his like-minded friends, develops "feeling." One sees in Mendelssohn how closely aesthetics and psychology are connected—and with intellectual historical justice!—for in Germany, the bourgeoisie first expressed its newly liberated life of feeling almost exclusively in art. Eighteenth-century German art, together with the theory of art in Lessing, Mendelssohn and their spiritual kin, is the *grande révolution* of the German bourgeoisie. In this revolution, Mendelssohn participates decisively indeed. The feeling for "beauty" and the "sublime," for the "pleasurable" and "unpleasurable" now receives altogether its due in general consciousness. It is no longer merely the prerogative of the ruling circles. Lessing continued to polemicize: "Art follows bread." But, with a clear affinity to Schiller, Mendelssohn already demanded that art clothe the lessons of truth in the garments of beauty, in order to maximize their effectiveness. Kant was now able to draw the philosophical parallels and Mendelssohn's initiatives found fertile soil in the progressive philosophy of art and feeling contained in Kant's *Critique of Judgment*.

Mendelssohn's two-sidedness gained dramatic expression toward the end of his life in his famous conflict with Jacobi about whether Lessing had been a Spinozan. In answering the question affirmatively, Jacobi rejected Lessing; Mendelssohn vindicated him with his negative reply. The question belongs to that category of intellectual historical issues that must be interpreted according to their broader meanings and for which it is difficult to render a final, objective judgment. Jacobi saw in the philosophy of Spinoza an atheistic system in which knowledge is gained solely through rational means. In accepting this system Lessing, according to Jacobi, sacrificed completely the most valuable side of life—that side namely that derives without mediation from suprarational sources of belief. In attacking Lessing, Jacobi launched the first great attack on the part of romanticism, the intellectual counterrevolution, against the bourgeoisie's attempt at political and social conquest. The bourgeoisie's most important weapon is science, and that is precisely what Jacobi sought to discredit. Mendelssohn addressed his famous verdict on Jacobi to Kant:

> For his part, he ultimately takes refuge behind the canon of belief and finds salvation and security in the bastion of the beatific Lavater, out of whose 'angelically pure' mouth he cites consoling words at the end of his text. But they afford me no consolation, because I do not understand them. This text by Mr. Jacobi is altogether a rare mixture: the head of Goethe, the body of Spinoza and the feet of Lavater.

The intellectual historical irony here consists in the following: one's literary sympathies belong to Mendelssohn, who fought more elegantly, while it cannot be denied that it was Jacobi who in fact hit upon Lessing's intentions in accusing him of the rationalistic spirit (of science). Moreover Mendelssohn in his defense of Lessing, and Jacobi in his attack, aspired to something fundamentally similar. Both wanted to save the existence of the spiritual as something provable. Mendelssohn made his attempt as yet with the tools of rational scholasticism; Jacobi already enlisted the irrational emotional forces of romantic thought.

In conclusion, a turn to the personal. In studying Mendelssohn, I am occasionally inclined to think of Goethe's remark on Hamlet: "A great deed laid upon a soul that was not equal to it." Mendelssohn is one of the most charming figures in German intellectual history; elegant in polemics, suggestive in presentation, penetrating and yielding at once in oral and written exchanges of opinion, accessible to even alien suggestions and prepared to accept them. But only a genius of unheard of capacity would have been truly able to recognize, to unite and, in a technically satisfying presentation, to clarify the intersecting and contradictory tendencies which came together in Mendelssohn's work. Thus does his philosophizing frequently fail to surpass evasion. He spoke excitedly, for example, of French philosophy, but meant only Rousseau, not exactly a sufficient representative. He commented wittily on the superiority of English thought over French, and meant at bottom merely the blissful emotionalism of a Shaftesbury. He seized upon the title of a Platonic text, whose spirit is that of the victorious consciousness of a gloriously dominant class, but conveyed with it, in essence, the mere appearance of immortality to a bourgeoisie eager to assume it that itself shares very insufficiently in the fruits of the good life. But perhaps we commit an historical injustice in calling to mind a genuis who could never have existed. Perhaps Mendelssohn was as he was because "Young Germany's" phrase, "Germany is Hamlet," applied already to his time.

2

Salomon Maimon

Maimon's most relevant book today is his *Autobiography* (edited by Jakob Fromer, Georg Müller Press, Münich). It was originally edited by Karl Philipp Moritz, the well-known writer of the German Enlightenment, whose Bildungsroman, *Anton Reiser,* represents the rationalistic counterpart to *Wilhelm Meister.* And, in fact, the motive which led Moritz to edit Maimon's autobiography is not in the slightest aesthetic, but bourgeois revolutionary in the true sense of the Enlightenment. Moritz believed Maimon's life to be an example of the power of human knowledge and will—victorious even within oppressive social relations:

> What gives this book particular worth in yet another respect is its nonpartisan and unprejudiced presentation of Judaism, of which one can justifiably maintain that it is the first of its type. It is, then, especially at present, when the formation and enlightenment of the Jewish nation has become an object of reflection in its own right, that it deserves attention of the first order.

In reality, Maimon's autobiography is the documentary result of an eastern Jew's attempt to penetrate the rational cultural world of the German bourgeoisie just before 1800. It is not, after the model of Augustine or Rousseau, a confession which strives to bring to light the hidden and secret, that which has till now been kept from the world and from the self. Much more, it manifests once again a life that is already manifest to all: the life of a person uprooted, cast to and fro and tragicomic, insecurely alternating between seriousness and ridicule of others and himself, the whole performed with the grimace of an astonished clown. Maimon's life takes one of the forms characteristic of the attempt by eastern Jews to break through to Western Europe (a process, by the way, that in the 1920s has not yet reached its end). One path to the West was the more or less forceable demand for social equality, of which Lassalle was an example.

Another drew on the powerful craving for conquest on the part of the cultural heritage of idolized Western Europe; so it was in the case of Salomon Maimon.

Maimon broke free to Europe, because he simply could no longer stand his life at home. His father was a Jewish barkeeper, forced into the misfortune of his calling by the miserable Polish legislation on Jews. Maimon's childhood memories tremble with the derision of Jewish family life everywhere apparent in his Christian environment. In this hell of inferiority and rejection there arose in him, as a decisive formative experience, a Jewish spiritual pride, which gilded in a thousand ways the suffering of the present with the special position of the Jew in his world of the future. This messianism at first seemed purely cabalistic and haggadistic, but it possessed at the same time an unfathomable disdain for the schematic pedagogical structure and narrow-minded logic of life in the Heder. At that point, through the despotic banishment of his parents from their residence, he was graced with a true teacher who awakened in him a love for the systematic logic of the Talmud. Fantastically gifted was this youngster who, at eleven years of age, could already have become a rabbi. But instead, a mark of distinction for his knowledge, he was married. The marriage threw the erotic aspects of his character development irretrievably into disarray, and to the end of his life his sexual experiences were exclusively helpless and comical. With the deepening of his knowledge came an interest in the German alphabet and the German book, and specifically in medical texts, which he studied thoroughly, afterwards regarding himself as a trained physician and providing his neighbors, near and far, with housecalls and prescriptions:

> Since my general circumstances became worse and worse—because I no longer wanted to devote myself to my usual activities and therefore found myself everywhere out of my element—and since, on the other hand, I could not satisfy my pet inclinations for studying science in my home, I decided to take myself off to Germany to study medicine and, in this connection, the other sciences as well.

At 25 years of age he arrived in Königsberg. The newly emancipated Jewish students, who wanted nothing whatever to do with rough and unkempt, slang-speaking eastern Jewish emigres, made his life miserable. Sent to Berlin, he was taken for a free thinker by the Jewish orthodox and expelled once again. He begged his way to Posen, where a leading Rabbi took an interest in him and arranged for him to work as a private tutor. But after only three years—by deriding a superstition popular in the Jewish community in Posen—he again made himself unwelcome. He arrived once again in Berlin, but this time he quickly found respectful acceptance in the circle around Moses Mendelssohn. He attempted to establish himself by learning the pharmacist's trade, but very soon suffered yet another calamity, applying to his trade far too little of his practical capacity, and to the extravagant pleasures of the metropolis Berlin, far too much.

Maimon then emigrated to Amsterdam. After initial successes, he again made himself unpopular among the orthodox and was driven into the street with stones. Following that incident, he made his ridiculous attempt at suicide. Bending his upper body over the water, death already mirrored there before him, he could not manage to cause his legs to follow—a fitting expression of the wretched situation of Salomon Maimon, the enlightened eastern Jew who wanted to live among the unenlightened Jews of the West in the region of the bourgeois German Enlightenment. Thus is it understandable, since he believed in nothing anymore, that in Hamburg he was even ready to have himself baptized. But because he believed in nothing, the church rejected him as well. Once again he was underway—from Berlin to Breslau. His wife, accompanied by a twenty-year-old son, found him there and demanded a divorce which she was granted according to a paragraph from the Schulchan Aruch:

A vagabond who abandons his wife for many years, does not write her and sends her no money, is to be forced to divorce her legally once he is found.

The "vagabond" once more made his way to Berlin. He wrote a treatise on Kant's *Critique of Pure Reason,* which reached Kant by way of his Jewish friend, Markus Herz. Kant answered enthusiastically, granting that no one among his enemies had yet understood him and his central problems in so distinguished a fashion, and he spoke of Maimon in the words of the highest respect. With that, Maimon's circumstantial fate took a turn for the better. His book on Kant was printed, periodicals accepted his essays, and, seizing the opportunity, Maimon wrote his autobiography. In one blow, he became known to all of intellectual Germany, all the way up to Goethe and Schiller. To be sure, he did not manage to maintain himself in this favorable position for long. As earlier among the Jewish orthodox, he made himself unpopular in bourgeois Christian circles by his rude and unrefined behavior. The Christians were willing to put up with the Jewish literati only given the polish, charm, and conciliatory ease of a Moses Mendelssohn. Finally, toward the end of his life, he once more found peace through the offices of Count Kalckreuth, who allowed him to live on his estates. More indulgent and lacking in the snobbery of the Berlin bourgeoisie, the aristocrat tolerated the bad manners of the great writer and thinker. When, in 1800, Maimon died, he was buried as a heretic.

It is not possible in brief to characterize Maimon's philosophical views comprehensively, but reference can be made to one point. The boundary of scientific investigation was set epistemologically by Kant with his unknowable thing-in-itself. Maimon's tendency was to attribute substance to that which, in purely formal terms, is unknowable, or to do away with the unknowable in order to allow metaphysical content to assume the place of merely logical construction. Thus he anticipated a post-Kantian philosophical stage by allowing for the possibility of overcoming the limitations of a theory of knowledge with substantive metaphysics.

3

Heinrich Heine

Why did Heine become a Christian?

We can exclude the otherwise common reasons to be baptized. Heine hoped for no financial advantage from this step. In constant conflict with his relatives and his publishers and forced to struggle with economic necessity until the end, Heine early on saw through the power of money and despised it. As a young man he wrote:

> But—to speak once again in the key of Frankfurt—are the Rothschilds and the Bethmanns not long since *al pari?* The businessman the world over has the same religion. The counting house is his church; his desk his prayer bench; his memoranda book his Bible; his warehouse his Holy of Holies; the bourse clock is his angelus; his money his God; and credit his faith.

And a few years later:

> . . . however, I would consider it beneath my dignity and a stain on my honor, if, to gain a post in Prussia, I were to have myself baptized.

But nor was it conviction that made it possible for Heine to become a Christian. The mere idea of such disgusted him:

> I don't know what I should say. Cohn assures me that Gaus preaches Christianity and seeks to convert the children of Israel. If he does so from conviction, he's a fool; if as a sham, then he's a scoundrel.

And once again, also to his friend Moser:

> I am now becoming a proper Christian; I sponge, namely, off the rich Jews.

15

But neither was it hatred of Judaism, toward which baptism would then be something like a frivolous affront. Immediately after his baptism he spoke with friends about his "Rabbi von Bacharach" and claimed, with light ridicule, that he would be "entirely misunderstood in the Christian world."

Once again, we may ask what made a renegade of this Jew who was driven to baptism neither by egotism nor by any presumable acknowledgment of the faith, who indeed immediately after the baptism wrote sadly to his friend:

> I am now hated by Christian and Jew. I regret very much that I've had myself baptized. I don't agree at all that things have gone better for me since; on the contrary, since then I've had nothing but misfortune.

Heine gives us the complete answer himself as he states, "The baptismal certificate is the ticket of admission to European culture."

We will return to that thought in just a moment, but what immediately becomes clear is what Christianity means to Heine. Christianity is nothing more than an empty platform, an accidental historical given, on the way to something entirely different. Christianity is nothing but the consecrated outer vestment of a modern European culture otherwise completely foreign to it. The dogma, the core of Christianity, is for Heine nothing—a mere historical fact that he glosses with ridicule and nearly with disdain one has only to recall the famous, pitiless lines from "Disputation." Heine submitted to Christianity in order to be able to destroy it in a messianic rage, which he had already anticipated at the moment of his conversion. Just before his baptism, he wrote:

> This collapse of Christianity—at last—is everyday more manifest to me. Long enough has this foul idea maintained itself. I call Christianity an idea—but what an idea! There are dirty families of ideas that take up lodgings in the chinks in this old world—the forsaken bedstead of the divine spirit—like families of bugs take up lodgings in the bedstead of a Polish Jew. If one tramples upon one of these idea-bugs, it leaves behind a stench than can be smelled for millennia. One such is Christianity, already trampled eighteen-hundred years ago, which, ever since, has been poisoning the air for us poor Jews.

This much the angry words certainly demonstrate: that it was not Christianity which Heine sought to acquire through the baptism. But what does "European culture" mean to Heine? To Heine European culture means the Europe of the French Revolution; it means the possibility of a joyful, free and full life. Heine sought in European culture the desire for concrete, this-wordly, earth-bound life. That this signified the greatest possible remove from the meaning of life-denying Christianity, is, indeed, completely self-evident. But it is a horrible historical irony that this specifically Jewish side of Heine, this love for a worthy life of free persons, is what drove him out of Judaism.

This love of life was enormously pronounced in Heine. We sense it over and over in his poems, in serious, but mainly in ironic turns of phrase. It is also characteristic of Heine that among his works is found a whole volume of travel descriptions, just the kind of literary document that occupies so much space among the works of the lifeloving Goethe.

Why Heine did not find in Judaism the possibility of a genuine life must yet be discussed. Why he believed it possible to find his life via the detour of baptism and European culture is a question to which the history of the Jewish spirit frequently gives a direct answer. It is the desire to rip asunder all historical, confessional, national, cultural ties, to cancel the "sociological conditions of our existence," as Georg Lukács once expressed it. It was fundamentally this messianic drive that impelled Heine to baptism. The longing, raised to an intolerable pitch, for a pure, real, beautiful life— a life, in fact, of which Heine was allowed to experience only little and of which he therefore dreamt all the more longingly—made it possible for him to change religions like a suit of clothes without having to change his conviction. This drive propelled him not only from one religious shrine into another, but also from one country to another. He, whose love for Germany perhaps followed immediately on his love for Judaism, turned his back on Germany to live in France, the country which he regarded as the appointed historical pioneer of freedom for mankind. This change derived as little from his love for France as his baptism derived from his love for Christianity. Both resulted from that strong messianic impulse to relativize all borders, to let all historical substance remain historical and always to place himself where he believed truth and freedom resided.

The baptism avenged itself bitterly. In his later years his hatred of Christianity broke through once more in passionate despair, but only with equal desperation could he seek a connection to historical Judaism. Heinrich Heine's "Confessions" belong to the most moving of documents that ever issued from the mouth of a Jewish renegade:

> The reawakening of my religious feeling I owe to that holy book; the same was for me every bit as much a source of salvation as an object of devout admiration. Strange! After having prowled for the whole of my life through all the dance halls of philosophy, having yielded to all the orgies of the spirit, having made love to all possible systems, without finding satisfaction, like Messalina after a dissolute night—now I find myself suddenly sharing the standpoint of Uncle

Tom, that of the Bible, and I kneel down beside the black bigot in the same devotion . . .

Earlier, I did not love Moses especially, probably because the Hellenic spirit was predominate in me and I did not excuse the lawgiver of the Jews his hatred of everything pictorial and of sculpture. I did not see that Moses, despite his emnity toward art, was himself an artist and possessed the true artistic spirit. Only in his case, as in the case of his fellow Egyptians, this artistic spirit was oriented solely toward the colossal and the imperishable. But, unlike the Egyptians, he did not form his art works out of brick and granite, but built pyramids of human beings and chisled human obelisks. He took a poor tribe of shepards and created of it a people that was to brave the centuries, a great, eternal, holy people, a people of God that could serve for all other peoples as a model, indeed, as a prototype for all humanity: he created Israel! . . .

As about the master of the work, so I've always spoken of the work, the Jews, with insufficient awe—all this due, no doubt, once again to my Hellenic nature, to which Jewish asceticism was always repugnant. My preference for Hellas has meanwhile diminished. I see now that the Greeks were only beautiful adolescents, while the Jews were always men, powerful, unbending men, and not just then, but up until the present day, despite eighteen centuries of persecution and misery. I have since learned better to honor them. And were not all pride of birth a foolish contradiction among the camps of the revolution and its democratic principles, then the writer of these pages could be proud that his ancestors belonged to the noble house of Israel, that he is a descendant of those martyrs who gave the world a God and morals and who struggled and suffered on all the battlefields of thought.

This, then, is the story of Heinrich Heine the *Christian,* which is, indeed, in reality the story of a *Jew.* And, thus, might we once again and legitimately raise the question of the Jewish Heinrich Heine.

The Judaism into which Heine was born and with which he had to come to terms as a maturing man was the Judaism of the German reform. This was, to be sure, no longer the reform, creative in its way, of the generation of Moses Mendelssohn, but already in part the reform of the Sunday Jews. Heine hated these abuses growing out of the reform movement and he condemned them in the sharpest of terms. He found in them nothing other than a veiled, unacknowledged or unexpressed inclination toward the Christian. How he was able to ridicule that!

Others want an evangelical Christianity in a Jewish style and make themselves a talles [prayer shawl] from the wool of the Lamb of God, make themselves a jacket from the feathers of the holy dove of the spirit and underclothes from Christian love; and they go bankrupt. And the progency calls itself "God, Christ & Co."

The path of radical reform was not the path of Heine the Jew. Certainly, he admired Moses Mendelssohn, but he also misunderstood him in part.

In Mendelssohn he found a responsible, unsentimental and strong love for Judaism, which he frankly did not expect of David Friedländer and Eduard Gans. Heine's misunderstanding of Moses Mendelssohn is yet further proof of Heine's deep Jewish instinct. He was of the opinion that Moses Mendelssohn had done away, at least in Germany, with the Talmud—"that Jewish Catholicism." It is known that Mendelssohn did not want to do so, even if he perhaps helped to bring it about. In this connection, Heine thought that Mendelssohn wished to maintain the Jewish ceremonial laws for reasons of rational insight, rather than sentimentality. "As the kings of the material world, so must the kings of the spirit relentlessly oppose familial sentiment; nor on thought's throne may one submit to easy geniality." This principle, that what matters is knowledge, the sovereignty of thought, places Heine in the line of the most representative of Jewish thinkers. Such was, after all, also Maimonides' essential motive: to cleanse Judaism of all sentimentality, superstitions, atavisms, and psychological contingencies; and to establish forever as Judaism's duty the acknowledgment of the one, unknowable God. Without in any way making the risky suggestion of a comparison, one may say that Heine's hatred of all dogma and all religious fanaticism was shared by Maimonides, and it is in this context that the following takes on its deepest meaning:

> My devotion to the essence of the Jew has it roots simply in a deep antipathy for Christianity. Indeed, I, the despiser of all positive religions, will perhaps one day go over to the crassest rabbinicalism just because I view the latter as a proven antidote.

To be sure, it never went beyond this "perhaps," but Heine does in fact fall victim to the great historical error committed by the reform in identifying historical Judaism with Catholicism as respective expressive forms of dogmatic religion. Heine always knew only of the danger of legalistic Judaism, of its cumbersomeness and stiffness, and nothing of its vitality, nothing of its capacity for lively development. He completely overlooked the historical context internal to Judaism, the lively continuity between its oral and written lessons, between the Torah and the Halacha. For him, the Talmud belonged in the same historical context as Catholicism.

> In fact, the Talmud is the Catholicism of the Jews. It is a gothic cathedral, overloaded, to be sure, with childish ornamentation, but which still astonishes us through its enormity reaching to the heavens. It is a hierarchy of religious laws, often concerning the most curious, ridiculous subtleties, which are nevertheless so ingeniously set over and under one another, which support and carry one another and work so terribly consistently together that they form a horribly defiant, colossal whole. After the decline of the Christian Catholicism, the

Talmud must decline as well. For the Talmud will have then lost its meaning; it serves, namely, only as a bulwark against Rome.

This passage essentially echoes the same historical misperception that drove Heine to baptism, namely, the idea that Judaism could be periodized and classified without qualification alongside European cultural history and that, therefore, Jewish forms were definable and variable in accordance with a European point of view.

Yet the weakest point in Heine's ideas is simultaneously the strongest; for if he held false historical *theories,* he also possessed a deeper historical *intuition.* In his theories of the history of Judaism during the European middle ages, it sometimes appeared as if Heine subscribed to the views of modern Jewish nationalism which, in a grotesque lack of understanding, frequently makes of the history of Judaism from the destruction of the second temple up to the time of Pinsker and Herzl a *quantité négligeable.* But Heine is saved from such historical absurdities by his love for Judaism. Especially in his youth, he undertook diligent and loving historical studies of the Jews in the middle ages.

Following his love for life, the second great authentic Jewish trait in Heine was his historical consciousness of a Jewish nation. He loved Judaism, everywhere, in every shape, form, and custom, indeed, in every farce that was Jewish. It was no sentimental love, but a genuine open-eyed love. Works like the *Rabbi von Bacharach* and the *Hebräischen Melodien* are undying testimonies of Heine's love for historical Judaism.

Only a representative, vital Judaism could have saved Heine from regarding *minhag* [custom] as the central aspect of Judaism. Thus in his surroundings and in his historical sources he constantly saw only the deification of the commentary or customs. And to the extent that he loved Judaism, he was forced by the principle of reason and knowledge to reject it. But this love had made him a national Jew; in *Jehuda Halevy* Heine's version of national Jewishness found its suitable expression.

How Heine's national Jewishness was expressed is once again characteristic of his Jewish intuition. He sensed the cohesion of Jewish history in all periods and customs, and in this the secret longing for the promised land. We have already seen what Europe, France, and Germany meant to Heine. He affirmed Europe. He loved the Harz mountains and Parisian society; as a good continental European, he hated the English. All of this he took utterly seriously. And yet—here he distinguishes himself in principle from the Jewish reform (and not only from that)—he did not experience life in Europe as life in his allotted homeland. He did not dream of a life in Europe in harmonious agreement with the other peoples as the Jewish ideal, but experienced life among the other peoples as *Golus.*

Jehuda Halevy, the splendid representative of occidental culture who lived in happy community among the Moorish peoples as a Jew, found no rest until he set out from the diaspora to his homeland on a journey which remains shrouded in mystery. In Heine, the European man of letters, there erupted over and over again—not in Jehuda Halevy's passionate determination to arrive at his goal, but in the melancholy brokenness of a poet—the longing for a home, the consciousness of homelessness.

Heine's love for Judaism found its most passionate expression in his relation to the Bible. Accustomed to making Jewish history of the middle ages the object of his conscious artistry, Heine increasingly withdrew as artist in those places where he spoke of the Bible. His poems demonstrate with what naivete and empathetic capacity he approached his Biblical material, but the older and more mature he grew, the more intimate and personal became his words about the Bible. His experience of the Bible is equivalent to that of the inadequacy of the artist. The longing for beautiful, genuine life that drove him to the baptismal, to France, into the arms of women, allowed him hope to find salvation and the meaning of life in artistic form. He was desperate, but also honest enough to understand that that could not succeed. As an artist he sensed that matters of artistic fact prevailed in the Bible, but he sensed as well that it was not artistic principles that had created them. The most flattering comparison that the artist Heine could bestow was the comparison of the Bible with Shakespeare, but in doing so, he did not lower the Bible into the sphere of art, but raised Shakespeare above it. Essentially Heine found in Shakespeare—in accord with the gift, not the reality—a secret alter ego. Shakespeare, the man, used artistic means beyond a mere artistic purpose to see through and disdain all dogmatism and fanaticism incorruptibly and without bias. This unconditional, comparatively speaking, messianic type held the mirror before European humanity, as Heine understood himself to do in his moments of greatest purity. His comparison of Shakespeare with the Bible, a comparison of style of the sort the artist is allowed to draw, demonstrates its confinement within a legitimate frame.

> Only in one writer do I find something that recalls the immediate style of the Bible. That is Shakespeare. In him as well the word sometimes stands out with that terrifying nakedness that startles and unnerves us.

When Heine compares Moses Mendelssohn to Luther who, like him, repudiated tradition and declared the Bible to be the source of religion, does he not become a Karaite? Does he not remind us of the sect that denied the oral tradition and recognized solely the Bible, but whose members were fundamentally the most unJewish of people? No! Ultimately the Karaites loved their Judaism as little as their spiritual grand-children, the Sunday Jews. Heine did love historical Judaism and its outward manifestations; it is simply that, as theoretician, he understood it wrongly or not at all. For the Karaites, the Bible was fundamentally an instrument of struggle against the nation of Jews that created for itself its living expression in the developing tradition. For Heine, the Bible was the quintessence of just that beloved people.

We began with Heine's position in relation to the reform and found that he too in part fell victim to that unhappy identification of Judaism with Catholicism. But what is decisive and significant for Heine is the appearance in those years of another conceptual pair which he distinguished cleanly and refined. I am speaking of reform and emancipation. In general, the reform conceived the emancipation of the Jews as liberation from unworthy living conditions and simultaneously as identification with the European ways of life. Heine took up the concept of liberation and understood it at first exactly as the reform understood it—as the liberation of the Jews from base servitude. But very quickly, this conception of Jewish, national liberation grew in him and became human liberation. If the great representatives of Judaism may be invoked once again in this connection, then one will remember the prophets, who formulated the concept of freedom as Judaism's central concept. Also recalled will be those who made of the national a social and universal human concept. As Heine writes:

> But what is this great task of our time? It is emancipation. Not merely the Irish, Greeks, Frankfurt Jews, West Indian blacks and other such oppressed peoples, but the emancipation of the entire world, especially of Europe, which has come of age and now tears itself loose from the iron reins of the privileged, of the aristocracy.

He was a critic of capitalism, but his criticism departed not from economic but from religious principles. Judaism was for him a symbol of liberation. To a symbol he was allowed to return, but not to a reality. He loved this symbol and suffered from it. For him Judaism was an illness, but it was an illness he affirmed.

The New Israelite Hospital in Hamburg

> A hospital for sick and needy Jews,
> For those poor mortals who are trebly wretched,
> With three great evil maladies afflicted:
> With poverty and pain and Jewishness.

The worst of these three evils is the last one,
The thousand-year-old family affliction,
The plague they carried from the grim Nile valley,
The old Egyptian faith so long unhealthful. . . .

Will Time, eternal goodness, some day end it,
Root out this black misfortune that the fathers
Hand down to sons? And some day will the grandsons
Be healed and whole, and rational and happy?

I do not know! . . .

(*The Complete Poems of Heinrich Heine*, translated by Hal Draper, Boston:
Suhrkamp/Insel Publishers Boston, Inc., 1982, pp. 398–99.)

Thus did the baptized defendant become the Jewish accuser.

4

Ferdinand Lassalle and Karl Marx

Marx, more than any other figure and to a very profound extent, succeeded in filtering and refining the whole genetic and psychological legacy of his Jewishness into a universalistic, theoretical worldview. Lassalle, on the other hand, succeeded least in drawing on his inherited Jewishness for the development of a transpersonal, universalistic worldview. A word of caution: There can be no question of taking a substantive stand on the life work of a Marx or a Lassalle. We are approaching our problem neither as politicians, nor economists, nor citizens or proletarians. Rather, we consider solely the relation of these Jewish figures to their Jewishness, and how their inherited Jewishness had a specific effect on their lives.

The point of departure for such a treatment must be Heinrich Heine. In countless documents from the life and literary activity of Heinrich Heine there occurs the passage of the Jewish personality into a realm of thought, an orientation toward the world that is fully universal, even if the universality bears with it the tragic aftertaste of Heine's failure to integrate Judaism in general and his own Jewishness in particular into the worldview. And if, as I will attempt to show, Heinrich Heine viewed things and formulated his reactions to them almost literally as Marx did later, then his purer and more intuitive character will offer us immediate access to Marx and Lassalle as personalities. Was it not also the case that both had personal contact with Heine? I maintain the incorruptibility of Heine's character, in spite of a widespread legend among his contemporaries, as well as literary historians of today, of a Heine who was morally unreliable in the extreme. When one takes a look at the documents responsible for this idea, one sees that in reality it often derived from resentment on the part of people to whom Heine once spoke the truth without qualification, or from whom, because he considered them unready or unworthy, he kept

24

his truths to himself. It is precisely his relations with Marx and Lassalle, in particular what Marx expressed to his friend Engels about Heine and what Heine said about Lassalle, that provide the best testimony of Heine's inner purity and incorruptibility and the best witness of his secure judgment of people, only possible, after all, given the integrity of character on the part of the judge.

If one wants to do justice to Marx and Lassalle from a Jewish point of view, then one must discuss, above all, the difference in their heritage. Marx came from a respected Rheinland family and lived in the liberated atmosphere produced in his homeland by the Napoleonic law on the Jews. Lassalle's father came from a small place in Poland; Ferdinand Lassalle was born in Breslau. Lassalle bore an enormous number of the characteristics of this heritage; his biography is simultaneously a contribution to the psychology of eastern European Judaism. Naturally, things today have essentially changed. One has to imagine conditions in Breslau and in the province of Posen as they were 100 years ago. There the Jew lived in conditions of extraordinary repression. The remnants of the ridiculous legislation on Jews hung on most tenaciously, disappearing completely only in 1848. Ferdinand Lassalle, born in 1825, knew thoroughly the feelings of the Jews just emerging from the constrictions of the ghetto. The relation of eastern European Jews, melded together into narrow bands, to their free environs or to the spirit of the world at large produced quite various types. The deepest manifestation of this relation was the mysticism of eastern Jewish Hassidism. In its ceaseless craving to rise, its ceaseless breach, or longing to breach, of established external and internal boundaries, Hassidic mysticism pushed unremittingly from within to burst the ghetto character. A second type, already then much more worldly, was represented by Salomon Maimon, whose attempt to break through occurred in the realm of the intellect and culture and whose all too rapid conquest of German science and Kantian philosophy was itself another document of the longing to escape from constriction. Ferdinand Lassalle was the classic example of the type known as *the social,* whose attempts to break through have not, even today reached an end. The life of Ferdinand Lassalle is eastern Judaism's attempt to overcome the barrier to Western European society. His formative experience, therefore, is the social subjugation of his people.

Since modern psychology has accustomed us to search for and find decisive experiences in a person's childhood and youth to explain his later life, we will have to concern ourselves especially with Lassalle's younger years. These experiences will give us the key to his life and personality. At 15 the Leipzig trade school pupil wrote the following words in his diary:

In fact, I believe I am one of the best Jews there is, disregarding the ceremonial laws. I could, like that Jew in Bulwer's *Leila,* wager my life to free the Jews from the oppression of their present conditions. I wouldn't even spare the gallows, if I could make them once again into a respected people. Oh, when I indulge my youthful dreams, so was it always my favorite idea to be on the side of the Jews, weapons in hand, restoring them to independence.

To make of the disrespected a respected people—that was Ferdinand Lassalle's most powerful Jewish experience. It is from the angle of this kind of experience that one must seek to understand his personality. What was always decisive for him was not some kind of precise theoretical conviction, some kind of thought derived from his manifold studies. It was rather always a personal, passionate experience. Expressed concretely, it was always the personal perception of disrespect and the drive to make up for and surpass it, that he felt above all as a Jew. As strange as it sounds, this experience of the disrespected people makes Ferdinand Lassalle, in a very personal if also very one-sided sense, a Jewish nationalist. For that, indeed, was essentially Herzl's experience as well, to return the disrespected people to a position of respect. But for Herzl, the sensitive, refined Vienna journalist, this experience was immediately transparent and transformed itself into a definite economic and political theory and practice. For Ferdinand Lassalle, the eastern European Jew who had been powerfully oppressed, then suddenly released to freedom, this nationalistic feeling erupted in an enormous transport of rage and violence, which sought, at any price, to avenge the disrespect of his people. Thus he writes a few months later in his diary:

> This evening the brother of the Madame Director brought me the report on the Jews in Damascus. Oh, it is terrible to read, terrible to hear, without my hair standing on end and the feeling in my heart transforming itself to rage. A people that bears this is terrible whether it avenges itself or suffers the treatment. Was there ever a revolution more just than that if the Jews of Damascus would rise up, set it afire from all directions, explode the powder keg and kill themselves along with their tormentors? Cowardly people, you deserve no better lot! The trodden worm writhes, but you just bend more deeply! You do not know the meaning of just revenge; you do not know to bury yourself with your enemies, and still tear them to pieces in the mortal struggle. You are born to slavery.

And again, three months later, this idea of the disrespected people had bored even more deeply into him, so that he could write:

> That from all corners of the world there come forth these accusations [concerned are accusations of ritual murder], shows me that the time will soon be ripe for us in fact to help ourselves through Christian blood.

This statement, to be sure, is shocking. But it is written by a 15-year-old boy who writes from within the terrible agony of a modern European. He experiences as abominable the conditions under which he, as a Jew, lives.

The story of the socialist Ferdinand Lassalle is then nothing other than the story of a Jew avenging the disrespect of his people. He becomes a socialist not out of deep economic judgment, but out of his experiences, seated in biology, as a Jew. Nor, however, can the story of the socialist Ferdinand Lassalle be separated from the story of the Ferdinand Lassalle who conducted the trial of Countess Hatzfeld and who wanted to marry the well-born Helene von Doenniges. But all of these stories—his socialism, his trials, his engagements to marry—were nothing more than his tragic attempts to transcend the disrespect of Jewishness. To be sure, he did not succeed in carrying out his struggle for respect within Judaism and with the weapons of Judaism (and this sheds equal light on the situation of contemporary Jews who pressed no satisfactory intellectual weapons into the hands of his highly able man and on the extravagent and unbridled nature of Lassalle). Rather, exactly the opposite transpired.

The experience of the terrible fate of the Jews led him, to be precise, to a terrible but also understandable rebellion against Judaism. It was not love of the Jewish people that made him able to feel disrespect for Judaism; rather, the disrespect for his person, for his individuality, made him suffer as a Jew. And so it was that the original Jewish hatred of Europe and Christianity became disdain and unkindness toward Judaism itself. He writes:

> I do not love the Jews at all; indeed, in general, I abhor them. I see in them only a very degenerate son of a great, but long since vanished past. During the centuries of slavery, the people have taken on the characteristics of the slave; for that reason I am ill-disposed toward them in the extreme. I have no tie to them whatsoever.

Without Judaism and, when necessary, against it, Ferdinand Lassalle attempted at any price and with all his might to break through into European society. His socialism, on the one hand, and his engagement, on the other, were only different expressions of his constant intention to enter into the splendor of European history, whether by destroying a bad Europe as a socialist, or by transfiguring himself through his noble marriage. The boundless ambition and the exaggerated vanity that ruled this man, "the violence of his being," as Heine once very correctly characterized it, stood thoroughly in the service of that craving for the idols of Europe. But that was not all Heinrich Heine saw. He not only saw his violence, not only his "egoism incarnate," as he once said of Lassalle in anger; he also saw the enormous tragedy laid bare in this man. In a conversation that was preserved between Heine and the then 21-year-old Lassalle, Heine predicts a great future for Lassalle in Germany:

> "What do you mean by a great future in Germany?" asks the young man. "To be shot by one of your disciples!" cried Heine. "I want to become the Mirabeau of Germany," returned Lassalle. "You aren't pockmarked," said Heine. "You are too handsome a young man. Were you a poet like Goethe, then all the pretty Frederikas and every ugly Mrs. von Stein would run after you. But, as you are, I see in you only an actor-to-be. One day you will be captured by an itinerant heroine of the stage."

Here Heinrich Heine referred in his ironic fashion to what was always decisive for Lassalle, the genetic and the psychological. Certainly, Ferdinand Lassalle is a revolutionary, a socialist, a founder of the General German Worker's Association. But he is all of these, if one looks at him closely, over and over again only out of that impulse to succeed as a Jewish figure in a world that tries to keep the Jews down. And just as a story of Karl Marx must in the main always be a political or intellectual story, a biography of Ferdinand Lassalle must above all analyze his psychology. If one wants to understand how it came to deep disagreements and finally to a break between Marx and his friend Engels, on the one side, and Ferdinand Lassalle, on the other, then one must necessarily recognize how much it had to do with Marx's arming of himself against the adventurous aspects of Lassalle's nature, and how that led him to conduct the trial of the Countess Hatzfeld. Marx sensed that Lassalle's reasons for being a socialist were not the ones that tirelessly drove Marx himself—the universal impulse for knowledge and liberation. He sensed instead how there lay behind the political tactics and behind the political views of Ferdinand Lassalle something of a more personal nature that did not derive from impersonal theoretical views of a socialist.

It is well known that the theoretical conflict between Marx and Lassalle centered on the role of the state in the realization of socialism. Ferdinand Lassalle championed the thesis that the state had to be the tool—placed in the hands of the right people and equipped with appropriate constitutional powers—that fulfilled the initial condition of the socialist struggle for emancipation. For Lassalle, therefore, the conquest of the state by the working class was equivalent to the victory of the workers over the bourgeoisie. In this thesis too, it occurs to me that the psychology of Ferdinand Lassalle is of utmost significance. The state—above all as conceived by Otto von Bismarck, himself nearing power, in whose advantage Ferdinand Lassalle took an extraordinary interest and with whom Lassalle would so gladly have engaged in high politics—this Bismarckian state represented a splendid peak of European development, especially if one had the romantic bent Lassalle had acquired in his early childhood. Lassalle's love for the state is the love of Jews legally deprived of rights over generations for the culmination of all strivings for power it represents. And insofar as the idea of the state has not yet entirely played out its role in modern Zionist ideology, it can be traced back to the same tendency toward romantic infatuation in the idea of state power that we find in Lassalle. Once again, an entry in the diary of the 15-year-old trade school pupil gives us an immediate key to Lassalle's theory, this time his theory of the state:

> I was in the theater. Löwe performed Fiesko. By God, a great character, this Count von Lavagna. I don't know—despite my present revolutionary-democratic-republican convictions—I still feel that in the position of Count Lavagna I would have acted exactly as he did and not satisfied myself with being the first citizen of Genoa, but instead have reached out my hand for the diadem. From that it becomes evident, when I examine the matter closely, that I am simply an egoist. Had I been born a prince or a count, I would be an aristocrat, body and soul. As it is, since I am merely a plain citizen's son, I will duly be a democrat.

In fact, one would have to say that this precocious young man already recognized himself completely. He was, or rather, he became a democrat and socialist *malgré lui,* but he really would have preferred to walk the splendid path of the aristocracy and the *haute bourgeoisie.*

Heinrich Heine, who took a certain aesthetic pleasure in the young Lassalle, later recognized the lack of inner authenticity in Lassalle with extraordinary accuracy. Significant is a conversation he had with a well-known doctor in 1848. As the conversation turned to Lassalle, Heine said, "Just imagine, one of his relatives had the insolence to say to me that I had recommended him for Berlin allegedly because I see in him the new redeemer. Woe unto the redeemed!" And this "woe" expressed by Heine for the falsely redeemed, applied yet much more to the purported redeemer, Lassalle himself. For this has to be the perspective: the state socialism, his friendship with Bismarck, the trial of the Countess Hatzfeld, his engagement to Helene von Dönniges—all of these could only be stages in the life of a doomed man. Ferdinand Lassalle was a tragic figure, the mark of decline already written on his face in his lifetime—that Heinrich Heine had already seen. Fanny Lewald tells of a conversation she had with Heine in the fall of 1855. Heine spoke much then of Lassalle's violent power and his stroke of genius. He wondered at the "rendezvous" in Lassalle of the best and the worst sides of his race, all of the good qualities and all of the defects. And he closed his remarks with the prophetic words, But it will come to no good end! In fact, it did not come to a good end, in psychological terms, because Ferdinand Lassalle essentially never got past the beginning. He never succeeded in taking his formative experience of the disdained Jewish people, filtering out the personal and the accidentally biographical, and recasting it into a pure idea. The failure becomes most apparent in the terrible finale. One who wants truly to comprehend Lassalle's personality must understand, much more than his writings, his diary entries as a 15 year old and, above all, the letters he sent to Helene von Dönniges toward the end of his life. He writes to his beloved:

> I have no thoughts other than you. I love you to insanity! Late Wednesday night, for the first, my love for you appeared to me in a terrible form as if from a revelation. First of all, my suffering sprung through the surface of the relative equanimity the happiness around me cultivates, and then my love leapt through in its terrible, gigantic shape. Politics, science, everything that otherwise fulfills me—all pales to a colorless shadow in the face of the single thought: Helene. I want to bless the brutality of your parents once I win you. For it was only this eternal suffering that consumes me for your sake which has made me conscious of what you really are to me. If I do not act for you, then I cry tirelessly every free minute the whole day long.

And on another occasion the following outburst:

> I no longer have any thoughts but you; to me everything else pales to colorlessness. Since Wednesday night, I love you to insanity.

We should not today reject the designation, "insanity." It must appear insane when a person who feels himself called to redeem oppressed humanity through his political and theoretical works can forget it all because of the passion of a personal experience. That is not how people behave who have a mission to accomplish. The only people who behave like that are the utterly broken in spirit who stand their ground in reference to themselves, to their ideas, to their surroundings, without qualification. Thus we cannot be surprised that this love, so passionate and fevered, grows not on the soil of an increasingly deep and internalized relationship, but is nothing more than an ultimately accidental eruption of a restless mortal. After an already lengthy period of acquaintanceship and infatuation, he writes to a friend: "In part, finally, to confess the whole truth, I knew not at all before our present separation how much I loved Helene. It is only since the night before last that I know it." It was then—when he lost his beloved, when he failed once again to make his way into a world that disdained him and his people, when entrance into that world would have been the highest triumph of the otherwise subjugated Jew—only then that he allowed himself to know something of the extent of his love. A few years earlier, he had sent a great confession to a young Russian woman whom he loved, claiming to have decided only with extraordinary dis-taste—because he sensed how misunderstood, how embarrassing, how degrading a step it was—to have himself baptized. Now even that had become completely indifferent to him. He concerned himself only with the purely technical questions: how baptism and marriage might be accomplished in the shortest possible time. The behavior of Helene von Dönniges is of no consequence whatever to our observation here. But from the following lines we draw a clear sense of the fundamental tragedy in Lassalle's character, which, in accord with the manifold futility of a violent and brutal emancipation, drove him to his death:

> Helene, if you could truly be faithless to me, could renounce me without regard for your vows, you would not be worthy of what I suffer for you. But I would kill myself anyway, for there is no further life without you, Helene. Calm me with a word!

To depend on the mood of a beloved woman and at the same time to be Ferdinand Lassalle essentially meant to wish for death, and the duel that then ensued in this connection was only the contingent expression of Lassalle's suicide. Lassalle wanted to fall in this duel, of that we have not the slightest doubt—one can prove it historically from what the eyewitnesses report of his last days. Lassalle, the complete contrary of his opponent, made not the slightest effort to check the weapons to be used or to practice with them. Lassalle's death was no nonsensical accident in the story of his life, however accidental the circumstances might have been. His death was only the execution of the unhappy resolution, which never escaped the bounds of the personal, that Lassalle found for his Jewish experience.

In his novel, *The Magic Mountain,* Thomas Mann draws for us in Leo Naphta a character who quickly evolves from his eastern European Jewish milieu through his early baptism into a dialectical defender of Catholicism. Leo Naphta is an extraordinarily clever person, schooled in thought, who developed himself as the consumate contrary to the figure of the idealistic and humanistic Settembrini. The intellectual struggle between the two gradually sharpened to the point of irritation which, in turn, led to a duel. Before it took place, Leo Naphta committed suicide. I have always interpreted the character of Leo Naphta as drawing on Ferdinand Lassalle. Both Lassalle and Leo Naphta had to commit suicide, because, they attempted to achieve a victory over the world that oppressed them and their ancestors by identifying with that world. It is part and parcel of the peculiarity of the Jewish situation of our time that it is usually non-Jews who familiarize us with such figures as Lassalle or Leo Naphta. Ferdinand Lassalle too has until now found no congenial Jewish biographer.

As we turn now to Karl Marx we can be briefer because, as we have already said, he, in opposition to Lassalle, is completely successful in transforming the original ground of his Jewishness into a universal world-view. Just as the key to Ferdinand Lassalle's theory is his life, so is the key to Karl Marx's life his theory. Karl Marx is the genuine continuation of the rationalization of Judaism that culminated in Maimonides. With grandiose one-sidedness and a dominating theoretical command, he moves forward along the line of the universal process of knowledge. Thus does the grandchild of a long line of rabbis—although born to baptized parents—become a true heir of the noblest rabbinical tradition.

If we want to investigate the life and work of Karl Marx from the angle of Jewish documents, then we really find only that one famous and notorious text, "On the Jewish Question," which he published in Arnold Ruge's *Deutsch-Französisches Jahrbuch*. And if we want to address something else of biographical significance for his position on Judaism, then it would be the documents of a cordial and friendly relationship to Heinrich Heine. They reveal a mutual esteem and respect, with no need for the painstakingly cautious strategy of observation that appeared necessary for their relationship to Ferdinand Lassalle. With friendly sympathy, for example, Marx concerned himself with Heine's literary worries. When Heine once came to Marx, inconsolable over a writer's attack on him, Marx offered consolation and sent him to his wife, who knew more than he of poetry. But not always, Karl Kautsky tells us, did Heine come seeking help; he also came to offer it. One case remained especially strong in the Marx family's memory.

Little Jenny Marx, an infant of a few months, was one day so afflicted with cramps that they threatened her life. Marx, his wife and her loyal assistant and friend, Helene Demuth, desperate and perplexed, stood watch over the child. Then came Heine, who looked at the child and said, "The little one needs a bath." With his own hands, he prepared the bath, lay the child in the water and, as Marx said, saved Jenny's life. Heine, a practical nurse for a child—to some the image might be suprising.

Marx was a great admirer of Heine. He loved the poet every bit as much as his works and judged his political weaknesses with utmost considera-tion. Poets, he explained, are odd fellows who must be allowed to go their own ways. One must not hold them to the same standards as ordinary, or even extraordinary, people.

The pamphlet, "On the Jewish Question," is a classic document of a type of anti-Semitism for which history has yet to be written, namely, Jewish anti-Semitism. This little text contains statements of great anti-Semitic harshness and pointedness, free of all concessions and all those loathesome compliments that non-Jewish anti-Semites like to apply to individual Jews. Two works by the radical theologian and young Hegelian, Bruno Bauer, "The Jewish Question," and "The Capacity of Jews and Christians to Become Free," provided Marx the occasion for this essay. Bauer defends the thesis that the Jews, in order even to be emancipated by the state—a Christian state, after all—have first to give up their religion and their national character. Here Karl Marx applied his critique. In very clear, dialectical statements, Marx showed how the political emancipation of the Jews, which Bruno Bauer was defending, would be an extraordinarily pernicious and one-sided affair, because it would be only a very partial emancipation and liberation. All depended, argued Marx, not on the political emancipation of one or another individual, but on human emancipation—the liberation of the whole of humanity from the burden of domination. For Marx the two most important instances of domination were the state and religion, which, finally, were only instruments of power in the hands of an exploitative stratum of capitalist masters. His strongest opposition to everything that was considered religion is expressed in this connection:

> We no longer see religion as the *basis* but simply as a *phenomenon* of secular narrowness. We therefore explain the religious restriction on the free citizens from the secular restriction they experience. We do not mean to say that they must do away with their religious restriction in order to transcend their secular limitations. We do not turn secular questions into theological questions. We turn theological questions into secular questions. History has been resolved into superstition long enough. We are now resolving superstition into history. The question of the *relationship of political emancipation to religion* becomes for us the question of the *relationship of political emancipation to human emancipation*. We criticize the religious weakness of the political state by criticizing the political state in its *secular* construction, *regardless* of its religious weaknesses. We humanize the contradiction between the state and a *particular religion*, for example Judaism, by resolving it into the contradiction between the state and *particular secular* elements, and we humanize the contradiction between the state and *religion in general* by resolving it into the contradiction between the state and its own general *presuppositions*. (Karl Marx, *Early Writings*, New York: Vintage Books, 1975, pp. 217–18.)

In this passage, a high point in universalistic Jewish thinking seems to have been achieved. Whether we measure the history of Judaism against the principles of its philosophy of history, or the social situation against the principles of a free society, we always deal with the method of universalistic critique. We are always concerned with the conflict between the dark realm of ignorance—of superstition, violence, and lust—and the enlightened realm of knowledge and justice. Idolatry or capitalism are symbols, but at the same time the contents of that dark realm; only the perception of this double function makes possible a struggle which is not mere tilting at windmills. When Marx proclaims, in his famous "Theses on Feuerbach," "The philosophers have only *interpreted* the world in various ways; the point, however, is to *change* it," attention should be directed, not only at the final phrase, but at the "only" in the first. (Karl Marx, *Early Writings*, p. 423.)

Once this much has been granted, the question of Marx's anti-Semitism remains open. Jewish historiography has almost always interpreted him literally (but literally in very imprecise terms), its anathema upon Marx remained firm. Unfortunately and fortunately, the non-Jewish world passed judgment more shrewdly and objectively. "Marx was a Jew," writes Robert Wilbrandt of Tübingen;

> He was one of those great Jews, deeply shaming anti-Semitism, who are much more passionate and profound anti-Semites themselves. . . . As eternal haggler and money-lender, as a Judaism eating its way into our society, as a Jewification of our life—thus the nature of this noble Jew as prophet perceived and designated the profit of our capitalist business life as greed. And I believe this sensibility derives from the same blood, the same purity and love intensified through contrast, as did the Old Testament prophets' wholly analogous sensibility . . .

Wilbrandt does, in fact, refer here to the ethos of a Jewish anti-Semitism—inaugurated in the nineteenth century by Moses Heß and supported, at times passionately, at times sarcastically, by Heinrich Heine—which reached its climax in Marx. Behind his text is the thought: it must not be allowed that Judaism becomes the symbol for violence, for the deprivation of rights, for capitalism. That Marx is speaking out of his profound ignorance of Jewish cultural values when he fails to disintinguish loudly and clearly between Jewish possibilities and realities is certainly not to be overlooked. But there remains, in spite of it all, the twofold nature of his claim—on the one hand, the protest against the fact that Judaism can be the symbol of capitalism; on the other, the Jewish-universalist manner in which the protest is carried out.

> Emancipation from *haggling* and *money,* from practical, real Judaism, would be the same as the self-emancipation of our age. An organization of society that abolished the basis upon which haggling exists, i.e. the possibility of haggling, would have made the Jew impossible. (Karl Marx, *Early Writings*, p. 236.)

Indeed. And yet, as we may add in more intimate interpretations of Marx, it would have made possible the realization of Jewish principles of justice.

5

Hermann Cohen

The emancipation of the Jews in the nineteenth century entailed a process in their intellectual history which decisively rendered its most important aspects dependent on the general social situation. The philosophy of religion meets the same fate. Not only for the Jews but for bourgeois society as a whole, the nineteenth century spelled the final destruction of the absolutist order through the establishment of the capitalist economy and its attending political forms. Upon Hegel's death, it became completely clear that intellectual energies were no longer directed toward theoretical confrontation with an obsolete though still established general regime. Instead, they were aimed without mediation at practice, at the shaping of an immediate agenda and day-to-day struggles. Despite their isolation and the apparently disjointed specificity of their tasks, the positive sciences, political theory and journalistic work coalesced on the point of theological discussion and philosophy. Were these remarks to be restricted to the circle of Jewish writers, then it would only take a reference to such men as Heinrich Heine, Karl Marx or Paul Ehrlich to fortify the point.

Beginning at the turn of the century, there arose a countermovement against the positivist infatuation with fact. Positivist "materialism" and "naturalism" were attacked, and the betrayal of each and every idealistic orientation condemned. In short, just as in the times of the great systems and the movement of bourgeois Enlightenment in western Europe, philosophy began once again to claim priority over all theoretical and practical questions of the day. Yet, to be sure, the conditions in which philosophy now asserts itself are very different. Around the eighteenth century, it was a question of overthrowing feudal and absolutist domination and creating the preconditions of bourgeois society; in the decades just past, the role of influential currents in modern philosophy is inseparable from the new order of class society and its victorious wing, which welcomes a glorification of the existing. The contradictions of bourgeois society, promoted through the development of scientific and technical forces and revealed by social and political theory, are facts that philosophy now disregards as "mere" facticities in favor of a higher, more general being. Thus devalued, the facts are also protected against attack.

For the role of Jewish intellectuals in the dialectical development of capitalism, the relationship of Hermann Cohen's philosophy to the general philosophical situation as characterized above is telling. In his fine foreword to Cohen's Jewish writings, Franz Rosenzweig relates a conversation that took place in Marburg between Friedrich Albert Lange and Cohen. Lange asks, "Do our views on Christianity differ?" Cohen replies, "No, for what you call Christianity, I call prophetic Judaism." And to this conversation Cohen appends the remark, "Thus, with one blow, did ethical socialism unite us beyond the bounds of our religions." The Kantian Cohen felt himself impelled directly toward socialism; in his memory appeared dimly the name of Karl Marx, even if he interpreted the latter's theory, unidealistic in the extreme, in "ethical" terms. But alongside Kant and socialism, there appears Judaism as a third term. Indeed, Cohen's early conversation already contained the kernel of the whole of his later philosophy of religion. From the point of view of Kant's scientific usefulness, especially in relation to his significance for mathematics and the natural sciences, it may have appeared first as if a revival of Kant would necessarily remain alien to religion. It may have appeared that for the philosopher who was fascinated with the "pureness" of reason (for Kant, unlike for the theologian Moses Mendelssohn, not a "totalizer", but a "founder"), no connection would be found to the substantive concerns of theology. Would religion, would the religious substance of Judaism pass the test of the rational? Just a glance at Cohen's writings shows how pressing this problem was for him. Alongside the historical essay, "Die Ethik des Moses Maimuni" ["The Ethics of Moses Maimuni"], appears programmatically a treatment of "Innere Beziehungen der kantischen Philosophie zum Judentum" ["The Internal Relations of Kantian Philosophy with Judaism"]; alongside the text, *Der Begriff der Religion im System der Philosophie [The Concept of Religion in the System of Philosophy]*, apparently necessary solely on systematic philosophical grounds, appears, ultimately as Cohen's testament, *Religion der Vernunft aus den Quellen des Judentums [The Religion of Reason from the Sources of Judaism]*. Just the title of this work names three concepts of great value to Cohen. For during the whole of his life the biographical legacy of being a Jew remained more than merely that; it signified to him something much more like a duty, and lended to his otherwise merely accidental existence as an individual a missionary ordination. General obligation, the moral responsibility of human beings (through which, indeed, mere positivism was to be overcome), the duty posed by ethics—all of these he once boldly defined as the "science of man." And this science finds, at the very least, its point of departure in the claim of ethical obligation with which all religion makes its appearance. The concept of the truth, however, spans both concepts, and the truth can make itself known only through the process of humanity's acquisition of knowledge, only, that is, through that which is called reason.

With reason, therefore, the Jewish philosophy of religion begins. The substance of religion is conceived and the instruments with which it operates produced by reason. Thereby religion becomes a problem of philosophy, and the history of religion rather a criterion of the extent to which human reason has realized itself in history. This criterion applies equally to all religions, and for that reason they all participate in the religion of reason. Nor is reason the intellectual monopoly of any single nation. Here the philosophy of Cohen attaches itself to that of Maimonides, for whom the laws of reason were discovered mutually by all the peoples of the world. Reason, as the first concept of the philosophy of religion, is supposed to bar the door to all impure sources of religion. Mere instinct is left to the animals; pleasure and pain are the accidents of individuals. Nor can historical givenness be a source for a concept of religion that endures. Only through reason can religion acquire normative validity.

"Reason does not exhaust itself in science and philosophy." As a second foundational concept, religion itself makes its appearance. It must first endure a cleansing of all possible historically contingent defects. Religion is not a myth for which the individual, entangled in guiltless guilt as the legacy of his ancestors or the product of an overwhelming fate, settles upon tragically for eternal want of redemption. It is not pantheism, which glorifies all that exists indiscriminately, thereby justifying it and annulling the obligation of change. It is not polytheism which, in the colorful multitude of its figures, signs, and symbols never permits decision and exalts lawless caprice. Nor, however, is it ethics. In ethics the individual is only abstractly justified as a part of humanity; it provides solely a method by which it becomes possible to determine what of the individual and in the individual is of value. Ethics does not treat the individual in his particular reality; it does not concern itself with I and thou. But religion does concern itself with the individual. It identifies the individual by way of the sign that ties all individuals together, that is, by way of sin. Religion is founded in the individual's self-knowledge of his sins. Cohen finds an anticipation of this theological self-knowledge in anticipatory form in the prophet Hezekial and also in Socrates. Religion, therefore, discovers the tension between sin and virtue. The path between the two is broad but on the path a guide is discovered in the concept of God. "For that reason love for God should surpass all knowledge; with the concept of him it should join all things and all the problems of the world together." With that claim, Cohen sets forth the essential themes of religion: God, God and man, sin and suffering, one's people, humanity, redemption.

Now the way is open for a discussion of Judaism, the third concept in Cohen's title. Working from the philosophical basis sketched above, Cohen derived the idea of a possible religion of reason drawn from the sources of Judaism. This source is the literature—for Cohen, the Bible, the Talmud, and Maimonides—in which the classical theme is fundamentally always the idea of a single God. "Religious literature is the most significant source of the spirit of the Jewish people." Cohen attempted his derivation of a Jewish religion of reason by investigating in this literature the decisive concepts of religion named above.

The concept of God comes first. "As far as I am concerned, God can be what he likes, but he must be one." The higher reality of God, being altogether, is enclosed within this unity. "Monotheism is a psychological mystery. Whoever does not recognize that does not understand it in its profundity." And yet this mystery finds its solution. Not, to be sure, in that Cohen constructs a positive theology, but more in its immediate relationship to humanity; for in the unity of God, set off against the multiplicity and variety of the human species, there exists a basic tension. His being is only revealed in action. God is the archetype of action for mankind. Once God is fully removed from the sphere of the specifically determinable, and once the concept of supreme life and action replaces the concept of a supreme order, having an image of God is by necessity excluded from a philosophy of reason. But there exists also another reason for this prohibition. An image can be drawn only of something concrete. The polytheist remains with the singular, his Gods are figures. "It is the test of the true God, that there can exist no image of him."

The being of God is only comprehensible in its reference to human beings. The relation of God to man becomes the compelling problem of the philosophy of religion. In Cohen's terminology, it is the problem of the relation of *being* to *existence*. The individual is necessary for God as the vessel of his essence. But to understand this correlation mystically would be to commit a serious misunderstanding. It may be that the unity of God is a mystery; yet nothing is more clear intellectually than the relationship between God and the individual. Morality is the content of this relationship. Thus the relationship between God and the individual is necessarily extended through the relationship of individuals among themselves. Their relationship originates altogether and is established ethically only through the correlation between the living individual and God. The more clearly and deeply the individual delves into the meaning of this correlation—that is, the more ethically people behave—the more is reason realized. The complete realization of reason would be redemption. "The highest confirmation of the correlation between the individual and God lies in the acting together of the individual and God to accomplish the deed of redemption." The specific characteristic of Cohen's philosophy, indeed, its whole pathos, can only be understood through the interchangeability in principle of the ideal of theoretical truth and the ideal of the true ordering of life. There exists no human relationship sanctioned in this idealistic philosophy whose foundation does not rest on the recognition of the right. There exists no theoretical statement that stands as truth which cannot be confirmed by its application to the morality of human beings. "I cannot love God without loving him with my whole heart as it lives for my fellow creatures, without my whole soul as it follows all the impulses of the spirit of our age, without employing the whole of my powers for this God in his correlation with human beings." In this citation there also appears an indication of how Cohen conceives and constructs a Jewish source—the piece from "Schma"—into the foundational conviction of his philosophy. Substantively decisive in this conviction is that everything that transpires between God and man is in essence referred to what transpires on earth. Religion and ethics relate to each other not as the beyond and the here and now, but as fulfillment, on the one hand, and methodological instruction, on the other. "The correlation of man and God founds the realm of the ethical, the realm of God on earth."

Yet, to be sure, the way to this goal is broad, and religion, which identifies the individual in his sinfulness, cannot acknowledge him without qualification as a fully worthy member of the correlation. Sin is the foundational problem of religion for human beings. It refers without mediation to suffering, the foundational problem of all human existence. Sin and suffering refer reciprocally to each other. The justification of the existence of evil, theodicy, is not the justification of God, but the justification of human suffering before God. "For monotheism there exists no fate." The individual is guilty. But, for Cohen, the suffering of the individual refers not to his guilt, but to my own. This theological solution to the problem of guilt and sin is already to be found, according to Cohen, in the Talmud. Were all this not to be found in the midst of a philosophy of religion, one might speak of a secularization of religious questions. Guilt and sin are in no way referred to any kind of dogma, to any kind of positive theological substance, but solely and explicitly to human society. Human relations—the contradictions, the cares and suffering—is the theme of Cohen's philosophy of religion. In fact it had been the theme of the religious discussion with Friedrich Albert Lange in Marburg as well. "Ethical socialism" may well and justly be called the religion of reason. Guilt is not hardened in mysticism; it can be given up. It is the opening to a higher ascendance of the individual, at which point he can acquire the guiltlessness of purely ethical action. The demonic concepts of religion— destiny and fate—are dramatically transformed into the humanized concepts of judgment and redemption. The steps toward redemption are those of a deepening correlation with God.

For the religion of reason in Judaism, the precepts of the law provide a guide along this path. The law is not an expression of the self-judgment of a people that knows it better than other people, but an instrument by which truth is discovered in the ethical realm. It is an "instruction in repentance, in the assumption of one's place in the correlation with God." Repentance is the act that people, for the time being, perform among themselves. The everpresence of morality is already proclaimed in the words of the tradition that the individual is supposed to repent one day before his death. For Cohen, Yom Kippur expresses, as parable, the imperishable nature of the relation of God and man. For here repentance and reconciliation refer to each other, they guarantee each other. Repentance presupposes knowledge, but that which is to be inferred from knowledge is moral action, in other words, repentance. It must come to know reconciliation, or, the righteousness that arises from the reciprocation between knowledge and action and fills the relation between God, the individual, and others with love. God's love is not, therefore, an act of grace, it is the seal of theoretical and practical truth. The unity of righteousness and love can be expressed as the essence of God. "God knows no judgment without redemption as the end of judgment. Nor is there redemption in the absence of judgment's process."

One sees how this philosophy of religion uses the whole apparatus of theological and religious-philosophical conceptualization to take repeated aim at the relationship among human beings. Yet, in history, this relationship has never been satisfactorily fulfilled. And so the questions remain: does perfection exist at all? does redemption exist at all?

With these questions arise the fourth and final of Cohen's fundamental themes, that of redemption. But this theme, like the others, remains true to earthly existence, for it is connected to the concepts of a people and humanity. The religion of reason derived from the source of Judaism turns finally to its most immediate source: the history of the Jewish people. In contrast to other peoples, for whom suffering hovers on the horizon of their history, for Israel it arises in the center. It must, however, be mentioned that, as with all of Cohen's philosophical constructions of history, this one, too, is to be treated with caution. There is no absolute fate for humanity, for the history of humankind contains the contradictions of the groups they make up. For the lower classes, suffering has always occupied the center; for the victorious it has always remained on the horizon. Nevertheless, Cohen would reply to such an objection that, at least relative to the broadest time frame of Israel's existence, it has had to bear the costs of history. Moreover, he might add, it is not at all a matter of glorifying the past suffering of Israel, but quite precisely a matter of deriving from Israel's suffering the meaning which relates to the redemption of all people from suffering.

The suffering of the Jewish people includes no tragic moments. It began with the renunciation of the land, but this renunciation was a voluntary one, and the suffering on account of the lost land—yet more on account of not having established the state—possesses a universal meaning. Israel suffers, therefore it must be redemmed. But, in that it carries this need for redemption to all corners of the earth, it claims the good before the countenance and for the benefit of all peoples and all people. Thus does "messianism" become "the consequence of the single God"; thus is the history of Israel relieved of its darkness."

Hatred is excluded from the common task of all people and all peoples. Among the most moving of Cohen's expositions is the thoroughly idealistic dialectic by which he denies hatred: "What is hatred? I contest its very possibility. It is a vain word that would seek to designate such an idea." In the place of hatred, there appears peace. The results of hatred are chaos among the peoples and conflict. With hatred history gradually falls victim to false appearance. Peace is the sign of eternity." This idealistic view, which sees in world history and its battles not the competition of immediate interests but the struggle of right and wrong, good and bad, is possessed of unprecedented consistency. One might be critical of the endeavors of modern philosophy in its struggle against the positivism of the nineteenth century, and one might continually learn, from the history of the eighteenth century in particular, that that which is recognized as false does not, for having been exposed, decline and disappear. And, still, there would remain the innocent purity of a way of thinking that enlists all of the fundamental concepts of religion and philosophy in the service of an ordering of the life of mankind that is worthy of affirmation. Cohen's concept of redemption receives perhaps its most profound commentary when one puts in its place his concept of joy; of a joy that will dawn upon the people, once all people have become free and useful, once all share in theory and in science, in searching for it and acknowledging it, once all people share in these as they now share in work and in our daily bread.

6

Sigmund Freud

A few weeks ago, Sigmund Freud received the Goethe Prize from the city of Frankfurt [1930]. It would be a fate he did not deserve, if, along the lines of the many essays which labor over the theme "Freud and Goethe," he were now to be patched together with all possible cultural tendencies, historical figures, scientific disciplines, and religions through such an "and." And yet there might well be two exceptions—Goethe and Judaism. Freud is thoroughly doctor and scholar. His individual personality seems to disappear behind his profession and theory; or, better put, in his professional activity, in the problems and results of his research, Freud's true essence presents itself. Serious disappointment awaits those who read his *Autobiographical Study* in the expectation of any sensational personal revelations about the creator of psychoanalysis—that is, about the man who created an effective weapon in the battle against neurosis (one of the most widespread of illnesses) which is, at the same time, the most progressive and radical of psychological theories. His life appears much more to be a constant struggle, fortified by prudence, to gain insights.

A very extensive work by Freud, *The Interpretation of Dreams,* could be taken as a contribution to his autobiography. In this book, he essentially relates his own dreams and uses them as material to gain scientific knowledge for that which, until now, lay deeply hidden in the legends and notions of popular traditions, fairy tales, poetry, and primitive consciousness. Were one now to recall Salomon Maimon, who has also been treated in this series of essays, one would note the difference between Maimon's autobiography and Freud's *Interpretation of Dreams*. The religious, scientific, and philosophical exertions of the one appear as the background to a fantastic, adventurous, exaggerated, vain, and melancholy life. For the other, everyday life, because of the information it provides, is only the occasion to reap technical and scientific gains, which is what ultimately is important.

And it is precisely this book, *The Interpretation of Dreams*, that provides us ample reason for discussing Freud's relation to Judaism. In a series of dreams and interpretations, one learns how the experience of anti-Semitism, the experience of being different that was forced upon the Jewish child from Moravia, became an important stimulus of psychological attitudes. We are told of a youthful experience which, Freud acknowledges, continues to be expressed in many of his present day "emotions" and dreams.

> I may have been ten or twelve years old, when my father began to take me with him on his walks and reveal to me in his talk his views upon things in the world we live in. Thus it was, on one such occasion, that he told me a story to show me how much better things were now than they had been in his days. "When I was a young man," he said, "I went for a walk one Saturday in the streets of your birthplace, I was well-dressed, and had a new fur cap on my head. A Christian came up to me and with a single elbow knocked off my cap into the mud and shouted: 'Jew! get off the pavement!' " "And what did you do," I asked. "I went into the roadway and picked up my cap," was his quiet reply. This struck me as unheroic conduct on the part of the big, strong man who was holding the little boy by the hand.
>
> (Interpretation of Dreams, trans. by James Strachey (New York: Avon Books, 1965), p. 230.)

The examples could be multiplied from which it emerges time and again how strongly the difficulties of being a Jew marked Freud's consciousness and, as he reveals himself, his unconsciousness. He has been barred in his life from positions and distinctions which would have been bestowed automatically on another scholar of such extraordinary caliber anywhere in Europe. Thus the problems pursued him even into his dream life: "the Jewish question, the worry about the future of the children to whom one can give no fatherland, the worry of how to raise them so that they can become free."

And yet, it would miss the mark to see in these and similar reports and remarks a bitter complaint which Freud wants to make public. It is much more the case that these bitter personal experiences became for him simply material for his scientific investigations. One might even say that the embarrassing anti-Semitic experiences have for Freud the same value as the Jewish jokes that he frequently adduced or told in his book, *Jokes and Their Relation to the Unconscious;* those "funny Jewish anecdotes . . . which conceal so much profound, often bitter wisdom concerning life and which we are so fond of quoting in conversation and letters." It is namely both—reaction to the hostile environment and jokes—that are stripped of their personal note and welcomed as material by the discerning rationality, by the scientific consciousness. In this sense as well, Freud made use of the sources of Jewish literature available to him; here it suffices to recall his reference to the Pharoah's dream and the Song of Solomon.

It is well-known that Freud was cordially disposed toward the Jewish national movement. But it would be difficult to find a group in either the Zionist or non-Zionist camp that could claim Freud as its direct sympathizer or opponent. Certainly Freud's experiences contributed to allowing him to welcome an opportunity which offers socially or psychologically oppressed Jews a worthy existence. Yet, any tinge of the nationalistic or religious zealot remains, in this connection, alien to Freud. Indeed, if one wants to think at all of externalities which might be floating about in Freud's national Jewish attitude, then one might justifiably refer to the institution of the family whose conservation is of utmost importance to him and whose protection in certain circumstances it seems to him might have been secured in Palestine. For, to the researcher of psychological drives, the transformations of the wishes and ideas the human infant directs at the parents—processes which, following Freud, are termed the "Oedipus complex"—are our most important intellectual and cultural achievements. It is from this perspective of the promotion of human culture that one may also understand the beautiful letter Freud wrote for the opening of the Hebrew University in Jerusalem. According to Freud, the reason the Jewish state of antiquity survived for a relatively long time was due to the yielding by its members of priority to its spiritual treasures: religion and literature. And for that reason, he bestowed his good wishes on the university. Since it is an abode of science and research, the university provides a service to all humanity; the university's advancement of the sciences contributes to man's knowledge of the world and, in turn, to his ability to control it. One sees, then, how Freud's national Jewish sympathies, stemming possibly from purely personal experiences, first acquire their significance from his attitude as a scientist striving to reform life in a way that advances the interests of more and more people.

That which is valid for Freud's position on the national question also proves correct in relation to the Jewish religion. If he acknowledges that he always had "a strong feeling of solidarity with my people and nourished it in my children," he yet writes in the same letter, "I am as distant from the Jewish religion as from all other religions; that is, highly significant to me as objects of scientific interest as they are, emotionally I am not involved in them." The significance of religions for Freud the scientist, in fact, emerges from the many historical investigations of religion undertaken by himself and members of his school. In one of his last works, *The Future of an Illusion,* he discloses the results he derived from this historical and psychological research. This book won him more enemies than friends. Those who are living positively religious lives will not be eager to regard as sensible the circumstance that, for him, religion becomes an illusion, capable, perhaps, of offering people consolation for the misery of their social and psychological situation, but incapable, to be sure, of changing decisively the conditions responsible for it. And yet the best defenders of religion, including the Jewish religion, will not close themselves to Freud's fundamental conviction. He grants to science not merely preference but exclusive priority in relation to religion; but what he has ultimately at heart is "to learn something about the reality of the world, through which we increase our power and according to which we can order our lives."

If we want to speak of Freud's relation to Judaism without resting content with an appreciation of his scientific treatment of Jewish themes and experiences, then we must direct our attention to those qualities he displays in the whole of his life. We celebrate in Freud the great doctor: the helper to those in psychic need for whom there has been no remedy until now; the fighter against the terrible illness of psychic affliction whose medical treatments might remind us of Goethe's Iphigenia as she redeems the chaos of passion through human dialog. But we celebrate in him the great scientist as well. Especially as a psychologist, through his teaching, through his students and beyond his specialization, he furthers and stimulates sciences which, in conjunction with the practice of public life, help analyze and will one day do away with the primary causes of psychological misery for many people. We think of society, of teaching. Help and reconstruction for individuals and for society as a whole—that is the star that illumines Freud's life and work.

PART II

Lectures (1978–1983)

7

Adorno and his Critics (1978)

Adorno was a genius, and his work, which is now published in more than twenty volumes, encompasses the intellectual universe of Western civilization, concentrating on but not limited to philosophy; the social sciences, musicology, and significant events of public life. It would be absurd for me to try to convey a systematic summary of Adorno's unique enterprise. Rather, I shall discuss it in a fragmentary style. In doing so, I find myself in tune with Adorno's own approach: to disavow consistently any legitimacy for a system. The famous *Dialectic of Enlightenment,* written with his friend Max Horkheimer, has the German subtitle *Philoso-phische Fragmente* [Philosophical Fragments], which was unfortunately omitted in the English version. His first writings on Richard Wagner were entitled "Fragments on Richard Wagner," and many of his books were called "notes" or "essays" or something similar. Adorno looked to Nietzsche, Karl Kraus, and Walter Benjamin as models of this literary form. The style has a characteristic open-ended, probing quality, and its format is essayistic, aphoristic, or fragmentary. In Adorno's case it was justified by his famous philosophical *bon mot* on Hegel's system: "The whole is the false."

We met in late 1922, brought together by the eminent writer, philosopher, and sociologist Siegfried Kracauer. Ten years later we found ourselves working together in the Institute of Social Research in Frankfurt, and we continued a close association for about twenty years. Our relationship was stormy at times, as is almost unavoidable in a community of high-strung intellectuals. It fills me with emotion to find, for instance, that Martin Jay, who is by now the preeminent historian of our Institute, in an article called "Adorno and Kracauer: Notes on a Troubled Friendship" (a subtitle that ironically might serve as a proper characterization for the mutual relationships of all of us) noted that in 1927 Adorno "brooded over his chances for successful habilitation and complained about his rivalry with a mutual friend, Leo Lowenthal, in the ranks of the Frankfurt Institute''; or that four years later, in 1931, "possibilities of Kracauer contributing to the new Institute journal were discussed, with Adorno lamenting that his hands were tied by Leo Lowenthal, whom he described as 'king of the desert' [*Wüstenkönig*] at the Institute.''[1] Well, I never had a crown, and Adorno gained his professorial appointment.

Maintaining a fragmentary format, I would first like to discuss the areas and problems on which Adorno and I either engaged in brotherly collaboration or shared scholarly interests, and then I would like to make some observations on the frequently rebellious criticism raised by some of his students and disciples.

As some of you know, the Institute continued the publication of its journal—which originated in 1932 in Germany, where it lasted only one year—first in Geneva and then in New York as an essentially German-language outlet for our work. It was, in the true sense of the word, a joint enterprise, because all the major articles were subject to critical scrutiny by the entire group. To give a personal example, in 1937 I published an essay on Knut Hamsun with the subtitle "A Prehistory of the Authoritarian Ideology," at a time when Hamsun's membership in the Norwegian Nazi-Quisling Party was still unknown. Adorno wrote a lengthy footnote for my essay, in which he drew close parallels between Hamsun and Sibelius, whose music expressed similar elements of contempt for men oppressed in the glorification of a rigid, pantheistically colored concept of nature. Collaborative closeness is also documented by the first three theses on anti-Semitism that are incorporated in the *Dialectic of Enlightenment* and, above all, by our studies in the seductive and potentially dangerous devices of the American fascist agitator. This work culminated in my book *Prophets of Deceit,* to which Adorno anonymously contributed a draft of an introduction in addition to copious substantive comments and suggestions. Conversely, I had the privilege of participating in the original draft of the research plan for the famous *Authoritarian Personality,* on which Adorno was a senior author, and of contributing my own comments and suggestions on his chapters of this monumental work. In a similar spirit of collegial and intellectual solidarity, Adorno wrote the major text of a section in an essay of mine on popular culture, which we properly called "Some Theses on Critical Theory and Empirical Research."

It is indeed in this area of popular or mass culture—or, as Adorno called it, "the culture industry"—that our interests frequently converged. It is, by the way, not without irony that many topics for this symposium mention Adorno's work on mass culture, a term that he, with his discriminatory perception for linguistic nuances, intensely disliked. In 1967 he expressly stated this in a postscript to the essay published in the *Dialectic of Enlightenment* twenty years earlier.

> The term "culture industry" was perhaps used for the first time in the book *Dialectic of Enlightenment,* which Horkheimer and I published in Amsterdam in 1947. In our drafts we spoke of "mass culture." We replaced that expression with "culture industry" in order to exclude from the outset the interpretation agreeable to its advocates: that it is a matter of something like a culture that arises spontaneously from the masses themselves, the contemporary form of popular art. From the latter the culture industry must be distinguished in the extreme.[2]

I am proud that Adorno approved and used my shorthand definition of fascist agitation as well as culture industry as "psychoanalysis in reverse," that is, as more or less constantly manipulated devices to keep people in permanent psychic bondage, to increase and reinforce neurotic and even psychotic behavior culminating in perpetual dependency on a "leader" or on institutions or products. We both saw modern anti-Semitism and culture industry as ultimately belonging in the same social context even though at times they go different political ways. What is at stake here, as Adorno never grew tired of repeating, is the ever-increasing difficulty of genuine experience mediated primarily through art, whose independence and integrity has been increasingly sabotaged by the sophisticated apparatus of social manipulation and domination. Significant is the inexorable paralysis of productive imagination and artistic experience leading to a conversion of cognitive effects into sales psychology. Culture industry provides the inescapable commodity character of all its products and imperceptibly extinguishes the differences among these products themselves and the general or specific advertising purposes for which they are created. We agreed that the culture establishment refused to take any responsibility by ignoring completely the meaning of mass culture and conveniently indicting its technology alone for its miserable productions; we agreed that the dividing line between art and commodity culture must not be obfuscated and that the unholy alliance of social domination with the naked profit motive hardly promotes a state of consciousness in which, in Adorno's words, *Freizeit* would turn into *Freiheit*—leisure into freedom.

I would like to let Adorno speak with his own words, first in regard to the dividing line between art and culture industry.

> The entire practice of the culture industry transfers the profit motive naked onto cultural forms. . . . The autonomy of works of art, which of course rarely ever predominated in an entirely pure form, and was always permeated by a constellation of effects, is tendentially eliminated by the culture industry, with or without the conscious will of those in control.[3]

I might add as a melancholic personal comment that I find it ever more difficult to persuade my students, despite their predominantly radical persuasion, to accept these irreconcilable differences—another illustration of how the infamous positivist value-neutrality is affecting and infecting the best of us.

Adorno stressed the inescapable fate of people to succumb to the culture industry whether they want it or not:

> The phrase "the world wants to be deceived" has become truer than had ever been intended. People are not merely, as the saying goes, falling for the swindle—if it guarantees them even the most fleeting gratification, they desire a deception which is nonetheless transparent to them. . . . Without admitting it, they sense that their lives would be completely intolerable as soon as they no longer clung to satisfactions which are none at all.[4]

It was once a theoretical dream of our inner circle that, in addition to the social theme of authority, we would engage in a joint study of all aspects of the decay of the essence and concept of the individual in bourgeois society and its conversion to mere illusion and ideology. However, whereas the theme of authority received profuse elaboration in what are now almost classic books, that of the individual remained merely a guiding perspective. Adorno, for instance, continually emphasized the hollow cult of the so-called personality and the exultation of the allegedly autonomous individual in the era of monopoly capitalism. I pursued the same theme in my own studies on the literary genre of biography—in this country as well as in Europe—and its role as a sham device that pretended human specificity when in fact the true meaning of the particular has been perverted. When I wrote on the cultural changes in the selection and treatment of biographies in popular magazines, from what I called "heroes of production" to "heroes of consumption," Adorno admonished me in a letter of November 1942 to emphasize the theoretical function of biographies in present society and particularly within the context of mass culture. He said, and I could not agree more, that

> ultimately, the very concept of life as a self-developing and meaningful unity has as little reality today as the concept of the individual, and it is the ideological function of the biographies to conjure up the fiction on arbitrarily selected models that there is still such a thing as life. . . . Life itself in its completely abstract appearance has become mere ideology.

While my own emphasis in the analysis of this trivial genre was on the shallow solace it offered the politically impotent and historically disoriented middle classes in Europe before the advent of fascism, Adorno's profound reflections stressed the awesome paradox that the same apparatus of culture industry that extinguishes private idiosyncratic consciousness falls all over itself in an endless praise of personality and individuality. In his words, culture industry's "ideology above all makes use of the star system, borrowed from individualistic art and its commercial exploitation. The more dehumanized its methods of operation . . . the more diligently and successfully the culture industry propagates supposedly great personalities and operates with heartthrobs."[5] Narcissistic as it may sound to some of you, this report of brotherly collaboration and intellectual exchanges should be understood solely as a foil: I wish to bring into relief Adorno's great contribution to a critical understanding of modern society's inescapable network of domination and of its seemingly inescapable reinforcement of the psyche of man, without which this very mechanism of domination would cease to be effective. This theme inspired his continual admonition: "Don't participate"—arguably the leitmotif of his life's work, against which all the weakness of personality or idiosyncracies of life-style weigh very little.

Thinking about Adorno's merciless, but always theoretically founded, indictment of the social phenomena themselves, as well as their faulty, distorted, and manipulated pseudo-interpretations in bourgeois philosophy, social research, and literary criticism—just to name a few of the dubious intellectual enterprises—I cannot help but be reminded of the original theological meaning of the Greek term *skandalon*. Every thought he ever had and every word he ever said created a new *Ärgernis* [irritant] for his foes and friends alike.

At this point I would like to break off my brotherly tribute to this genius, whose much too early demise might not be unconnected to the *skandalon* he adhered to without compromise until the end at his post as Germany's most prominent academic teacher and outstanding citizen of the Western European avant-garde. He would have been the first to understand that the implacability implied in each of the intellectual positions he held needed constant refinement and defense against facile acceptance by followers and angry misinterpretations by adversaries. Nothing is more ironic than the term "Frankfurt School," which presupposes a body of learnable statements and doctrines that one could live with, comfortably or uneasily—whatever the case might be—henceforth. I truly believe that no one who, either directly or indirectly, belonged to our circle at its beginnings over a half century ago would ever have felt comfortable with this term. As a matter of fact, the by now indeterminably large corpus of books, articles, doctoral theses, symposia, and seminars has almost "industrialized" the Frankfurt School; many of these works seem to be little short of talmudic disputations about the meaning of this or that theorem at different periods or about the relation of this or that writer or scholar in this or another phase. When Adorno chose as the subtitle of his first major collection of fragments and aphorisms the words "Reflections from Damaged Life" he did not offer to repair such damage. But many, if not most, of his disciples—indeed, students of all shades of the school—could not and cannot accept the absence of political and cultural remedies. I cannot help but think that their call for action is not so far removed from the all-pervasive advocacy of fashionable pseudo-psychological cures that are about to poison many of our contemporaries. If I appear irate, you are not misreading me, but it is an ire grounded in compassion for the restless youth and the now equally restless middle-aged who have looked in vain to Adorno for salvation; he was not, and did not want to be, a messiah.

In stressing some of their collective misreadings, I may perhaps be able to add to an understanding of Adorno's intellectual heritage. I start with the *ad hominem* argument: Adorno as a human being. One of the most popular objections to radical thinkers has been the vulgar argument that they should practice what they preach—although they are not really preaching anything—by staying away from all the amenities of the good life. Brecht's comments on the financial resources of the Institute and the upper-class backgrounds of some of its principal members (which I believe to be in poor taste) are well known. I take more seriously the elegant observation of Lukács, who, in the preface to a new edition of his *Theory of the Novel* in 1962, commented as follows:

> A considerable part of the leading German intelligentsia, including Adorno, have taken up residence in the "Grand Hotel Abyss," which I described in connection with my critique of Schopenhauer as "a beautiful hotel, equipped with every comfort, on the edge of an abyss, of nothingness, of absurdity. And the daily contemplation of the abyss, between excellent meals or artistic entertainments, can only heighten the enjoyment of the subtle comforts offered."[6]

I have never heard that miserable living conditions and substandard nutrition are necessary prerequisites for innovative thought. If Marx and Nietzsche at times suffered insults of material deprivation, their theoretical creativity survived, not because of but despite such painful conditions. I might also add that Georg Lukács found his own ways of comfortable survival in a political environment where many other heretic Marxists, who were not privy to Lukács's strategy of adaptive behavior, had their heads chopped off. This is an example of an older contemporary, though, not of a "rebellious son." The sons' favorite outcry, to which all of us have been exposed at times, is against the cardinal sin of what they call "elitism." In a lengthy essay by W. V. Blomster entitled "Sociology of

Music: Adorno and Beyond" there is a section called "Adorno: ad personam":

> In an age when psychological interpretations of almost all phenomena are irresistible, it is astonishing that so few questions have been asked about the man Adorno and the degree to which his own psychological constitution might have conditioned—indeed, limited—his work in music. Although this may seem at best a peripheral concern within this study, several observations demand inclusion here . . . . There are moments of uneasiness in working with Adorno when one finds in his position the imprint of that "authoritarian personality" which he himself fought so vehemently. . . . Little remains to be said upon Adorno's elitism and snobbishness; precisely in his work in music, however, it is felt that a greater humility might have vastly increased his effectiveness.[7]

Blomster is in error. The litany about elitism has been sung for a long time in many quarters, young and old, particularly when it comes to the considerable demands made upon the reader to engage in great efforts to follow the thought but not the thinker. I will return to this issue toward the end of this essay. May it suffice for the moment that it is exactly this kind of biographical and psychological reductionism that Adorno always opposed in his extensive studies of the literary arts (I might say, I learned a good deal from him whenever I succumbed to an *ad hominem* shortcut in my own critical work in literature).

I take more seriously a second paradigm, according to which Adorno cut the connection between theory and practice so sacred to Marxist doctrine. Hans-Jürgen Krahl, for a short while a prominent spokesman of the German New Left before he died in a tragic accident, took Adorno to task for allegedly cutting this umbilical cord. Although, according to Krahl, Adorno understood the ideological contradictions of bourgeois individualism and his "intellectual biography is marked by the experience of fascism," he nevertheless remained entrapped in the very contradictions he overtly diagnosed.

> Adorno's cutting critique on the ideological existence of the bourgeois individual irresistibly trapped him in its ruin. But this would mean that Adorno had never really left the isolation that emigration imposed on him. . . . Production of abstract labor is mirrored in his intellectual subjectivism. This is why Adorno was not able to translate his private compassion for the wretched of the earth into an integral partisanship of his theory toward the liberation of the oppressed.[8]

It seems to me that Adorno gave the correct answer with his often-quoted sarcastic observation that he did not know that Critical Theory had given license to throwing Molotov cocktails. True, had Adorno and his friends

manned the barricades, they might very well have been immortalized in a
revolutionary song by Hanns Eisler. But imagine for a moment Marx dying
on the barricades in 1849 or 1871: there would be no Marxism, no advanced
psychological models, and certainly no Critical Theory. The call to arms
the ultraradical disciples directed at their teachers—legitimate as their
intentions may have been—has merely produced excesses, the consequences of which have become only too obvious in the troubled state the
New Left finds itself in today.

This leads to another, more serious, aspect of this perverted rebellion.
In an introduction to a short piece by Adorno called "Culture Industry
Reconsidered," Andreas Huyssen, an editor of *New German Critique*, in
fall 1975 endorsed Hans Mayer's misguided formulation about Adorno's
"secret hostility toward history."[9] I do not want to be disrespectful of
Huyssen, whose good intentions are shown in his praise of Adorno as
"one of the first to use critical Marxist thought to illuminate Western mass
culture, which for years had been dismissed by conservative culture critics
with elitist moralizing"; however, his reproach of Adorno, that he "consistently avoided historic specificity in his work," is plainly absurd. There
seems to be an attempt on the part of these youthful followers (or
nonfollowers) to demand an activist pseudo-historic participation, almost
on a day-to-day basis and in a spirit of team-dictated partisanship. At least,
that is how I interpret Huyssen's condescending remark that, although
Adorno's "thought unmistakably developed in reaction to critical events,"
his hostility to history was nonetheless severe: "This hostility in turn
reflects his rejection of the determinate negation as a key concept of the
philosophy of history and indicates his insistence on negativity and refusal
as crucial elements of a modern aesthetic."[10] This perplexes me! Every
member of the Institute's inner circle not only was immersed in Hegelian
philosophy and the classical aspects of Marxian dialectics but also continuously emphasized "determinate negation" as the key concept of any
critical theory. Huyssen himself, a few pages later, after the first outburst
seemed forgotten, correctly quoted the following words from Adorno's
essay "Culture and Administration":

> The authentic cultural object must retain and preserve whatever goes by the
> wayside in that process of increasing domination over nature which is reflected
> in expanding rationality and ever more rational forms of domination. Culture is
> the perennial protestation of the particular against the general, as long as the
> latter remains irreconcilable with the particular.[11]

I do not really know how to explain this vogue of vague accusations
except as what I suspect to be an understandable "morning-after" malaise

in the wake, and at the wake, of the student movement. When hope for radical political change in our day or tomorrow collapsed, Critical Theory offered itself to many of the young as a convenient scapegoat. To the great pain and sorrow of its creators and practitioners, above all Adorno, it was forgotten that critical thought itself is adequate practice. It clashes with and is resisted by the cultural and, in part, political establishment, which always wants to convert the *skandalon* of nonconformist theory into a mere scandalous aberration and to recommend—and, if possible, contribute to—the liquidation of leaders and followers of Critical Theory. In that respect, Adorno's work and life in post-Hitler Germany serve as eloquent testimony to his historical sensitivity and his knowledge that only by a determined no, which he so admirably practiced, could historical progress and regression be kept alive in critical consciousness.

The attempts to catch Adorno in his alleged contradictions caused by lapses in historical consciousness are a continuation of my theme of filial rebellion. The same Mr. Huyssen perceived an irreconcilable contradiction between an Adorno who spoke, in the *Dialectic of Enlightenment,* of the autonomous individual as "a phenomenon of the bourgeois past" and one who, in his later essay "Culture Industry Reconsidered," allegedly revived this "autonomous individual" as a "precondition for democratic society." But if one reads the text carefully, it becomes apparent that, first of all, Adorno never intended to "reconsider" his theory of cultural industry but rather, as the German text clearly states, to write a "résumé, that is, a summing up of what he explicated, with Horkheimer, in the original essay. Furthermore, Adorno expressly says at the end of the new essay that culture industry's anti-enlightenment and mass deception has "turned into a means for fettering consciousness." He then dialectically states that autonomous individuals would only develop if there were no culture industry "obstructing the emancipation for which human beings *could be"*—not, as a translator incorrectly renders it, *are*—"as ripe as the productive forces of the epoch permit." The point here is unmistakable: capitalism will not provide the emancipation that, according to every good Marxist, including Adorno, would technically be possible every day, since "the productive forces" would allow the termination of misery and domination. In contrast to his critic, Adorno remained rather melancholic, if not desperate, about the seemingly unresolvable—for the time being at least—intertwining of the establishment and its nonautonomous subjects (in the true sense of the term *subjection*). This is the opposite of a "retraction" of the original thesis of "enlightenment as an instrument of rationalized domination and oppression."

More painful even than the eagerness to trip Adorno in contradictions is the eagerness to take him to task for overlooking some very obvious historical phenomena. In a recent book by Otto Karl Werckmeister, *Ende der Ästhetik,* which, to my knowledge, has not been translated, we read:

> When Adorno until the very end defended modern art [meaning avant-garde art] against an imagined front of cultural conservatism, as if modern art still needed social certification, he missed the consequences of its complete assimilation in the late-capitalist culture. Culture and police both watch over the borderline of reality and art. On this side of the border, Adorno's negative-utopian glorification of art and the affirmative ideological function of art in bourgeois culture are much closer to each other than Adorno's concept of their absolute contradiction.[12]

To this schoolmasterly reprimand for having failed to do his homework, I can only say that the whole theory of avant-garde modern art, in which Adorno was really the leader of our group, consists precisely in defending the thesis that avant-garde art is the only reservoir of genuine human experience, and therefore of oppositional consciousness, which itself is in constant danger of being suffocated through the loving profit-tentacles of the culture industry. Indeed, nobody was more aware than Adorno of the enormous dangers to the survival of "auratic" art (to use Benjamin's term).

Let me give you one last example of this chorus of critics (some of whom, I am sorry to say, I cannot differentiate from Beckmesser in the *Meistersinger*). It is fairly well known that Adorno's work in musicology and the philosophy and sociology of music developed the theory of the indispensable unity of performance and the intent of the composition. In particular, he spent a good deal of his efforts demonstrating the distortion of serious music by the technology of electronic reproduction, including, but not limited to, broadcasting and recording. I am not a musicologist, but I know something about the necessary relationship of a work of art and the social frame within which it is presented or performed, and I must assume by analogy that the horrors of televised Shakespeare are comparable to the distortion of musical listening of which Adorno speaks. (It is, by the way, at this juncture that I would like to say that I believe in the superiority of Adorno's aesthetic theories over those of Walter Benjamin. But this is a topic for others to ponder.) In a slick German literary journal I found a review of volume fourteen of Adorno's writings in German— which, incidentally, came out not too long ago in English under the title *Introduction to the Sociology of Music*. The reviewer, Helmut Heissenbüttel, did not like Adorno's typology of the music listener, and he quickly expressed regret that poor Adorno did not live to the day when the recording industry permitted variations of musical interpretation through the plethora of available records. This, he believed, is now possible thanks to the enormous accessibility to recorded performances composers have provided of their works, which are codified in record catalog. Heissenbüttel cited with approval the so-called Bielefelder Catalog, "which appears every year with semi-annual supplements," and he reminded readers that in America the Schwann Record and Tape Guide appears every month. Missing heretofore, then, were reliable guides that listed not only what was available but also what to select and why to select it. This gap has now been filled. I quote from Ulrich Schreiber's *Schallplatten Jahrbuch I* [Record Yearbook I]:

> What is decisive for the listing of a record in this guide is not its market value but the contribution it makes to the formation of knowledge about the composer, about an epoch in the history of music, about musical interpreters and strategies of interpretation. Thus a record [*Schallplatte*] is here being taken seriously as an aesthetic, not an economic, phenomenon. For the first time, a comprehensive attempt is being made in German to assign to the record its significance in musical life and to use the medium "record" for a demonstration of changes in the history of musical tasks and consciousness. The records that we recommend for the reader of this guide do not add up to an eternal inventory of classical music, nor are they merely commodities for consumption. It is the essential task of this book to mediate meaningfully between false extremes.

I can only marvel at Heissenbüttel and his uncritical endorsement of Schreiber's thinly veiled industrial enterprise, this epitome of what Adorno called manipulated listening, *gegängelte Musik*. This naïveté is topped by an insult: Heissenbüttel spoke of Adorno as a caricature of the expert who has now been replaced by a true "leader," the *Schallplattenführer*—in short, Leader Schreiber. Some of us have always been critical of guidelines as predigested experience of works of art, enterprises that, of course, only serve the purpose of rendering the oppositional character of the artwork into a harmless, so-called aesthetic experience.

Let me juxtapose Schreiber's words on the merits of a *Schallplattenführer* with a Time-Life Corporation advertisement, which guarantees that

> though your time may be limited, you will be reading widely and profitably . . . books that are truely timeless in style and significance. This plan draws its strength from the fact that the editors spent thousands of hours finding the answers to questions that you, too, must have asked yourself many times. . . . It is part of their job to single out the few books that tower over all others. In each case, the editors will write special introductions to underline what is unique in the book, what impact it has had or will have, what place it has earned in literature and contemporary thought. . . . The books will be bound in durable, flexible covers similar to those used for binding fine Bibles and Missals.

I invite the audience to make a comparative content analysis between the shrewd public relations agents of the Time-Life Corporation and the Heissenbüttel-Schreiber alliance.

On this note I shall terminate my sampling of manifestations of oedipal rebellion against Adorno. I would like to say one final word about comments that persist from all quarters about the difficulty of reading Adorno.[13] It is true, Adorno's texts are very difficult. He never intended to make it easy for his professional and intellectual colleagues or for all his readers and listeners. He would not tolerate—another variation of the Adorno *skandalon*—that what he had to say should ever fit into a mode of easy consumption. On the contrary, the demands he made of himself and his audience are only another variation of his theme of striving for genuine experience in production as well as in received productive imagination. His sense of responsibility for language, his hostility to the all-embracing emergence of a one-dimensional, nonconnotative, unambiguous language of efficiency and predigested derivative thought that leaves no room for the unique and idiosyncratic, for productive imagination and the dissenting voice, reminds me of a letter Coleridge wrote to his friend Southey almost a hundred and seventy years ago, defending his style of "obscurity" and contrasting it "with the cementless periods of the modern Anglo-Gallican style, which not only are understood *beforehand,* but, being free from . . . all the books and eyes of intellectual memory, never oppress the mind by any after recollections, but, like civil visitors, stay a few moments, and leave the room quite free and open for the next comers."[14] I do not know whether Adorno knew of this letter, but I am sure he would have smiled with approval if I had told him about Coleridge's praise of "obscurity" as a witty rejection of linguistic consumerism. And so we come to another thinker who was, like Adorno, the embodiment of the *skandalon,* Friedrich Nietzsche. In his preface to *The Dawn,* he wrote:

> I have not been a philologist in vain; perhaps I am one yet: a teacher of slow reading. I have even come to write slowly. At present it is not only my habit, but even my taste, a perverted taste maybe, to write nothing but what will drive to despair everyone who is in a hurry. . . . Philology is now more desirable than ever before . . . it is the highest attraction and incitement in an age of "work," that is to say, of haste, of unseemly and immoderate hurry-scurry, which is intent upon "getting things done" at once, even every book, whether old or new. Philology itself, perhaps, will not "get things done" so hurriedly; it teaches how to read well, that is, slowly, profoundly, attentively, prudently, with inner thoughts, with the mental doors ajar, with delicate fingers and eyes.[15]

Those of us who knew Adorno will always carry this image of him with us: his "mental doors ajar," and touching everything he did "with delicate fingers and eyes."

Notes

1. Martin Jay, "Adorno and Kracauer: Notes on a Troubled Friendship," in Jay, *Permanent Exiles: Essays on the Intellectual Migration from Germany to America* (New York, 1985), p. 222.
2. Theodor W. Adorno, "Culture Industry Reconsidered," *New German Critique* 6 (Fall 1975): 12.
3. Ibid., p. 13.
4. Ibid., p. 16. (Translation emended.)
5. Ibid., p. 14.
6. Georg Lukács, *The Theory of the Novel*, trans. Anna Bostock (Cambridge, Mass., 1971), p. 22.
7. W. V. Blomster, "Sociology of Music: Adorno and Beyond," *Telos*, no. 28 (Summer 1976): 109.
8. Hans-Jürgen Krahl, "The Political Contradictions in Adorno's Critical Theory," *Telos*, no. 21 (Fall 1974): 164.
9. Andreas Huyssen, "Introduction to Adorno," *New German Critique* 6 (Fall 1975): 3; Mayer's charge is made in *Der Repräsentant und die Märtyrer* (Frankfurt am Main, 1971), p. 165.
10. Huyssen, "Introduction to Adorno," pp. 4–5.
11. Theodor W. Adorno, "Culture and Administration," *Telos*, no. 37 (Fall 1978): 97. (Translation emended.)
12. Otto Karl Werckmeister, *Ende der Ästhetik* (Frankfurt am Main, 1971), p. 31.
13. I am well aware that this criticism is often raised against Western Marxism as a whole.
14. Coleridge to Southey, October 20, 1809; in *Collected Letters of Samuel Taylor Coleridge*, ed. Earl Leslie Griggs (Oxford, 1959), vol. 3, p. 790.
15. Friedrich Nietzsche, *The Dawn of Day*, trans. Johanna Volz (London, 1910), p. xxviii–xxix. (Translation emended.)

8

Recollections of Theodor W. Adorno (1983)

What I have to say will come as a relief for those of you who have been participating in this conference for the last couple of days, for I will engage you less intellectually—tragedy is followed by comedy, and you will probably want to laugh about some of my remarks. But classical comedy always has a serious personal perspective, too. I am in a difficult situation, being asked as a survivor to talk about people who are no longer with us, because survival always poses the problem of distinguishing between an event of a purely biological nature and one that, considered from an intellectual standpoint, is not strictly arbitrary. My countryman Goethe frequently grappled with exactly this problem—if I may, for a moment, appeal to such a great standard.

A second personal remark: when one has lived as long as I have and belonged to a group that has gained such historical significance, one is constantly considered a kind of fragment of history. And indeed, in recent years I have experienced firsthand how history is actually written. Without wanting to cast aspersions on the integrity of friends in the audience who are historians, I must say that I am filled with increasing skepticism. Just recently a portrait of Adorno and myself was created on the basis of passages from letters;[1] that portrait, however, is less true to the relationship as a whole than the one I am going to sketch tonight—also on the basis of letters. This experience has led me to reflect on the question of documentation. One may reconstruct history from documents, or one may rely on memory; I, however, have the great fortune to possess both documents *and* a memory, and these serve mutually to correct each other. But this leads to a third personal problem: I am supposed to say something about my recollections of Teddie (it will be difficult to speak of "Adorno" the entire evening, since he is someone I knew since he graduated from high school), and when I speak of my recollections of Adorno, I certainly want to avoid the intrusion of a narcissistic tone. Yet, it is unfortunately impossible for Leo Lowenthal to remember Adorno without here and there mentioning a word (or two) about himself and his work. I would like therefore to ask at the outset for your understanding of such a contradiction.

I would like to present, essentially through letters, several aspects of the life we shared, especially in the 1920s, 1930s, 1940s, and 1950s. Obviously, this selection has a fragmentary character for the simple reason that we lived together so many years; in Frankfurt, in New York, now and then in California. The accidental, however, is not merely accidental.

I was introduced to Adorno when he was eighteen years old by Siegfried Kracauer, who played a major role in our friendship—a friendship with all the positive and ambivalent traits such relationships have. I start with a letter from December 4, 1921, which I have already published, in which Kracauer conveys the following impression of Teddie: "Something incomparable puts him in a position over both of us [Kracauer and myself], an admirable material existence [note a slight ambivalence: Adorno was a very spoiled young gentleman from a well-to-do family] and a wonderfully self-confident character [here now the positive]. He truly is a beautiful specimen of a human being; even if I am not without some skepticism concerning his future, I am surely delighted by him in the present."

Anyway, the Adorno of these years—I don't know whether there is anybody here who knew him back then, I certainly doubt it—was a delicate, slender young man. Indeed, he was the classical image of a poet, with a delicate way of moving and talking that one scarcely finds nowadays. We would meet either at a coffee house—mostly at the famous Café Westend at the opera, where intellectual *enfants terribles* met—or at one or the other of our parents' places. Naturally, I knew Adorno's parents well, also his aunt Agathe. It was an existence you just had to love—if you were not dying of jealousy of this protected beautiful life—and in it Adorno had gained the confidence that never left him his entire life. For a short period of time, however, my relation to his parents was disturbed by a dissonance perhaps not uncharacteristic for the history of assimilated German Jews. When I accepted my first paying job in 1923—I had just received my Ph.D., a year before Teddie—bearing the overrated title of "Syndic of the Advisory Board for Jewish Refugees from Eastern Europe," Oskar Wiesengrund told his son that Leo Lowenthal was not welcome in his house as long as he had something to do with Eastern European Jews.

There is a remarkable irony in the fact that Adorno asked me many years later, he himself being ill in Los Angeles, to give the euology at his father's funeral. A certain knowledge of the mentality of the German-

Jewish middle class, and particularly upper middle class, is required to entirely understand the atmosphere at the time. This might also account for why—this is how I explain it to myself—Adorno had such an incredibly hard time finally leaving Germany (we had to drag him almost physically); he just couldn't believe that to him, son of Oskar Wiesengrund, nephew of aunt Agathe, and son of Maria, anything might ever happen, for it was absolutely clear that the bourgeoisie would soon become fed up with Hitler. This kind of naïve unfamiliarity with the real world—particularly that of Germany and the at first complicated and then not-so-complicated relations of Christians and Jews—must be borne in mind if one is to fully understand Adorno's personal history.

For the moment, I would like to return to several experiences from an early period, when Teddie was about nineteen or twenty, making use of some passages from letters, to which recollections can so superbly be related. I have many recollections. For example, Adorno and Kracauer tell me about their reading of Ernst Bloch and Helmut Plessner; about Bloch they have as yet very little negative to say; Plessner, however, is said to write in an awful jargon, but nevertheless views many problems correctly. Soon they drag Benjamin over the coals in a way that will surprise you (more on that in a minute); I, too, am chided, because at that time I identified strongly with apocalyptic and messianic motifs. I had just finished writing an almost unreadable "master work," "The Demonic: Project of a Negative Philosophy of Religion"—I barely understand a word of it now—and, shortly thereafter, a dissertation on Franz von Baader, both composed in an expressionist style, which caused my friends to constantly poke fun at me. For example, on April 14, 1922, from Amorbach during a hot summer: "It would be a pleasure to take a bath [Bad], which doesn't mean that you have to plunge right into Baaderlake." And they also wrote to me that I was a professional apocalyptist, and for professional apocalyptists there was unfortunately no vacancy in Amorbach; but for the sake of a meeting they would be willing to try and find a room in the next town. That was about the tone in which we talked to each other. Yet openly friendly sentences, like this one, for example, from a latter from August 11, 1923, were heard as well: "Although you are constantly with us in our thoughts, it would naturally be nice to have your empirical person around also."

The year 1923 was when Adorno and Kracauer undertook a common reading of Goethe's *Elective Affinities* and subsequently the first draft of Benjamin's essay on the same work—to which I will return in a minute. On August 22, 1923, Adorno wrote that he was "so pleasantly tired that I don't even want to get down to *Elective Affinities*." But they were still reading Franz Rosenzweig's *Star of Redemption*, about which Teddie had made this comment: "These are linguistic philosophemes I would not understand even if I understood them"; and in that letter of August 1923 he added: "We would certainly have the real chance to recover if we did not have to fear the mighty dollar's putting a premature ending to our idyll." That was about six weeks before the upward evaluation of the dollar, so I understood his comment only too well. The day before the dollar was revalued I was, for the first time in my life, in Brenner's Park Hotel in Baden-Baden—back then it was called Hotel Stephanie (we were always bon vivants) or, as Lukács says, the Hotel Abyss; but only for a day, for when the dollar was stabilized, I had to clear out of the hotel and take the train back to Frankfurt—third class. Kracauer and Teddie had similar experiences at the time.

Back to more serious talk, though: Kracauer wrote again about Rosen-zweig on August 31, 1923: "As a thinker [he] is and remains an idealist . . . and even his star won't redeem him from that—just as I don't believe that his book will have great success in the future, in spite of Scholem and his brother Benjamin." And Teddie added: "I've finished reading *Elective Affinities* and agree with Friedel [Kracauer] on its interpretation"—and now follows a comment that will surprise you—"but definitely less so with Benjamin, who in fact reads into the text rather than extrapolates from it and essentially doesn't grasp the meaning of Goethe's existence." That's how impertinent we were!

Now, to give you another example of the combination of intellectual, wit, seriousness, and concern for each other's private lives, I would like to read from a letter written by Kracauer and Teddie together, which will conclude my selection from the 1920s. On December 8, 1923, Teddie wrote, on the occasion of my marriage: "I wish you and Golde [my wife] luck; at the same time [I wish] that, as a quiet bourgeois husband, you are less abducted by mail, telegraph, and train from the protected sphere of productive conversations than has been your habit thus far."

Kracauer, however, commented in the same letter on Teddie's remark:

Such pseudo-philosophical, noble rhetoric Teddie regards as naïve, and he prefers to make use of it in small talk, that is to say, in letters, seminars, and discussions with young ladies. His own literary style is, as you probably know, of such a quality as to . . . make Benjamin's . . . scurrilous language sound like . . . baby talk. However, the young philosopher wants it no other way, and I guess we will just have to let him have his way.

And here Kracauer made a lovely remark:

If Teddie one day makes a real declaration of love and gives up his perfectly sinful bachelor status . . . for the equally hypocritical state of marriage, his declaration of love will undoubtedly take such a difficult form that the young lady in question will have to have read the whole of Kierkegaard . . . to understand Teddie at all; otherwise she will surely misunderstand him and reject him, because there will definitely be something about a "leap" and about "belief through the absurd," and she will believe that Teddie the philosopher considers her to be absurd, completely the wrong thing to think.

I am sorry that dear Gretel [Adorno] cannot listen to this prophesy today, for in the end the story had a very different outcome. And Teddie responded to this in the same letter with extraordinary wit, alluding to Benjamin's famous last sentence in his *Elective Affinities* essay[2] and criticizing Kracauer thus: "You know him; for me hope remains only for the sake of those without hope, but it is still such a long time till then."

To conclude my account of the 1920s, I'd like to mention that this letter of congratulations arrived in Königsberg in a beautifully calligraphed envelope—Kracauer, the architect, was very good at these things. By the way, this reminds me of another one of those episodes—if I may interrupt my account—very characteristic of German Jews. My first wife was from Königsberg in Prussia. My father, an old Frankfurt resident who, like Kracauer, Teddie, and myself, had gone to school in Frankfurt, refused to accompany my mother to my wedding; when I had announced my wedding plans with a young lady from Königsberg he had told me: "You're crazy! Königsberg, that's practically in Russia!" As early as 1923 he had already anticipated the course of world history and so was not behind Teddie's father in his aversion to the East.

Anyway, this letter of congratulations came in an envelope decorated by Kracauer and with the return address: "General Headquarters of the Welfare Bureau for the Transcendentally Homeless"; and below, again in Teddie's handwriting: "Kracauer and Wiesengrund. Agents of the Transcendentally Homeless. General Management at Frankfurt Oberrad." That, of course, is an allusion to Lukács's *Theory of the Novel,* but at the same time it also anticipates what my friend Martin Jay emphasized [in his conference presentation] today:[3] the being-nowhere-at-home, the homelessness, the existential exile—all this was preformulated in this humorous envelope.

I now turn to the 1930s, which are characterized especially by our resettlement in the United States, but also by the founding of the *Zeitschrift für Sozialforschung* and by our persistent, and ultimately successful, attempts to get Adorno to come to the United States. We stayed in contact—all of us carrying a collective responsibility for the journal, although I was, for the most part, in charge of its management—largely because of the innumerable and extremely stimulating suggestions that Adorno constantly sent to us from Oxford—some to Horkheimer, and some to me as well—about articles we should do or contributions he himself was planning to make. I will give you an interesting example; in a letter dated August 19, 1937, he wrote me concerning an essay on Karl Mannheim (to which I will soon return):

> Personally, it matters a great deal to me not to function as a specialist for music, for example, but to be open to a broad range of themes; for this reason I would highly appreciate [this essay's] publication. For in principle I represent the antispecialist attitude, and in this vein I encouraged Horkheimer in his decision to write something about Raffael [the French Marxist] and about Sade, as I would like you perhaps to write something on mass culture in monopoly capitalism . . . Specialization indeed has its dangers, particularly in the isolated situation in which we find ourselves.

He thus not only divined the specific intellectual interests of each of us with an extremely subtle sympathetic understanding, but he also encourged us and identified with those interests. And he was ultimately successful: the essay on Sade in *Dialectic of Enlightenment* is essentially Horkheimer's work, and my book *Literature, Popular Culture, and Society* was published as the first volume of my collected works.

Here I come to an important point concerning the 1930s. Previously—and obviously in vain—I have tried to destroy a legend about whose background no one is better informed than I, since the other parties concerned are no longer alive: that we, using financial means, forced Walter Benjamin to comply with our editorial requests concerning his articles for the *Zeitschrift für Sozialforschung* and at times to forgo their publication. It might be news to you that Teddie's contributions were subject to the same "censorship"—but without our ever having denied him or Benjamin a penny. The essay on Mannheim he wrote of from London on August 19, 1937, was not accepted, nor was one on Husserl; and in several reviews we made major substantive changes. Thus, for example, I wrote to him on September 21, 1937: "I've had your reviews copied now, and in a form reflecting the consequences of my changes, with which, by the way, Marcuse agrees. . . . If you approve of the abridged versions I would like to ask you to submit the manuscripts . . . so that they can be prepared for typesetting." Teddie then wrote to me on October 31:

> That's how it is with my scribbling; it is, fortunately or unfortunately, formed in such a way that ridiculously minor changes can, under certain circumstances, mess up the whole thing. . . . I ask you to accept my proposals in this spirit, and not as an expression of pedantic self-righteousness. I believe that they can be executed almost entirely along the lines of your suggestions for changes. Only the deletions on pages seven and nine have major implications. The essay in its

current form has already, as you know, been rigorously abridged. . . . However, I understand very well the . . . considerations that have motivated you to make these deletions. Maybe you can insert a sentence containing the idea of what has been deleted without being offensive. Let me conclude by saying that God will reward you for your effort in such cases.

That's how it really was—we always negotiated our texts with one another. Indeed, two of my own essays were not published until much later. Like everything else, they finally appeared in print via our *Flaschenpost*.[4] For example, there was a long study of naturalism that was not published because Meyer Schapiro thought that it was superficial and distorted. Well, I told myself, if that's the way it is, forget it. And another longer essay on German biographies by Emil Ludwig and others was rejected because we didn't want to offend German Jews in exile. But we offended them later anyway! Such negotiations—among other things—led, of course, to arguments and disputes; but when you don't have arguments, then you'd better get a divorce. Finally, though, what counts is not the malicious remarks people occasionally make about each other, but rather the remaining opus.

I would like to pick out one more thing from the correspondence of the 1930s, because it illustrates what Teddie meant to me, and I guess also to Horkheimer, who once said to me, "One learns so much from Teddie." Whatever I now know about music, particularly modern music—which, of course, is already old music for you—I learned from him, and I was finally even praised by him as a result. Thus I wrote to him from New York in October 1937 that the Kolisch Quartet had very cleverly performed four concerts, on four consecutive nights, of the music of Beethoven—his late quartets—and of Schönberg, so that you really learned to interpret Beethoven through Schönberg and Schönberg through Beethoven. Teddie responded to this:

> I am glad that you also liked the first quartet of Schönberg so much. I think that it is most useful as an introduction to the mature Schönberg, along with the two major works from the same period, the chamber symphonies and the second quartet. . . . I am of the opinion (and Berg, by the way, was too) that once you have experienced the first quartet, not even the latest and strangest things of Schönberg remain totally unintelligible. I would like nothing better than to demonstrate such things to you *in concreto*.

And he meant it. Adorno was an extremely generous person concerning all these intellectual things. There was no "I don't have time for that"; when you turned to him for help, he gave you his attention.

Now a couple of words about the 1940s. This was when Adorno joined Horkheimer's exodus from the East Coast to the West Coast, going to live in Santa Monica, near Los Angeles. It was a time when we engaged in an extremely intense scholarly correspondence, which I don't want to go into now. It was when Horkheimer wrote *The Eclipse of Reason,* with Adorno as well as Pollock and myself contributing to its composition—it really was a kind of collective effort. The only correspondence in which changes were discussed was between Adorno and me, though, for Horkheimer and I talked about it on the phone. It was also during the 1940s that *Dialectic of Enlightenment* originated. Having the chance, on my frequent visits to Adorno's apartment in Southern California, to witness the two of them coin every phrase together remains an unforgettable experience for me, a singular experience—the production of a truly collective work where each sentence originated by joint effort. I, too, had the satisfaction of being able to contribute to some of the book's "Theses on Anti-Semitism." There was an atmosphere of serenity, calmness, and kindness (Gretel was also there quite often), not to mention hospitality, that felt like a bit of utopia—in any case, that's how it seems today. The collective works and discussions on various studies on anti-Semitism fall in the same period as well. I myself took part in the planning of *The Authoritarian Personality,* occasionally mediating between Teddie and his colleagues, American professors, and playing the role of the appeasing diplomat who does not take the quarrels of others seriously. I quieted Teddie, telling him that what the empiricists wanted was not so bad, we just had to be patient with them and make them familiar with what we understood as theory, then everything would come out all right.

Here is a particularly interesting personal reminiscence: Teddie wrote to me on December 6, 1942, probably remembering his former illusions about German domestic policy, "I don't want to finish without once again having stated that Hitler will be defeated!" This phrase is remarkable in that not all the core members of the Institute shared his confidence. Thank God Teddie was right.

Another correspondence was initiated the year both his parents and my father died—but I do not want to keep you much longer by going into this. I would like to point out only one thing from this frequent epistolary exchange, since it reminds me of Teddie's generosity. I was in the process of writing a book on popular culture; I had certain ideas for this topic and wrote Teddie on February 23, 1948: "Whatever thoughts you have about how to organize something like this would help me immeasurably. Do you still remember your extemporaneous reflections"—I remember as if it were yesterday—"when we drove down Sunset Boulevard on a Sunday in thick fog and you conjectured how you would organize a lecture on the sociology of literature? That is exactly the model I have in mind for my present study." Such was the nature of our intellectual solidarity, the imprint of which was so strong that one could live from it for quite some time.

Finally, a few words about the 1950s, when Adorno had returned to Frankfurt. First, some personal remarks; on August 5, 1959, he wrote to me: "In about ten days we hope to move into our own apartment, Kettenhofweg 123 [which is still Gretel's address], very close to the university and where the Institute will be located. Right now, they are removing, in a frightful din, the rubble from the lot on which the Institute will be constructed." By that time several members of the Institute, some of whom are here tonight, were still working in the basement of the destroyed building, located near the corner of what was then Victoriaallee and Bockenheimer Landstraße. I read to you from this seemingly unimportant passage because it is so intimately personal and therefore expresses something of the almost symbiotic relationship we maintained, even over a great distance. A second personal document is relevant only for me; thirty years ago I was here in Frankfurt for a longer period of time, to give a talk in the Institute, and Teddie sent me a telegram on September 25, 1953: "Reservation Hessischer Hof. Most cordially. Teddie." Here I am again at the Hessischer Hof, on almost the same day thirty years later, but this time no Teddie was there waiting for me.

Teddie came back to Frankfurt for the first time in 1948, full of deep longing but also with a certain anxiety about having to teach German students again. He told me about it on January 3, 1949:

> I cannot keep secret from you the fact that I was happily overwhelmed by the European experience from the first moment in Brittany [where he had spent his vacation] and that working with students excels everything you would expect—even the time before 1933—in intensity and rapport. And the contention that the quality of the students has sunk, that they are ignorant or pragmatically oriented, is mere nonsense. Instead, much suggests that, in isolation and estranged from politics, they had plunged into intellectual matters with an unequaled fanaticism. The decisively negative factor that is everywhere in evidence derives from the fact that the Germans (and all Europe, in fact) are no longer political subjects, nor do they feel themselves to be; hence, a ghostlike, unreal quality pervades their spirit. My seminar is like a Talmud school—I wrote to Los Angeles that it is as if the spirits of the murdered Jewish intellectuals had descended into the German students. Quite uncanny. But for that very reason it is at the same time infinitely canny in the authentic Freudian sense.

Just let this important letter take its effect on you.

In order not to exhaust your patience I will limit myself to just one more remark. This affects me particularly and expresses an opinion that I share and by which I have been moved throughout this entire conference. Teddie wrote to me on December 2, 1954—sorry to be slightly narcissistic again—

regarding the essay I mentioned earlier on the genre of biography that was so popular before Hitler. It was by now perfectly acceptable to publish the essay because we no longer had to show special consideration for formerly exiled Jews, so we planned to include it in an attempted revival of the *Zeitschrift für Sozialforschung* in the 1950s. This plan came to nothing, however, and instead a series of sociological studies arose, to be published by the Institute; its first volume was the festschrift for Max Horkheimer's sixtieth birthday, in which my essay finally appeared.

"Concerning the study on biography," Teddie wrote in December 1954.

> I am of the firm opinion that it should be published. Not only because I think it is necessary that you make an *acte de présence* in the first issue, but also because I believe that the topic has the same relevance today as it did before. The genre is inexterminable, the love of the German people for Stefan Zweig and Emil Ludwig has undoubtedly survived the Jews, and the biographical essays that inundate illustrated magazines (often still featuring Nazi celebrities) derive in large measure from this kind of writing, the dregs of the dregs. Your arguments are so striking that we shouldn't do without it. And your work has methodological significance as well, insofar as it represents a very legitimate parody of the official practice of *content analysis*. To enumerate sentences of the sort 'Never before has a woman loved like . . .' [I had put together innumerable phrases in which each person states about everybody and everything else that he, she, it, is the greatest thing that ever happened to the world] is quantification rightly conceived.

And now I turn to the passage for the sake of which I selected this letter in conclusion: "Finally," Teddie continues, "I would like to say that I fundamentally do not adhere to the conviction that our works will become outdated for external or thematic reasons a couple of years after they are written; for the emphasis of what we are doing lies, I would think, in a theory of society and not in ephemeral material." I have the same response to some of the criticisms launched during this conference, which allege that the agenda of classical Critical Theory is no longer relevant today. No, I agree with Teddie, who continues his letter: "We, at least, should not pursue the kind of modernity that consists in making abstract chronology the standard for relevance and that thus represents the exact opposite of the truly progressive." I would like to add here, with a certain hope and without aggressiveness, that I've heard as well in the critical melodies of the outstanding papers of this conference a distinctive theme that may resonate longer than our critics would like to concede.

Notes

1. See Martin Jay, "Adorno and Kracauer: Notes on a Troubled Friendship," in Jay, *Permanent Exiles: Essays on the Intellectual Migration from Germany to America* (New York, 1985), p. 219.

2. The phrase referred to is from the essay "Goethes *Wahlverwandtschaften*" (*Neue Deutsche Beiträge* 2, no. 2 [January 1925]: 168): "It is only for the sake of those without hope that hope is given us."

3. Martin Jay, "Adorno in America," in *Permanent Exiles*.

4. Critical Theory's efforts have often been described as a *Flaschenpost*, or a "message in a bottle," a phrase coined by Adorno in *Minima Moralia: Reflections from Damaged Life*, trans. Edmund F. N. Jephcott (London, 1974), p. 209. The full phrase is "messages in bottles on the flood of barbarism."

9

Walter Benjamin: The Integrity of the Intellectual (1982)

Walter Benjamin ends his essay on surrealism with the image of "an alarm clock that in each minute rings for sixty seconds."[1] The essay appeared in 1929 and bore the subtitle "The Last Snapshot of the European Intelligentsia." I can hardly find a better way to express the feelings that accompanied my preparation of these remarks in memory of Benjamin. As I studied his work once again, it seemed indeed as if a clock were incessantly sounding an alarm: Benjamin's immediacy today set off uninterrupted shocks in my mind and demanded constant alertness.

Although I begin my lecture with similarities that link Benjamin and myself both biographically and intellectually, I am quite conscious that by drawing such parallels I may appear to be equating myself with him. This is not my intention. Being only eight years his junior, I might be tempted to overestimate the value of mere survival and thus see things with which I myself am associated as more important than they are in the context of the fate experienced by a generation of German and German-Jewish intellectuals. When I speak of the past, that is, of Benjamin's *oeuvre* and the memory of his person, this past becomes entirely present. Benjamin's fundamental themes—and it is not by coincidence that I mentioned his essay on surrealism first—have accompanied me throughout my life.

While the mere fact of outliving someone cannot alone legitimize a memorial address, I do not feel too uncomfortable with my task. In the relationship Benjamin and I had—direct or indirect—there was no discord. Elsewhere, I have spoken out with indignation against insinuations from some quarters concerning allegedly humiliating dependence and intellectual suppression in Benjamin's dealings with the Institute of Social Research. Gershom Scholem, who was to speak to you today, no longer lives. In his memory, I would like to read a few words from his long letter to Benjamin dated November 6 and 8, 1938. Scholem mentions a visit to our Institute in New York, and he reports: "I think the people of the institute have every reason to frame you in gold, even if only in secret. In our brief but harmless encounters, I had the impression that people like Marcuse and Lowenthal realize this as well." There could never be any doubt on that score.

The extent of my involvement with Benjamin's publications in our *Zeitschrift für Sozialforschung* is meticulously documented in the notes to his collected works. I will refer here to just one episode regarding his essay "The Paris of the Second Empire in Baudelaire," published posthumously by Rolf Tiedemann in 1969.[2] As managing editor of the journal, my main concern was to publish this essay—part of a planned book on Baudelaire belonging to the Arcades Project—as soon as possible. There were repeated delays, owing in part to Benjamin himself and in part to the complex correspondence between Adorno and Benjamin. On August 3, 1938, Gretel Adorno wrote to Benjamin from the Adornos' vacation address: "And now to the most important matter, to Baudelaire. Leo Lowenthal was visiting us here for a couple of days when your letter arrived. We thought it best to show him your letter right away. Lowenthal was beside himself [about the delay] and declared that he absolutely must have the essay for the next issue."[3]

Then, when the essay arrived, Adorno and I had an argument, which I lost. In a letter to Benjamin dated November 10, 1938, Adorno wrote: "The plan is now to print the second chapter ("The *Flâneur*") in full and the third ("Modernism") in part. Leo Lowenthal in particular supports this emphatically. I myself am unambiguously opposed to it."[4] At that point—and this played a role in the subsequent attacks on Adorno—the essay was not accepted for publication, undoubtedly through Adorno's influence.

He presented his objections bluntly, as the correspondence between him and Benjamin shows. Although Adorno's criticism upset him at first, Benjamin did put it to use very productively. On the basis of the revision suggested by Adorno, a new, independent essay emerged, "Some Motifs in Baudelaire," which we published in 1939, in the last German-language volume of the journal. In his essay, Benjamin explicitly connected his themes of the crisis of aura and the loss of experience, which he had treated separately in his "Storyteller" and "Work of Art" essays.[5] This decisive shift of emphasis in turn gives the first Baudelaire essay, whose publication I had supported, a weight of its own.

No one who is familiar with the German intelligentsia in the Weimar Republic and in exile will be surprised to learn that my circle of friends and acquaintances overlapped extensively with Benjamin's, among them

Adorno, Hannah Arendt, Ernst Bloch and Kracauer, Horkheimer and Lukács, Buber and Rosenzweig. These names also signify both definite identity and confrontation, for example in early relations with the Jüdische Lehrhaus initiated by Buber and Rosenzweig. There was another almost tragicomic parallel between our two biographies: Benjamin's *Habilitation* [qualification as lecturer] for the University of Frankfurt in 1925 was rejected on the basis of objections by German philosophy professor Franz Schultz and could not be rescued, even by the intervention of Hans Cornelius, philosopher and teacher of Horkheimer and Adorno. A year later the same thing happened to me. In 1926 my *Habilitation* as well—it was in the philosophy department—was prevented by Schultz in his capacity as dean, although Cornelius supported it most warmly.

As far as I remember, I did not yet know Benjamin personally in 1925, although the themes of our work already overlapped at important points. Benjamin was greatly interested in Franz von Baader, whose religious philosophy of redemptive mysticism and solidarity with society's lowest classes is evident in Benjamin's "Theses on the Philosophy of History."[6] I wrote my dissertation in 1923 on Baader's philosophy of society. Today I gather from Benjamin's review of David Baumgart's biography of Baader,[7] and from his correspondence with Scholem,[8] that the vanguard position of this conservative, Catholic philosopher of religion—particularly his political morality and his affinity to those who suffer in this world, to the *Proletärs,* as he called them—had similarly attracted us both. Although at the time I was very radical politically, I did with a clear conscience write my dissertation about a conservative thinker. It strikes me as an additional confirmation that Benjamin had also been engrossed in this man's writings.

Another more important convergence of our intellectual interest lies in the unyielding critique he conducted in 1931 of the enterprise of literary history and criticism. My first essay in the first issue of the *Zeitschrift für Sozialforschung* in 1932 had borne the title "On the Social Situation of Literature." It passed judgment in its own way on the then-reigning university and literary establishment with its apolitical, *lebensphiloso-phischen,* and ultimately reactionary categories. It is hardly a coincidence that these same philologists whom Benjamin had taken to task were not treated gently in my essay either. I am ashamed to admit that I was not then familiar with Benjamin's essay, which had appeared in *Die literar-ische Welt.*[9] Otherwise I would certainly have cited it positively, if not considered my own essay superfluous. Benjamin was quite familiar with my later socioliterary work. I know for example that he was at first hardly enthusiastic about my essay on Knut Hamsun, in which I analyzed Hamsun's novels as anticipations of fascist mentality. But he did appreciate my study on the reception of Dostoevsky in Germany. In these and other studies, I had essentially begun to formulate the now familiar questions of reception theory and *Wirkungsgeschichte* [the history of effects], admittedly with clear emphasis on the critique of ideology. That coincided with Benjamin's interests. He wrote to me from Denmark on July 1, 1934:

> In the few days since my arrival in Denmark, the study of your Dostoevsky essay was my first undertaking. For a variety of reasons it has been extremely productive for me, above all because after your preliminary reference to Conrad Ferdinand Meyer, I now have before me a kind of reception history that is precise and in its precision—as far as I know—entirely new. Until now such attempts have never gotten beyond a history of the literary material because a sensible formulation of the essential questions was lacking. An early and interesting venture, which admittedly has little to do with your observations, would be Julian Hirsch's "Genesis of Fame," with which you are probably familiar. In many ways, Hirsch never gets beyond the schematic. In your work one is dealing with the concrete historical situation. One is, however, surprised to learn just how contemporary the historical situation is in which the reception of Dostoevsky has taken place. This surprise gives the reader—if I may infer from myself to others—the impulse that sets his own thinking into motion. . . . A certain continuity of class history right through the world war has been made visible for Germany, as has its mythic apotheosis in the aura of cruelty. In addition, illumination came for me from a remote source, falling all the more revealingly on figures and trends from which literary history's usual point of view was able to derive but little. I found that the discourses on naturalism confirmed what you had intimated to me in Paris; they met with my unqualified agreement. What you say about Zola is particularly interesting. . . . To what extent has this German reception of Dostoevsky done justice to his work? Is it not possible to imagine any other based on him, in other words, is Gorky's the last word on this subject? For me, since I have not read Dostoevsky for a long time, these questions are presently more open than they seem to be for you. I could imagine that, in the very folds of the work into which your psychoanalytical observations lead, elements can be found that the petitbourgeois way of thinking was unable to assimilate.

My essay on C. F. Meyer and his reception as ideologue of the German national *grande bourgeoisie* appeared to Benjamin of some importance in another context as well. In his efforts to have an article about our Institute in New York published in the culturally conservative émigré journal *Maß und Wert,* it occurred to Benjamin to stress the aesthetic contributions as politically unthreatening and yet secretly to point out their political significance to those who knew how to read between the lines. As he informed Horkheimer on December 6, 1937, he wanted to try to introduce, through the back door so to speak, the radical critique of the present that informed the *Zeitschrift.* He wrote, "The closest we might come to it [the sphere of actuality] would be to approach it in aesthetic disguise, i.e., by way of Lowenthal's studies on the German reception of Dostoevsky and on the writings of C. F. Meyer."[10]

But the most profound contact between Benjamin and myself lay in our shared fascination with the dichotomy, which has never been resolved and indeed resists resolution, between political, secularized radicalism and messianic utopia—this thinking culminated in Benjamin's concept of *Jetztzeit* [now-time], which was intended to explode the homogeneous continuum of history and the notion of unending progress.[11] In this messianic-Marxist dilemma, I am wholly on Benjamin's side; even more, I am his pupil. Like him, I initially came into close contact with the idea of the complementarity of religious and social motives through Hermann Cohen's school in Marburg; but also just like Benjamin, I later realized that the way of Hermann Cohen's neo-Kantianism leads into a bad infinity.

The Jewish assimilation into the liberal philosophical tradition (with or without socialist bias) was all the more futile because intellectual liberality remained something foreign in Germany. Just as the German university and later the fascist state drove him away, Benjamin was from the outset never at peace with the institutions of the cultural establishment. Was it prophetic instinct that the school desk, the first institution he confronted, suggested to him the law that would govern his life? In the section "Winter's Morning" from his book *A Berlin Childhood Around Nineteen Hundred,* he writes: "There [in school], once I made contact with my desk, the whole tiredness, which seemed to have vanished, returned tenfold. And with it the wish to be able to sleep my fill. I must have wished that wish a thousand times, and later it was actually fulfilled. But it was a long time before I recognized that fulfillment in the fact that my every hope for a position and a steady income had been in vain."[12]

In a letter to Scholem dated June 12, 1938, Benjamin says of Kafka: "In order to do justice to the figure of Kafka in its purity and its peculiar beauty, one must never forget: it is the figure of one who has failed."[13] These words apply to Benjamin himself, not only in the tragic sense that he took his life when he was not yet fifty years old (is this his childhood wish to sleep his fill being tragically fulfilled?), but also in the more positive sense that in Benjamin's life and in his work the suffering of the species— of which he spoke in his most significant book—is constantly reproduced. It is impossible to determine—and it makes no difference today—to what extent Benjamin consciously or half-consciously brought about his failure and to what extent it was determined by the historical space in which he had to live. World War I, inflation, expulsion, exile, and internment in France—these facts outline the historical context clearly enough. But his integrity as an intellectual remains decisive in the motif of failure. He was never really able to decide on a bourgeois profession. The educated bourgeoisie, and even the less well educated, could have asked maliciously: what in fact was Benjamin's profession? Even the attempts he made in this direction are not really believable; perhaps he did not quite believe in them himself. He certainly did not follow his father's wish that he establish himself in the business world. His *Habilitation* was turned down, he never held a steady position as editor for the *Frankfurter Zeitung* or for any publisher, and finally an attempt to secure a position at the University of Jerusalem went awry. The thought of leaving, by the way, was never without ambivalence for him. And so from 1933 on, he repeatedly promised Scholem that he would move to Jerusalem, and he repeatedly put off going. He stayed in France until the last minute. In his letters to Adorno and to Horkheimer, it becomes clear that he conceived of the Arcades Project as a commitment that could be brought to completion only in Europe, in fact only in Paris. Would the only refuge he seemed once to have decided upon, the home that beckoned, namely membership in the Institute of Social Research, the emigration to the United States that had been planned to the last detail, the move in with the rest of us in New York, would that have been a satisfactory solution for him? He did not live to see it. What a cruel allegory of failure!

Were there a Benjaminian fate, it would be that of the radical intellectuals of the Weimar Republic and that which followed. He himself was most aware, not only in terms of his own person, but also in his theoretical-political analysis of the intellectual, that there was no such thing as "free-floating" intellect—an idealized concept fashionable at the time in Karl Mannheim's coinage; no such thing as the so-called classless intellectual; no such thing as the "organic" intellectual à la Gramsci; nor even any such thing as the so-called intelligentsia (a word Benjamin thoroughly disliked). He knew that, in a bitter sense, the intellectual is homeless. As a German intellectual, he experienced that homelessness firsthand and paid tribute to France, in whose intellectualism he trusted. In a brief note in the *Literarische Welt* in 1927, he said the following about the French Association of Friends of the New Russia: "The problematic situation of the intellectual, which leads him to question his own right to exist while at the same time society denies him the means of existence, is virtually unknown in France. The artists and authors are perhaps not any better off than their German colleagues, but their prestige remains untouched. In a word, they know the condition of floating. But in Germany, soon no one will be able to last whose position [as an intellectual] is not generally visible."[14] In his programmatic essays about French intellectuals—for example, in the essay on surrealism cited above or in the article first printed in our journal, "On the Current Social Position of the French

Author"[15]—Benjamin criticized attempts to restore to intellectuals an independent status without commitment, stressing by contrast experiences of radical politicization. One must grasp the paradoxical definitions together: "untouched" and "largely visible." The latter points to the necessity of taking a political stand, the former to maintaining the integrity of the intellectual. In the crisis, the intellectual remains "untouched" in his integrity when, instead of withdrawing into the ivory tower of timeless values, he takes a stand.

"Untouched" in the sense of *noli me tangere* is a fitting word for Benjamin's social stance as an intellectual. His urbanity concealed a willfulness of commitment that used even his urbanity as a weapon. In the genteel elegance of his manner and his epistolary style, Benjamin let his readers know that lines had been drawn, lines that would not allow an infringement on his integrity. He had to pay for that. The intellectual marketplace in both Western and Eastern Europe understood Benjamin's intentions precisely. The *Frankfurter Zeitung,* in spite of its liberality and the occasional hospitality it showed the avant-garde, refused to publish the polemic essay "Left Melancholy,"[16] in which Benjamin settled accounts with pseudo-radicals. For him, their radicalism was nothing more than "leftist theater" for the consumption of the educated bourgeoisie, who used this radicalism-by-proxy to put distance between themselves and society's real political and moral problems whenever they paid their conscience-money—which committed them to nothing at all—at the box office and the book store. Benjamin received similar treatment from the other side as well: the truncation—tantamount to rejection—by the *Great Soviet Encyclopedia* of his marvelous Goethe essay,[17] the genuine radicalism of which was unbearable to the manipulative Soviet cultural policy, speaks volumes.

Was he a pariah? The ragpicker (no one wants to "touch" him), about whom Benjamin has a good bit to say, especially in the Baudelaire essay, knows no disguise, plays no roles. The ragpicker is as he is, stigmatized and yet independent. What he has given up, and what society would not allow him, is mimicry, playing up to the stronger of opposing forces, to those who dominate in society. Mimicry is, as I see it, one of the most perceptive categories for categorizing what is phony, false—false consciousness, false politics, cowardly attempts to find cover. Just think of that passage in his review of Kästner's volume of poetry, which sparked his essay "Left Melancholy," in which Benjamin in a single breath pinions both the feudal mimicry of the lieutenant in the Imperial Austrian Reserves and the "proletarian" mimicry of the disintegrating "leftist" intellectual: the reserve lieutenant of the bourgeoisie, crushed after World War I, who finds a futile resurrection in the Nazi empire; the leftist melancholic who fetches his tidy fees from the bourgeois press while trying to secure the sympathies of radicals internationally, and who ultimately disappears quite helplessly in the witch's cauldron of the 1930s—these are far removed from the failure of Benjamin with his Angelus Novus-like view of the ruins of history. Benjamin remains on the side of marginality, of negativity; he remains the figure on the fringe who refuses to take part. With his persistence in saying no—the "the salt of refusal," as he called it in his essay on Stefan George[18]—he becomes what I am tempted to call the esoteric figure of the intellectual. Most of what has been said about the definition of the intellectual—sociologically, anthropologically, and in terms of cultural politics—amounts to nothing before the figure of Benjamin, who is exactly what intellect should be: independence in a self-imposed exile. Hence every attempt to reduce him to a formula in order to fit him into someone's convenient set of categories, rushing to label him messianic or Jewish or Marxist or surrealist, was bound to fail. To use a fitting expression of W. Martin Lüdke's, what remains is the "difference," the idiosyncratic, the endless searching; what remains is the unrelenting, sorrowful gaze.

That can be seen precisely in his essay about Karl Kraus.[19] In less than flattering terms, Kraus rejected the essay as a psychological portrait of himself. In reality, though, Benjamin's essay is autobiographically inspired: it is testimony for marginal existence and against mimicry; it is testimony of the relentlessness of the everwatchful court of judgment, of the daily Last Judgment. What a shame Karl Kraus did not understand it.

The following words on Kraus appear in that essay: "Kraus accuses the law in its substance, not its effect. His charge is the betrayal of justice by law."[20] The linguistic tensions between *Recht* [right] and *Gerechtigkeit* [justice], *Recht* and *Gericht* [court], that perpetually convening "Last Judgment," are decisive for Benjamin. Perhaps I can make that clearer with two quotes. The first is Schiller's sentence, which has been quoted to death: "World history is the world's court of judgment." The other is by Ibsen: "Writing means holding a day of judgment, judgment over oneself." Neither Schiller's nor Ibsen's formulations could have been acceptable to Benjamin, for they are overcome dialectically. If history is the world's court of judgment (and Hegel agrees that it is), then the victors have not only won the spoils, but they have also declared themselves on the right side of the law. In Benjamin's great formulation, "History has always been written by the victors." Schiller's bourgeois idealism, according to which the world court will have the final word, but only as an "idea," has always been reconcilable—tragically, as they say—with the continued existence of bourgeois society. And that is what Max Horkheimer and Herbert Marcuse mean with their concept of affirmative culture. Surely

Ibsen's phrase about holding a day of judgment is an indictment against the ideology of the individual in individualistic, bourgeois society. But since he assigns to writing and to the writer a role in which the writer preempts truly autonomous human existence, and thereby the passive observer or reader as recipient of his guilt appears to be redeemed with him, the monadic isolation of class society is neither converted nor overcome in revolutionary form.

Burkhardt Lindner, to whom I showed a first draft of this paper, wrote me, adding:

> Benjamin's use of "court" stands in radical rejection of "right" (law). He criticizes so-called positive right as a rationalization for dominance and violence; it lays claim to justice only erroneously. Justice must be applied to the individual, to the particular. Justice is the messianic emergence or the purifying, profane power of revolutions. Correspondingly, Benjamin also rejects the notion of world history as world court. Only the revolutionary interruption of history or the messianic cessation of history can disrupt the repressive continuum and pass judgment over what has been.

In the concept of "court of judgment" of which Benjamin becomes the advocate, the motifs of political radicalism and historical materialism are combined with the messianic element of Judaism. This constellation of political radicalism, messianism, and Judaism is characteristic of Benjamin. In the volume of material on his theses "On the Concept of History,"[21] one finds passages like this: "Each moment is a moment of judgment upon certain moments that preceded it." Or this: "Without some sort of test of a classless society, the past is nothing more than a jumbled collection of facts. To that extent, every conception of the present participates in the conception of the Final Judgment."

At this point, I would like to return once more to the association between Walter Benjamin and the representatives of Critical Theory. Sometimes it even extended to similarities in formulation. As an example, in Horkheimer's programmatic article "Traditional and Critical Theory," published in the *Zeitschrift für Sozialforschung* in 1937, these words occur:

> The intellectual is satisfied to proclaim with reverent admiration the creative strength of the proletariat and find satisfaction in adapting himself to it and in canonizing it. He fails to see that such an evasion of theoretical effort (which the passivity of his own thinking spares him) and of temporary opposition to the masses (which active theoretical effort on his part might force upon him) only makes the masses blinder and weaker than they need be.[22]

Nearly ten years earlier, in 1929, Benjamin had written: "The intellectual adopts a mimicry of proletarian existence without this linking him in the least with the working class. By doing so, he tries to reach the illusory goal of standing above the classes, especially to be sure that he is outside the bourgeois class." And later, in his 1938 essay about our Institute in *Maß und Wert*, he cites that passage from Horkheimer's essay, adding: "The imperial nimbus in which the expectants of the millennium have cloaked themselves cannot be dissipated by the deification of the proletariat. This insight anticipates the concern of a critical theory of society."[23]

Benjamin, like the rest of us, had to go through the painful process of recovering, theoretically and emotionally, from the disappointments dealt us by the history of the Soviet republic and the Communist movement from the mid-1920s on. As I formulated it once before, we felt that we had not abandoned the revolution, but rather that the revolution had abandoned us. Thus arose the disastrous situation of which Jörg Drews speaks in a review of the Benjamin-Scholem correspondence: "The cruel dilemma, namely through what categories and by means of which future-directed group the antifascist intellectual might find orientation, was the central problem for Benjamin after 1930."[24] It was the central problem for all of us.

Here it once again becomes clear why Benjamin's original confidence in Marburg neo-Kantianism, which attempted to unite Kant's moral system with a socialist conception of progress, ultimately had to be disappointed. Because I underwent a similar development myself about ten years later, I am particularly moved even today by what Benjamin says about that. There is a passage in the drafts of the theses "On the Concept of History," from which I quoted before, in which Benjamin connects the critique of neo-Kantianism with his critique of social democratic thought—linking them in the concept of endless progress, the ultimately quietist attitude of the average socialist. By contrast, Benjamin holds up his certainty of the always-waiting presence of the messianic spark:

> In the notion of the classless society, Marx secularized the notion of the messianic age. And that was good. The trouble arises in that social democratic thought raised that notion to an "ideal." That ideal was defined in the neo-Kantian teaching as an "endless task." And this teaching was the school philosophy of the Social Democratic Party. . . . Once the classless society was defined as an endless task, then the empty and homogeneous future was transformed, so to speak, into an anteroom in which one could wait more or less sanguinely for the appearance of the revolutionary age. In reality there is not a single moment that does not carry with it *its own* revolutionary opportunity.[25]

Benjamin had already spoken of the necessity of overcoming neo-Kantianism in his significant short review, dated 1929, called "Books That Have

Stayed Alive."[26] He cites *History and Class Consciousness* by Lukács, among others, and about Franz Rosenzweig's *Star of Redemption* he says: "A system of Jewish theology. As remarkable as the work itself is its genesis in the trenches of Macedonia. Victorious incursion of Hegelian dialectic into Hermann Cohen's *Religion of Reason*."

Here we come once more to the third element I spoke of, which joins the messianic and the political: the Jewish. Some of us long denied its essential role in our development. In retrospect, this must be corrected. After all, Benjamin in his time and I in mine came into contact with positive Jewish influences as a result of our protest against our parents— Benjamin through his encounter with Scholem, I through the friendship of the charismatic Rabbi Nobel, the Buber-Rosenzweig circle, and the Jüdische Lehrhaus, which later became important for Benjamin as well.

The utopian-messianic motif, which is deeply rooted in Jewish metaphysics and mysticism, played a significant role for Benjamin, surely also for Ernst Bloch and Herbert Marcuse, and for myself. In his later years, when he ventured—a bit too far for my taste—into concrete religious symbolism, Horkheimer frequently said (and on this point I agree with him completely) that the Jewish doctrine that the name of God may not be spoken or even written should be adhered to. The name of God is not yet fulfilled, and perhaps it will never be fulfilled; nor is it for us to determine if, when, and how it will be fulfilled for those who come after us. I believe that the essential thing about practical socialism that so shocked us is the idea that one is permitted to plan for someone else. The notion of something perhaps unattainable, perhaps unnameable, but which holds the messianic hope of fulfillment—I suppose this idea is very Jewish; it is certainly a motif in my thinking, and I suppose it was for my friends as well—but quite certainly it was for Benjamin a shining example of the irrevocable commitment to hope that remains with us "just for the sake of the hopeless."

In the sixth of his "Theses on the Philosophy of History," Benjamin writes: "Only that historian will have the gift of fanning the spark of hope in the past who is firmly convinced that *even the dead* will not be safe from the enemy if he wins. And this enemy has not ceased to be victorious."[27] Now that the edition of Benjamin's collected works is completed, the publishing house and the group responsible for it can collectively regard themselves as the writers of Benjamin's history. It will remain a concern to all of us, especially the younger generation, to defend from the enemy his gift to us (and Benjamin never made that easy for us—which is a gift as well). The enemy comes in many guises, such as the paltry accusation that the appearance of a classic-type edition is a burial ceremony that puts Benjamin firmly and finally into his coffin—and we all know that, particularly in Germany, although a classic may mean hours of nostalgic leisure-reading, it also means ritual quoting and being forgotten. Yet the philosopher of a negative theology, the architect of history as ruins in temporal and atemporal space, the thinker of the contradiction (whether intentionally or not, he himself is not free of contradictions), the traveler on Hegel's path of positive negation, is entirely safe from the fate of a German classic. This fate cannot touch Benjamin, and indeed, he has already survived the enemy.

Notes

1. Walter Benjamin, "Surrealism," in Benjamin, *Reflections*, trans. Edmund F. N. Jephcott (New York, 1978), p. 192.
2. This essay can be found in Benjamin, *Charles Baudelaire: Ein Lyriker im Zeitalter des Hochkapitalismus* (Frankfurt am Main, 1969); and in English translation in *Charles Baudelaire: A Lyric Poet in the Era of High Capitalism*, trans. Harry Zohn (London, 1973).
3. Walter Benjamin, *Gesammelte Schriften*, 5 vols. (Frankfurt am Main, 1972–1982), vol. 1, pt. 3, pp. 1084–85.
4. Adorno to Benjamin, November 10, 1938; quoted in Theodor W. Adorno, *Über Walter Benjamin* (Frankfurt am Main, 1970), p. 142. Also in Benjamin, *Gesammelte Schriften*, vol. 1, pt. 3, p. 1098.
5. All three essays can be found in English in Walter Benjamin, *Illuminations: Essays and Reflections*, ed. Hannah Arendt, trans. Harry Zohn (New York, 1968). The last two also appear in Benjamin, *Gesammelte Schriften*, vol. 1, pt. 2.
6. In Benjamin, *Illuminations,* and *Gesammelte Schriften*, vol. 1, pt. 2.
7. Benjamin, *Gesammelte Schriften*, vol. 3, pp. 304ff.
8. *Briefwechsel Walter Benjamin–Gerschom Scholem, 1933–1940* (Frankfurt am Main, 1980).
9. Walter Benjamin, "Literaturgeschichte und Literaturwissenschaft," *Die literarische Welt 7*, no. 16 (April 17, 1931); also in *Gesammelte Schriften*, vol. 3, pp. 283ff.
10. Benjamin to Horkheimer, December 6, 1937; in Benjamin *Gesammelte Schriften*, vol. 3, p. 682.
11. For a good account of Benjamin's complicated concept of *Jetztzeit*, see Richard Wolin, *Walter Benjamin: An Aesthetic of Redemption* (New York, 1982), pp. 48ff.
12. Walter Benjamin, *Berliner Kindheit um Neunzehnhundert* (Frankfurt am Main, 1950), p. 38; also in *Gesammelte Schriften*, vol. 4, pt. 2, p. 248.
13. *Briefwechsel Benjamin–Scholem*, p. 273.
14. Walter Benjamin, "Verein der Freunde des neuen Rußland—in Frankreich," in *Gesammelte Schriften*, vol. 4, pt. 2, p. 486.
15. Walter Benjamin, "Zur gegenwärtigen gesellschaftlichen Standort des französischen Schriftstellers," *Zeitschrift für Sozialforschung 3*, no. 1 (1934): 54–73.
16. Walter Benjamin, "Linke Melancholie: Zu Erich Kästners Gedichtbuch," *Die Gesellschaft 8*, no. 1 (1931): 181–84; also in *Gesammelte Schriften*, vol. 3, pp. 279ff.

17. Walter Benjamin, "Goethes *Wahlverwandtschaften,*" *Neue Deutsche Beiträge* 2, no. 2 (January 1925).
18. Walter Benjamin, "Rückblick auf Stefan George," in *Gesammelte Schriften,* vol. 3, p. 397.
19. Walter Benjamin, "Karl Kraus," in *Reflections.*
20. Ibid., p. 255.
21. See *Materialien zu Benjamins Thesen "Über den Begriff der Geschichte,"* ed. Peter Bulthaup (Frankfurt am Main, 1975).
22. Max Horkheimer, "Traditional and Critical Theory," in Horkheimer, *Critical Theory: Selected Essays,* trans. Matthew J. O'Connell et al. (New York, 1972), p. 214.
23. Walter Benjamin, "Ein deutsches Institut freier Forschung," in *Gesammelte Schriften,* vol. 3, p. 522.
24. Jörg Drews, "Katastrophen Abgerungen: Zum Briefwechsel Zwischen Benjamin und Scholem," *Süddeutsche Zeitung* 194 (August 8, 1980).
25. Benjamin, *Gesammelte Schriften,* vol. 1, pt. 3, p. 1231.
26. Walter Benjamin, "Bücher die lebendig geblieben sind," *Die literarische Welt* 5, no. 20 (May 17, 1929).
27. Walter Benjamin, "Theses on the Philosophy of History," in *Illuminations,* p. 255.

10

Goethe and False Subjectivity (1982)

My original enthusiasm for the invitation of the city of Frankfurt to deliver the commemorative address on the occasion of the 150th anniversary of Goethe's death soon gave way to a state of depression. I thought of Walter Benjamin who, exactly fifty years ago, on the 100th anniversary of Goethe's death, wrote: "Every word about Goethe spared this year is a blessing." I then came across Thomas Mann's caustic remark made on the 200th anniversary of Goethe's birth in 1949, in his address "Goethe and Democracy": "I have nothing new to say to you." And as if this were not enough, Leo Kreutzer only recently told us that "there is no longer any idea connected with Goethe which might still be capable of playing any significant role."

Slowly, as I made myself more familiar with contemporary secondary literature I came around. I found formulations such as that of "cultural surplus value" in *Wilhelm Meister,* or the announcement of a "Psychogram of a great man and poet," and innumerable excursions into mythological, hermeneutical, existential, structuralist and post-structuralist realms.

I therefore reconsidered the question of my legitimation. And as I was once a pupil at the Goethe-Gymnasium in Frankfurt, who wrote his graduation essay on the theme "To what extent is *Tasso* a fragment of a great confession?," and since I also happen to own a somewhat tattered doctoral hat from Johann Wolfgang Goethe University from the year 1923, and finally, as I also counted as one of the founding fathers of the so-called Frankfurt School, I found myself courageous enough to stand now before you.

In the history of his reception, Goethe has played much too often the role either of a pontificated chief witness or of a much maligned scapegoat, both of which actually conceal the lack of an authentic historical consciousness or sensitivity to tradition. The absurdity, if not the immorality involved in the marketing of this much-quoted but largely unread genius is perhaps best revealed in the saying from World War I, that each German soldier carried a copy of *Faust* and *Zarathustra* in his knapsack. One thing is nevertheless beyond doubt: Goethe and Nietzsche did have one thing in common: a steadfast avowal of world citizenship and a critically reserved attitude towards "fatherland." In Goethe's words: "The fatherland (is) nowhere and everywhere."

Chronological fate has it that Goethe celebrations, marking his birth and death in fifty and 100 year cycles, have heretofore always coincided with critical moments in German history. In 1849, 100 years after his birth and shortly after the failure of the bourgeois revolution, there was hardly any mention of Goethe. In 1882 and 1889, during the founding years of the German empire and its boast as "self-healer of the world" (*Weltgenesens*), his reputation was immersed in the dishonest undertow of the Wilhelminian transfiguration. One may read in connection with the latter date Stefan George's angry poem "Goethetag." And as far as the former date is concerned we must shudder—since we know what later transpired—as we hear what the director of the newly founded Goethe Society announces in his first address: "A great national empire knows how fully to appreciate the value of its greatest poet; the foundation and preservation of our people's political greatness goes hand in hand with the cultivation and furtherance of its intellectual goods." In 1932 the "Goethe Year" took place on the eve of the period of absolute sinfulness—I will return to this year—and in 1949 in the aftermath of the shock of complete destruction.

In August of 1949 Frankfurt University organized an international scholar's conference in honor of the 200th anniversary of Goethe's birth. The president of the university at that time, Franz Boehm, for whom I have the highest respect, delivered the welcoming address, which I happened to find in Leo Kreutzer's heretical book *Mein Gott Goethe*. In a very courageous manner Franz Boehm demolishes the ridiculous way in which Germans have quoted *their* Goethe during the stylized celebrations of national triumph or defeat, as a glorification of exploits or a covering up of crimes. Franz Boehm said "The call: Back to Goethe! does not convert us into a politically free people. It converts us into people who are destined to end up in a concentration camp should a regime of terror return once again. There is no path that leads from Goethe to National Socialism, nor to a liberation therefrom," and Boehm warns against the much touted supreme ideal of the culture of the self which "cannot achieve permanency if it does not have the power to produce out of itself a corresponding world of social and political culture." I believe that this refusal of the cult of inwardness can help us to a contemporary understanding of Goethe and thereby to a greater self-understanding. I mean to say that Franz Boehmn stands closer to us today than the great historian Friedrich Meinecke, who, immediately after the collapse of the National Socialist regime in 1946, wrote about the "German catastrophe" (the title of his book), and in his perplexity could find no other consolation than to conjure up Goethe. He speaks of "turning again to the altars of our fathers" and demands exactly that which should not be demanded and what in fact fully contradicts the spirit of his chief witness Goethe, when he exclaims: "Today everything depends on an internalization of our existence. Over the ruins of the Bismarck period we must find the path to Goethe's time." The program which he lays out at the conclusion of his book calls for "every German city and large locality to have their own Goethe community" whose task it will be on Sunday afternoon of each week (in a church if possible) "to transmit to the heart of the listener audibly the most living testimonies of the great German spirit." This anti-political cult of inwardness, proclaimed after the collapse of the Regime of Terror, reminds one of Ortega y Gasset's search for a "Goethe within" in 1932. Even if—as in both of those cases—it is recommended by two *homues de bonne volonté*, this cult blocks any historically specific and thereby moral relevance for our time or any other. Regarding such proclamations, which quickly transform Goethe from a spiritual rarity into an article of mass culture, the *Frankfurter Allgemeine Zeitung* stated in its Feuilleton section of August 18, 1979 on the occasion of Goethe's 230th birthday: "His portrait still serves as the coat of arms of the German spirit." Indeed, the entire organized West German export of culture takes place in his name: he vouches for the quality of German products. Goethe is used as a brand name like Mercedes, Karajan or Siemens.

This official advertising cult celebrated one of its most painful moments on the eve of National Socialism. Just listen how Goethe was celebrated in Weimar Germany on March 22, 1932. The Weimar correspondent of the *Berliner Tageblatt* describes it as follows:

> The minister-presidents of nearly every German *Land,* numerous ministers from Austria, Hungary and some Balkan states, many ministers of culture from German *Länder,* representatives from the world of science, noteworthy Goethe specialists (from abroad as well), representatives of the central government, of the army, navy and parliament had taken their places on the stage.

And the President of the Goethe society, Julius Peterson, the Berlin University professor of German literature (a Nazi sympathizer) proclaimed, "It is not without anxiety that we face a new century which announces itself in apocalytpic signs. Hope, however, can free us from the prison of the present. Inspired by it the Poet bursts open the gates to the future and strides before us into the darkness.'' And at the same evening (and in the same mood), Walter von Molo had the impudence to refer to the festivity in Weimar as "an hour of the *Volksgemeinschaft"* and to characterize "the entire German people as Goethe's family.'' While official Germany, either unsuspecting or conspiratorially and without shame, betrayed and buried everything Goethe stood for, within the left opposition the tragi-comedy between Social Democrats and Communists was repeated once again. In the Communist Party magazine *Der Rote Aufbau* of July 1, 1932 one read that "the unprecedented Goethe cult" had also seized Social Democracy, whose leadership, "that petty bourgeoisie drilled in prep schools and universities representing the elite of social fascism," had no idea what Goethe represents. Of course, quite the opposite is true for the Communists, who maintained: "he is *ours;* as dialectical artist, as the greatest linguistic creator of the world of form and content which finds its home today in the upper reaches of cultural history's spiral development—in the highest achievements of proletarian revolutionary literature.'' Hardly consistent with Carl Sternheim's statement of ten years earlier appearing in the left-wing radical journal *Aktion:* "we no longer understand Goethe's thought nor poets like him. We need once and for all a different artistic quality. The bourgeoisie can keep Goethe!'' But did the bourgeoise want him? Not Alfred Krupp anyway, who let his cultivated bourgeois facade down in a private letter written shortly before his death in 1887: "I ask neither Goethe nor any other man in the world what is right; I know myself what is right and I place no one so high that he might know better. Goethe may have been a great philosopher . . . that hardly concerns me . . .''

Enough of attempts to make Goethe into a positive or negative cultural hero; enough of attempts to find a substitute religion in his work. Goethe as helpmate for one's personal life, Goethe as model, as an inexhaustible source of quotes for daily life, with Goethe through the year, hour by hour? Goethe deserves more than to be treated merely as a miracle cure in the healing business of alienated mass culture—or, worse yet—as a symptom of the bourgeois world's malaise. In view of such rites of invocation one is tempted to say that one can indeed also live without Goethe. At any rate he is not to be saved by ultramodern theater productions, political or religious programmatic explanations, or diligent philology. But in this searching and fumbling around Goethe, in this absence of an historical literary consciousness which other West European nations possess, one should find perhaps an indication as to what Goethe could mean today. Perhaps he should serve as an inducement to reflect on authentic tradition and the reasons for its absence in one's own cultural life, and perhaps we should utilize this day in order to occupy ourselves with a Goethe who points to the problematic of modern alienated man. Not in the sense of a cure, but as critical reflection. And I believe that this is the manner in which one must approach Goethe. Discussion about the lack of a seamless system, of the contradictory nature of Geothe, is of course one of the conventions of the secondary literature; sometimes it is criticized and at other times praised. From my political perspective Goethe appears as a negative philosopher of history, as a critic with relevance for today, who touched the nerve points of that modern society which, justly or unjustly, we still refer to as bourgeois.

The history of critical consciousness in Germany is inconceivable without Goethe. His entire life work is a denial of a closed system, of final answers. As he lets his cosmopolitan view roam over continents and historical epochs he frees himself from the "pain" of any ethonocentric residue: He was German but more than German, European but more than European; herald and model of a democratic image of a man, herald and partisan for a liberal philosophical anthropology of—in his own words— "the free trade in concepts and feelings," world citizen (one must pronounce the word slowly; *citizen of the world*), who demands the necessity of strong moral laws and principles for the "international community." Insofar as his work represents at the same time the only and last document through which German culture attempted to establish for itself a world tradition, Goethe reminds us of the never realized historical consciousness of the Germans. One could say perhaps that, viewed in the light of the present day situation, the Germans stand closer to America and its ultimate lack of a historical tradition than to any other civilization. The unmastered past—one of those popular catchwords used again and again to describe the German identity crisis of the last twenty-five to forty years—is perhaps itself an essential feature of that which bourgeois society has become. It has not mastered its past but merely overcome it. It wants no tradition; yet while it refuses tradition it damages and endangers the life of the individual in whose very name it appears.

To clarify the discussion of this problem let me quote from the English historian J. H. Plumb's book *The Death of the Past,* 1969, where he states: "Unlike merchant, artisan or agrarian societies modern industrial society has no need for the past. Intellectually it is oriented not to preservation but to change, exploitation and consumption. The past therefore becomes a thing of curiosity, of nostalgia and sentimentality."

There is no reason not to take this diagnosis seriously. Had Goethe been able to read it I have no doubt he would have accepted it. It leads us to consideration of what Goethe already recognized in his time—and he was certainly not alone—that is, the nascent consumer and conformist society at which he directed his anger both privately and publicly. Although the concept could not have been his own, there is a dialectical structure in Goethe's critique of society. Goethe foresaw what has been the dilemma of modern bourgeois society, in its timeless historicity, up to the present day: on the one hand a consumptive and conformist mode of behavior, a phony egalitarianism, which undermines nuance and prohibits individualism and idiosyncracy. On the other hand a false conception of subjectivity, of an individualism which does not comprehend the individual as constituting a demand for a solidary, moral, and intellectual way of life with others, but rather as a private kingdom where one follows one's own ends. And in the under- or overestimation of what one really is there is at the same time the danger of losing one's self in mass society.

Around August 8, 1797 Goethe wrote in his autobiographical report *Reise in die Schwiez,* and in nearly the same words in a letter from Frankfurt to Karl August:

> How odd that it has occurred to me just how the public of a large city actually lives; it lives in a constant frenzy of getting and spending. All forms of entertainment, even the theater, are meant for distraction, and the general inclination of the reading public towards newspapers and novels is due to the fact that the latter always, and the former mostly, add distraction to distraction.

And in the letter to Karl August he adds that in Frankfurt people grumble about the extremely high cost of living, yet they continue to spend money to accumulate the very luxuries about which they complain.

Goethe's relationship to Frankfurt was not without ambivalence. To be sure, he wrote that "we Frankfurt patricians have always considered ourselves the aristocracy's equal," and he denied that his elevation to the ranks of the nobility may have meant anything to him. At the same time he expressed himself in a somewhat unfriendly tone in a letter to Zeller, written in 1803, where he says: "the gentlement of Frankfurt value nothing but money." Nonetheless, Goethe himself was not beyond financial self-interest; in a letter to his acquaintance Friedrich von Luck dated June, 1822 he wrote: ". . . as far as myself is concerned I tell you confidentially that I removed my assets from Frankfurt and gave up my rights as a citizen, in order to relieve myself of the burden of local taxes." Thus, the local patriotism of our fellow Frankfurter Goethe had its limits!

To return to more serious matters—who upon hearing of the "constant frenzy of getting and spending" would not be reminded of that famous passage in *Faust* where the individualist, seduced and rent by distraction, says:

> I stagger from desire to desire
> And in pleasure I yearn for desire.

Frenzy and distraction remain for Geothe in the realm of the fortuitous, of caprice and false subjectivity. This is not to say that the idea of synthesis, the concept of authentic individuality and humanity, is missing in Goethe. He is not far from Pascal's famous definition of authentic subjectivity when he speaks, shyly, of poetic production: "Poetry demands, indeed, it commands concentration and self-composure; it isolates the person against his will, it repeatedly forces itself upon him and in the wide, open world it is as uncomfortable as a faithful lover." Thus genuine isolation, for Goethe mediated through art, for Pascal through religious contemplation, is at the same time a way back to oneself, away from the world of distraction and capricious subjectivity.

William Wordsworth (as well as many others) shows an affinity with Goethe's and Pascal's critique of popular culture and its distraction. The opening lines of his sonnet, written in 1807, read like a poetic translation into English of the passages in Geothe's diaries and letters quoted above:

> The world is too much with us; late and soon,
> Getting and spending, we lay waste our powers:
> Little we see in nature that is ours . . .

Goethe saw a danger as well for the artist who falls victim to the hypertropy and hubris of a self-reflecting narcissism. Referring to the style of correspondence exemplified by his literary predecessors Klopstock and Gleim, Goethe delivers the following warning in the 10th book of *Dichtung und Wahrheit:* "even the most excellent of persons lives ephemerally and leads only a most miserable existence if he is too introverted and lets the fullness of the outer world bypass him, where alone he could find nourishment for his growth and at the same time a measure thereof."

The bourgeois revolt in 18th century Germany—as distinct from those in Western Europe—had only the artist as spokesperson for an autonomous individuality. But in the course of the nineteenth century the artist begins to realize that the price for identification with a society which now openly invites him in can be exactly as high as the price of resistance. Indeed, there is concealed here a more serious danger to his individuality (precisely because it is more subtle). The artist has the inner freedom to declare war against a decaying social class with a clear conscience. Yet what sort of society is it which claims to work on behalf of its members, yet secretly is able to poison the work of the artist, to impose upon an artist of excellence its own criteria of excellence, the criteria of the market, forcing upon him consent and conformity? And this is due precisely to the fact that the social milieu appears to favor artistic autonomy.

It was already the case in Goethe's Germany that the artist could not be the most important spokesperson of his generation: he was forced into a defensive posture and had to compete with what Goethe called "the weak, sensitive and mawkish newer publications." Goethe was well aware of the literary traditions of other Western societies. He wrote to Eckermann:

> With him [Molière] there is nothing distorted, nothing artificial. He mastered the mores of his time; in contrast our Iffland and Kotzebue [i.e., representatives of popular culture in Goethe's time] let themselves be mastered by the mores of their time, and as a result they were their prisoners, their dependents. Molière chastised people by depicting them as they truly are.

The category which includes both conformism and false subjectivity is that of dilettantism, for Goethe an important concept. A letter speaks of an investigation into dilettantism, planned in collaboration with Schiller, as a "task of greatest importance." It is difficult at first to determine the cause of Goethe's intense interest. The sources suggest that it was meant as a critique of artists and artistic production not meeting high aesthetic standards. The fragmentary "Scheme of Dilettantism" worked out by both is limited to listing all the arts from poetry to dance, with a notation about the usefulness and harmfulness of each artistic practice, the latter being defined as lacking competence. Little is mentioned regarding "usefulness" but under "harmfulness" we find expressions like "amusement," "sociability," "mediocrity," "conceptual emptiness," and "insipidity." It seems reasonable to interpret these negative concepts as specifications of "distraction," which for Goethe—as we have seen in the reports from Frankfurt—was the essential characteristic of the city dweller's need for relaxation. At the same time the charge of dilettantism refers to the would-be artist, the bungler, who convinces himself of being something special, yet is only one among many. Here too the connection between false subjectivity and mass culture becomes visible. This outbreak of anger against dilettantism becomes a critique of the sinking level of culture which is exemplified in second-rate so-called artistic practices.

The dialectical scheme presents itself again: bad generality, bad subjectivity, and the counter-image of man developing in a context of authentic tradition and culture. This explains perhaps Goethe's puzzling words in a letter to Schiller dated June 22, 1799:

> It is only now that I view with horror, after we have researched the matter thoroughly and have given a name to our brainchild, that artists, entrepreneurs, buyers and sellers and lovers of art have been completely drowned in dilettantism. When someday in the future we open the sluices it will result in the fiercest quarrels, for we shall inundate the whole lovely valley where the bunglers have so happily settled. Now since the main characteristic of the bungler is incorrigibility, and since especially our contemporary species is afflicted with bestial

arrogance, they will cry that their settlements are spoiled and, when the water has subsided, will put everything back together again like ants after a downpour. But nothing can be done about it—let there be a mighty deluge!

(We know that unfortunately things turned out differently!)

Goethe was inclined to render this piece on dilettantism in poetic form. Thus it becomes even clearer that in Goethe's classical philosophical anthropology—as in Schiller—the genuinely artistic is equated with what is genuinely human and true. The beautiful is the good because it is the true. And it is true because it has been preserved and has proven itself in historical tradition, in an inherited cultural context. The dilettante is the opposite of the creative; dilettantism is in the last instance passivity incorporate which, as Goethe expresses it, "completely gives itself over to the material instead of mastering it." And he adds in his *Italienische Reise* that historical consciousness is the most important means for combatting dilettantism. "Anyone who is serious sees that in this area [art vs. dilettantism] no judgment is possible except if it is placed in the historical context of development." Critical historical consciousness is always with Goethe. He wrote to Zelter on May 17, 1815: "The true can only be unfolded and preserved through its history, the false can only be debunked and dissolved through its history."

By now I have realized that despite my original intention my remarks have taken on the character of a ceremonial speech. Yet, on closer inspection Goethe succeeded in pronouncing in an exemplary fashion the afflictions of modern man: false collectivity, false subjectivity, and the defeat of the utopian idea of—in his words—the complete human being. Consonant with the concept of false subjectivity which I introduced earlier Goethe speaks of the "false striving of the individual who wishes to glorify himself." People produce slipshod work "without knowing it" . . . "Nowhere does one encounter a genuine striving to put the self in the background for the sake of the whole and for the matter at hand." This sounds at first as if it refers only to art and distraction, yet it concerns the world as a whole.

So I come back once again to my graduation essay whose theme, *Tasso* as a fragment of a great confession, I could adequately treat only today, more than sixty years later. By association with a book title of Rousseau Goethe plays a trick on us; actually his autobiographical epigram denotes just the opposite: against the sentimental, cultic outpour of feeling, against the orgy of irrational inwardness of self-centered individualism of Rousseau and his disciples, Goethe by implication teaches us that the work of art (as well as the man himself) must justify symbolically and actively its own specific subjectivity in the light of the *whole,* in other words, human society in all its contradictions throughout history.

Earlier I alluded to inwardness as an always present focus of disease of the German situation. I feel strengthened in my analysis when I find nearly the same expressions in Goethe. In a conversation with Eckermann on January 29, 1826 he said of an acquaintance: "he suffers from a common illness of today, from subjectivity." And he adds: "I would like to cure him of it." Critical consciousness has searched for two hundred years for a way of curing this illness, but it has not been found. The world has merely denied its existence. In his fine essay *Goethe's Concept of World Literature* Hans Joachim Schrimpf, in reporting on Goethe's critique of inwardness, observed astutely: "Goethe attacked those spreading tendencies which—as we can see today—had their fateful effect in the subsequent course of the 19th century and, as Goethe correctly predicted, far beyond the sphere of art on the social and political life of Germany." And I would add that up until the present day this has not changed. False subjectivity conceals itself behind many masks in modern society: in the competitive capitalist, in the pragmatic patriot, in the poet and novelist of the new inwardness who yearn nostalgically for soul and nature, and especially in the pretensions of the citizen who believes he owns his own secret, personal kingdom. Goethe said once in one of his maxims: "The Germans should avoid using the word 'Gemüt' for a period of thirty years, then perhaps 'Gemüt' would eventually re-appear." I believe that his *bon mot,* this educational advice, is by all means called for today.

A narrowed concept of self, of one's life, of one's conduct and philosophy of life, remain essential phenomena to be judged critically, for Goethe's time as well as our own. With subtle irony he spoke of how a subjective nature "has soon pre-empted its little inwardness." He said it in the same context in which he spoke of the general illness of the contemporary period, of subjectivity. And he expanded the discussion of this phenomenon, previously illustrated by reference to second-class poets, to the world-historical by adding, in a conversation with Eckermann on October 29, 1826: "all epochs in a state of regression and dissolution are subjective, in contrast all progressive epochs have an objective direction . . . our present time is a regressive one since it is a subjective one." And he closed with the following reflection: "On the other hand every competent endeavor turns from the inside out into the world, as you observe in all great epochs which were actually in a state of striving and progress and which were all of an objective nature." Against the hypothesis of the subjective he placed the concept of experience. In speaking of himself he noted how what he achieved amounted to little to boast about, since he had merely gathered the experiences of other men: "I had nothing more to do than to help myself to the harvest which others had sown for me." The awareness of a historical context, which is constituted through personal history as critical reexperience of mankind's history, constitutes the most serious critique of the present day situation, as well as of his own time. Quite some revolutionary force is contained in a statement from the same conversation when he said "Basically we are all collective beings. For it is very little that we really own and are which we call in the strictest sense our own property.""Our property"—this central category of bourgeois, of capitalist society, was diametrically transformed by Goethe into a symbol of genuine subjectivity and at the same time of an authentic awareness of tradition.

As I arrived at this point of my reflections on Goethe's negative philosophy of history I began to have certain doubts. Is this critical attitude which I have attributed to Goethe actually a projection of my own position, that of critical theory to which I remain committed? I think not. It is certainly correct that Goethe was a member of bourgeois society. It is just as correct that he subjected this society to immanent criticism. It is senseless to speak of eternal values, but to make the past contemporary is not. And I agree with my late friend Theodor Adorno when he said in an essay on Karl Kraus: "Despite all the talk to the contrary nothing has changed in the fundamental basis of bourgeois society." And it is this basis about which I have attempted to say a few words, this social conditioned, false and basically anarchic individualism which Goethe understood as firmly established in bourgeois society. In this sense Goethe the bourgeois is the great antibourgeois, the great nay-sayer. "Despite the immense literature which has been produced about Goethe, "writes Benjamin in his encyclopedic essay on Goethe, "the bourgeoisie has been able to make this superior mind serve its purposes only minimally—not to mention the questionable extent to which they have been able to explore his intentions. His entire work is full of reservations toward this class. And whenever he placed one of his sublime creations in this class he turned his face aside." As I began to work on Goethe in the late 1920s he appeared to me as the great representative of the rising bourgeoisie. The historical experiences of the last half century have helped me to understand Goethe also as a critic of bourgeois "progress."

Goethe's attack, as I have attempted to show, was directed at a false concept of individuality which is a key component of bourgeois—and especially German bourgeois—ideology, today as during Goethe's lifetime. When I spoke at the beginning of how Goethe commemorations always coincide with critical periods in German history, this holds for the present day as well. An enlightened world citizenry is needed more than ever for defining authentic membership in a nation, in a national culture, and for community-oriented individuality. I find it moving that fifty years ago Thomas Mann in his Weimar address on the 100th anniversary of Goethe's death remembered the latter's dictum: "From the heights of reason life resembles a horrible sickness and the world a madhouse." Without a doubt, at that hour, the imminent hour of Weimar's demise, Thomas Mann remembered the metaphor of the sick society just as I remember at this hour Goethe's pronouncement on the modern sickness of false subjectivity. Only reason can guide human activity, and only critique could become the praxis of human solidarity in order to prevent Goethe's diagnosis from becoming a prognosis or, worse, a prophecy.

11

Caliban's Legacy (1983)

"The burning of books is, ultimately, the burning of human beings."[1] This quotation from Heine, which serves as the motto for this colloquium, has an antecedent in Shakespeare. In *The Tempest,* Caliban urges Trinculo and Stefano not only to kill Prospero, but also to burn the library that the humanist brought with him into exile:

> . . . 'tis a custom with him
> I' th' afternoon to sleep: there thou
>   mayst brain him,
> Having first seized his books; or with a log
> Batter his skull, or paunch him with a stake,
> Or cut his wezand with thy knife. Remember
> First to possess his books; for without them
> He's but a sot, as I am, nor hath not
> One spirit to command . . .
> Burn but his books! (III.ii. 85–93)

Goethe also provides testimony on book burning. In the fourth book of the first part of *Dichtung und Wahrheit,* he reports how, as a young man in Frankfurt, he had to be "a witness to various executions," and he continues, "it is worth mentioning that I was also present at a book burning. There was really something terrible about seeing punishment exercised on a lifeless being."[2] Like Heine and Shakespeare, Goethe associated the annihilation of books with that of human beings.

Often the association was not just metaphorical. In 1559 during the Protestant–Catholic religious wars in France, a Protestant bookdealer was burned; next to him stood a gallows on which the Bible and New Testament were hanged and afterwards also burned.[3] Often during the *ancien régime* Parliament ordered a condemned book to be burned by the public executioner—in addition, of course, to punishment for the author himself. An

98

especially abhorrent manifestation of the simultaneous destruction of book and human being was the procedure, not uncommon during the religious wars, of thrusting pages from the forbidden Bible into the mouth and wounds of the slain Protestant.[4]

Caliban's calendar has many entries. The first great book burning of the Western world was probably the destruction of the Jewish library during the revolt of the Macabeans in 168 A.D.[5] The first Roman emperors ordered the writings of republican spokesmen burned, together with all prophecies and oracle books. Diocletian and Constantine competed in the burning first of Christian and then of heathen literature.[6] During the Middle Ages Hebrew writings were destroyed in an unparalleled orgy of burning. On May 13, 1248, twenty wagonloads of Jewish books were burned in Paris. Something must have survived, however, for in 1309 another three wagonloads were burned.[7] The wagons remind one of the truckloads of books hauled and burned by Nazi students in 1933. In addition to the above-mentioned Protestant and Catholic book auto-da-fés in the sixteenth and seventeenth centuries, in the eighteenth century works of the Enlightenment by Voltaire, Diderot, Rousseau, Helvetius, and Holbach were burned. The *Encyclopedia* was also supposed to be burned, but since it had cost so much money, the Church and government locked it away like a dangerous poison.[8] Even the French Revolution was not free of these adventures in the "pornography of power," as Peter Brown, in a conversation with me at Berkeley, called the destruction of books; in 1794 the commissar of the army of the lower Rhine ordered that all Hebrew books be eradicated in an auto-da-fé.[9]

I will content myself with these few particulars. The longer I have investigated this phenomenon, the more I have been struck by the plenitude of examples. They are not restricted to the European world. In the third century B.C., for instance, the founder of the Chin dynasty, Shih Huang Ti, ordered the burning of writings by Confucius and other philosophers and historians.[10] Whenever so-called Christian nations came into conflict with other cultures, the destruction of books was on the agenda. In the sixteenth century, the first bishop of Mexico burned the literature of the Aztecs, and one generation later a representative of the bishops sentenced the literature of the Mayas to a firey death.[11] Around 1500, after the defeat of the Arabs, Cardinal Ximenes, the opponent of the Moor Almansor (who figures in Heine's tragedy, from which comes the quote, "the burning of books is, ultimately, the burning of human beings") ordered, in the course of exterminating Moorish culture, over a million books burned in a public square in Vivarrambla.[12] The Inquisition periodically pursued such courses of action.

One would accordingly assume that the burning of books—meaning organized and prolonged terrorism against the life of the intellect—is an important subject of research in history and political science. Astonishingly, however, there is a dearth of intensive historical investigation into this problem. Is a psychological defense mechanism at work here? A significant literary event has brought me to this supposition. Hans Friedrich Blunk, the first president of the National Socialist *Schrifttumskammer* had the insolence to write in his 1952 memoirs, *Unwegsame Zeiten (Difficult Times)*, that he had not been annoyed by the "rumors" of book burnings, adding "such things happen in all revolutions."[13] Perhaps with that remark Blunk ushered in the revisionist histories of Nazi Germany not uncommon in the 1950s. Note how he proceeded: at first he claimed that it may have been just a rumor, but he immediately added the excuse that in all revolutions the burning of books is routine.

At the other end of the political spectrum is Günter Steiger, who in 1967 published a book in the German Democratic Republic about the Wartburg Festival in 1817. Entitled *Aufbruch (Departure)* the book trivializes the May 1933 book burnings as manifestations of "the class interests of the most antiprogressive faction of German finance capital." On the occasion of Wartburg book burnings, which I will discuss later, Steiger seems almost dismissive: "The public burning of books . . . as the expression of particular contempt has a long history and was well known to contemporaries."[14]

For both Hans Friedrich Blunk and Günter Steiger, the history of book burning functions as a moral alibi ("It's not all that important and anyway, historically it's an everyday event") and as evidence of social repression. No one has yet attempted to write a critical analysis of this phenomenon. In sketching out the following three aspects, I will attempt to make a start in this direction: 1. The erasure of history; 2. The contemporary extermination of carriers of illnesses and epidemics hostile to the prevailing political system (hygenic cleansing); 3. The liquidation of the subject.

The Erasure of History

This is a relevant and delicate topic especially now, when modernist trends, emanating from tendencies to problematize historicism, often put history itself into question, essentially and conceptually and even begin to liquidate it, as is the case with more than a few proponents of structuralism and poststructuralism. As an academic exercise, this may be harmless, as long as it involves polemical quarrels between traditional historians and postmodernists. The issue becomes more serious when it concerns what Helmut Dubiel and Günther Frankenberg in *Die Zeit* (March 18, 1983) accurately called "die Entsorgung der Vergangenheit" ("the clean-up of the past")—attempts to repress, relativize, or even deny the past, especially when that past is a horrifying one. I do not say this in order to suggest hastily that the frequent postmodernist unfriendliness to the historical is equivalent to annihilation in the material and social world. That would be absurd.

Let us return to the book burnings of ancient China. Shih Huang Ti, who had all the books that preceded his reign banned and burned, built the Great Wall. Jorge Luis Borges, in his brief, profound "note" (as he calls it), "The Wall and the Books," suggests that it was perhaps no coincidence that the same emperor who ordered the building of the Chinese Wall also ordered the burning of the Chinese past. In Borges's words, "nor is it banal to pretend that the most traditional of races does not renounce the memory of its past, mythical or real."[15] What happened in the Chinese, as well as in all totalitarian and most authoritarian societies, was the mad attempt to found anew the history of the world, to devise a new creation myth, the genealogy of a new history of salvation, which disowns, destroys, and erases all that precedes a new arbitrary calendar.

In his study of book destruction in antiquity, Wolfgang Speyer wrote that one will clearly "recognize that the burning of heretical books is in general just as little the arbitrary result of a church-influenced decree of the state as was the burning of Christian books by a heathen emperor. Because of the spiritual assumptions of their secular and religious outlook, heathens, like Christians, could not tolerate these books, which assumedly posed a danger to the welfare of their existence."[16] Erasure affected names as well as texts. No longer were they allowed to be named, not then and not 2000 years later: Jews, those of partially Jewish descent, and those related to Jews were excluded from the *Reichskulturkammer* (Office of Cultural Affairs). For the German press, works by Jewish emigrants did not exist.[17]

The ages-old procedure of burning is of particular importance. I entirely agree with George Mosse, who in his important book on the nationalization of the masses connects the burning ritual with combat against demons.[18] Burning is the only means to wreak complete destruction. Natural events like earthquakes, or historical phenomena like the destruction of cities, leave ruins behind, and ruins allow the reconstruction of the past. But only the mythical phoenix emerges from ashes, as the power-elites of all eras have known.

Certainly there are great differences between the social mechanisms that lead to book burning—between, on the one hand, regimes whose authority is consolidated, for instance, whose upper class neither needs nor tolerates mob action; and on the other hand, for example, the Nazis during the taking of power. As a manipulated actor, the mob steps onto the stage of history. It must so completely repress the knowledge of its inferior status in society that it simply cannot grasp the difference between it and power. The mob was included as a noisy or silent partner in the Nazi rituals of annihilation that embodied the perverse new creation myths of the thousand-year Reich; erasure of the past was the predominant theme of Goebbels's speech at the auto-da-fé in Berlin on May 10, 1933: "Thus you do well, at this nocturnal hour, to commit the evil spirit of the past to the flames. That is a great, powerful, and symbolic act . . . that will show the world: here the spiritual basis of the November Republic sinks to earth, but from these ruins, the phoenix of a new spirit will rise victorious",[19] and so forth. It is apparent that it is from the utter ashes of the past that the phoenix will emerge, *creatio ex nihilo*.

Ironically, it is from Communist and Jewish ashes that this Nazi phoenix shall rise. What an invitation to a psychoanalytical interpretation! Present becomes past. History begins now, at this moment, as Hanns Johst already stated in 1932, "The National Socialist state and culture are identical." No culture exists before National Socialism; afterwards, however, culture no longer exists. What matters is the celebration of the new in the erasure of the old. This celebration, in which mob and power unite, is utterly typical of and specific for the ritual character of the authoritarian mode of behavior. What is needed is the festival, the celebration—something altogether unknown in the Middle Ages and antiquity. As late as 1945, the howling "werewolf [radio] station" boasted in the grotesque spirit of *"Götterdämmerung"* during the final period of saturation bombing, "The enemy, which strives to destroy Europe's future, has only succeeded in destroying the past, putting an end to all that is old and worn-out . . . now that everything lies in ruins, we are forced to rebuild Europe." This is an absurd psychological projection, which blames the opponents for the thwarted liquidation of history.

The American science fiction writer Ray Bradbury, who wrote about book burning in his well-known novel *Fahrenheit 451,* also popular in Germany, portrayed the celebratory character of book destruction ("It was a pleasure to burn," it begins). The protagonist, Montag, who certainly thinks better of it later, is initially described thus: "The blood pounded in his head, and his hands were the hands of some amazing conductor playing all the symphonies of blazing and burning to bring down the tatters and charcoal ruins of history."[20] When Montag is finally on the path to conversion, it becomes clear to him that "a man was behind each one of the books."[21] But his leader, a science-fiction Ximenes who is captain of the fire brigade on which Montag serves, knows otherwise: "Let's not quibble about individuals with memoriams. Forget them. Burn all, burn everything. Fire is bright and fire is clean."[22] This unspoken dialogue between Montag, who becomes an individual as he perceives the character of the individual behind every book, and the fascist, who orders forgetfulness, could also serve as a motto for this conference.

Hygenic Cleansing

Here I can be rather brief. The erasure of the purportedly unhealthy in the present goes hand in hand with the erasure of the historical, the darkening of its horizon. The book is already destroyed or under lock-and-key like a poisonous substance. (This sort of poison-chest would involve a chapter in itself. All arsonists have made use of it, from ancient China up through Stalin and the Nazis. One wonders whether it represents a magical or perverse deed of re-insurance, an esoteric caprice, theft, or compulsion to collect. In any case, the idea of the sacred erasure of history is somewhat profaned and marred by the use of the "poison-chest.") The proscribed writer is already in the concentration camp or dead in exile, his name forgotten, erased. What remains is the possibility of infection. Now an orgy of anality begins. The idea of racial purity, religious purity, cultural purity is carried out through the symbolism of cleansing, for which the book is simultaneously bearer and symbol of infection. Goebbels, in the same speech in which he speaks of the erasure of history, talks about the Jewish asphalt-literati's garbage and filth, which fill the libraries. Garbage and filth cause illness. In the Middle Ages, during the Inquisition and the religious wars, an analogy with the plague was always at hand. For example, when humanist citizens of Venice and Florence tried to persuade Cardinal Ghisilieri that he might indeed prevent book burning, he answered that when the plague struck the princes ordered the burning of household goods where there was danger of infection, and that everyone was willing to bear this loss in order to protect the city. The same, the Cardinal continued, must therefore apply to the plague of heresy, which is spread by books.[23]

The impulse to cleanse also has a long history. Already in antiquity there is the concept of fire as a means of sterilization, which lifts the curse of contamination by dangerous literature. Fire cleanses. In Speyer's words, "it frees the community from the infectious swamp of blasphemous books and cleanses it."[24] At the boorish orgies on the Wartburg (Heine called it "idealistic rowdiness") and in 1933 all over Germany there was talk of cleansing, destroying, and fighting the source of infection. The *Völkische Beobachter* reported on May 12, 1933, "columns of smoke announce the death by fire of the infectious plague." How does Goebbels express it in his "reckoning" with intellectuals? Away with "this parasitical vermin who crowd the splendid boulevards of our great cities." The apparent goal is to excite disgust. One must become disgusted by Jews and pagans, by the books of Jews or pagans. And the indictment of what was disgusting in the past, which no longer exists, and of what is disgusting but nevertheless still exists, this synthesis of the diachronic and synchronic programs of annihilation forges the weapon which prepares the way for the final onslaught—the liquidation of the subject.

The Liquidation of the Subject

I return now to Caliban. His ferocious plan to rupture domestic tranquility by destroying books, murdering the heads of the households, dishonoring the daughters of the house, is emblematic of the context in which book burnings take place: the expunging of memory, the expunging of the specific; the declaration of war on the individual; the relapse from the continuity of meaningful history into nothingness, chaos; and finally the transformation of historical space into brute nature. It may seem odd that I apply these precise and very angry words to cultures which are often solemnly cited, but in every dictatorship individuality, the idiosyncratic critical subject, is intolerable. Those in possession of absolute power want to exterminate everything that interprets history either religiously or rationally, that signifies the historical anchoring of the past, present, and future. Whether it is Stalinist reaction or the reactionary Chinese cultural revolution, it is always the same. Shi Huang Ti had all those who hid forbidden books either executed—often by burying them alive, a magical symbol of extreme de-individualization—or branded and damned to work on the Great Wall for the rest of their lives. Even those who dared discuss forbidden books in private were condemned to death. Similarly, in the absolutist phase of the Roman empire, private ownership and even just the reading of condemned books was branded a crime—so profound was the invasion of the intimate sphere.

The same applied to the time of the Inquisition. One historian expresses it thus: the thoroughness of this house-cleaning surpasses every fantasy.[25] For example, a censor spent eight hours a day for four months in the library of a rich Spaniard in order to clear out the forbidden. And anyone who even printed without permission was punished with death! A university professor who quoted from banned books was sentenced to four years in prison and was forbidden to teach for the rest of his life.[26] Such practices are not restricted to the Inquisition. According to Article 58, Section X of the USSR penal code, anyone who sells, produces, or distributes "literature of this kind" is charged with "individual counter-revolutionary crime" and threatened with "remission of freedom" for an unspecified amount of time.[27] The Stalin regime burned millions of books by authors who had become "non-persons" often in every sense of the word, their individualities expunged.[28]

I wish to suggest the following theoretical consideration: an end must be made of all witnesses to any and all evidence of enduring human accomplishments which are manifest in history; this must be done in the name of a bad subjectivity, which makes use of the Führer-myth as well as the manipulated sensibility of the people, in (Adorno's phrase) a *"Jargon der Eigentlichkeit"* ("jargon of authenticity"), according to a vulgar philosophy of life that permits no abstractions and no mediations. It is significant that this magic orgy of destruction turns on the book and therefore also on that people traditionally imagined as the people *of* the book—the Jews—whose liquidation stands for the total liquidation of all intellectuality and all intellectuals, from Hegel's *objektiver Geist"* ("objective spirit") to—one is tempted to say—Karl Popper's "World III." Hostility against the written, against the text, is directed against the freedom of a pluralist, hermeneutic, that is, individual interpretation. It is the screaming of the leader that creates the charisma of an unmediated direct connection and cuts off any discourse between autonomous subjects.

In the last year of the Nazi regime, I wrote an article in which I speculated on the fate of the individual in a time of terror.[29] The modern system of terror seemed to me to demonstrate the successful atomization of the individual. The dehumanization put into effect by terror consists above all of the total integration of the population into a collectivity that paralyzes every communication between people—despite or rather because of the huge apparatus of communication to which people are now exposed. Today I would add that book burning is an important mechanism in this process of mass psychology. One of the conditions of terror is that the individual is never alone and always alone. He is numbed and paralyzed, not only in relation to others, but also in relation to himself. Fear prevents him from spontaneous emotional and cognitive reactions. The act of thinking becomes an act of folly; it is life-threatening. It would be dumb not to be dumb, and consequently a generalized dumbness grips the terrorized populace. People succumb to a state of paralysis and numbness equivalent to a moral coma. Certainly, the transformation of a person from an individual—whose essence entails continuity of experience and memory—to a mere bundle of fragmented reactions has more far-reaching consequences among the imprisoned, defenseless victims of terror than among the so-called "free" people in a totalitarian society. The difference, however, is ultimately only one of degree. The lives of all become a chain of shocks—anticipated, avoided, suffered—and these fragmented experiences lead to a fragmentation of the individual. In a terrorized society, where everything is most carefully planned, the plan for individuals is that there be no plan, that there must be no plan. The human being becomes a mere object, a bundle of conditioned reflexes, with which he learns to react to innumerable manipulated and calculated shocks.

I do not wish to be misunderstood, and perhaps I have already brought about a misunderstanding in my attempt to indicate, through the introduction of several general perspectives, that the Nazis' destruction by fire of intellectual goods is not an unprecedented event. I by no means intend to relativize, much less excuse, the uniqueness of the Nazi ritual by placing it in a general historical context. It is also a matter of a specific German experience—not that I wish to introduce a theory of the German "national character," in which I do not believe. Nonetheless it is worth consideration that both the Wartburg Festival and the book burnings of May 10, 1933 hark back to Luther's burning of the bull of excommunication, as if it were a matter of a legitimate continuity of consciousness with a quasi-religious coloring. If one looks more closely at the Wartburg Festival, one finds that despite the quite different ideological rationalizations, extraordinary similarities mark the self-styled liberal and anti-absolutist *Burschenschaftsbewegung* (student association movement) and the National Socialist Führer-ideology. The ritual of book-burning, accompanied by anti-Semitic outbreaks, the screaming student choirs, the infamous participation of university professors who aided in inciting this ill deed at the Wartburg Festival as well as in German university towns in 1933, are expressive of the similarities between 1817 and 1933. One of the spokesmen of the Wartburg Festival, the Germanist Hans Ferdinand Massmann spoke at the book auto-da-fé much as Goebbels did at the Berlin book burning: "We also want the flames to censure the recollection of those who have shamed the Fatherland by their speech and deeds, who in their lives and writings have tyrannized freedom and denied truth and virtue."[30] One of the main speakers and active ideologues at the festival was the anti-Hegelian Jacob Friedrich Fries, agitating both onstage and behind the scenes; Goethe called him "the skeleton of a tiger,"[31] and Hegel "the general of a shallowness that calls itself philosophizing."[32] A year before the Wartburg Festival, Fries had already published an article "about the danger the Jews pose to German welfare and character." Just before the beginning of the festival, Goethe recorded his premonitions about the disastrous event[33] that he later described with disgust as "the nasty stench of the Wartburg fire."[34]

Indeed, a direct route connects the irrational roar of students at the Wartburg Festival to the directed and manipulated anti-intellectual and antirational politics of the book burning festival on May 10, 1933. The similarities are too great to avoid expression of the fear that these events involve tendencies that, although they are not unknown in other countries, have in Germany again and again taken frightening form. In the Roman empire, teachers, intellectuals, rhetoricians, and academicians decided to risk their lives in protest against the emperors' destruction of books, whereas in 1933 not a single university protested publicly. In 1933 the analogy to the Wartburg Festival was clearly on the agenda. For example, the *Münchener Stadtchronik* reported on May 10, 1933:

> Torchlight parades . . . of the collective student body . . . to a public celebration at the Königsplatz. Following the example of the "Wartburg Festival," writings—Communist, Marxist, pacifist (many from a Jewish pen)—were burned as a symbol of the rejection of the non-German spirit.[35]

An evil continuity!

As the last survivor of the first generation identified with Critical Theory, my most urgent task is still the critical analysis of the past out of concern for the present. At the outset of my talk I referred to the mechanism of repression that has historically characterized book burning; it is therefore most appropriate for this colloquium to break out of this devilish circle. Perhaps a good topic of discussion would be the question of why scholars and intellectuals who are professionally bound not to allow us to forget have themselves forgotten for so long to analyze historically the social and political function of forgetting. At the end of Bradbury's *Fahrenheit 451,* an old man says,

> We know all the damn silly things we've done for a thousand years and as long as we know that and always have it around where we can see it, some day we'll stop making the goddamn funeral pyres and jumping in the middle of them. We pick up a few more people that remember, every generation.[36]

It is not appropriate to close the introduction to a colloquium like this with an optimistic remark. Nonetheless, as an incorrigible pessimist who simultaneously cherishes a spark of utopian expectation, I—with Tacitus—do not give up the hope that the continuity of this evil history may now finally be broken. In the *Annals,* Tacitus tells how a historian, in effect a former colleague, who had fallen from favor politically, was brought to trial by the emperor Tiberius, sentenced, and driven to suicide, his books burned. Tacitus, an intellectual and historian who did not forget and who thus serves as a paradigm for us here today, commented:

> This makes one deride the stupidity of people who believe that today's authority can destroy tomorrow's memories. On the contrary, repressions of genius increase its prestige. All that tyrannical conquerors, and imitators of their brutalities, achieve is their own disrepute and their victims' renown.[37]

This paper was presented at a conference on Nazi culture at the Academy of the Arts in Berlin (Germany), marking the passage of fifty years since the Nazi book burnings in 1933.

Notes

1. Heinrich Heine, "Almansor: Eine Tragödie," *Samtliche Werke,* ed. Hans Kaufmann, vol. 4 (Münich: Kindler, 1964), pp. 143–216.
2. Johann Wolfgang von Goethe, *Dichtung und Wahrheit, Samtliche Werke,* ed. Edvard von der Hellen, vol. 22, introduction and annotation Richard Meyer (Stuttgart and Berlin: Cotta, n.d.), pp. 176–77.
3. Cf. Natalie Zemon Davis, *Society and Culture in Early Modern France* (Stanford, Calif.: Stanford University Press, 1965), p. 322 n. 81.
4. Cf. Davis, p. 157.
5. Cf. for example Clarence A. Forbes, "Books for the Burning," *Transactions and Proceedings of the American Philological Associations* 67 (1936), pp. 118–19.
6. Cf. Forbes, *passim;* W. Speyer, "Büchervernichtung," *Jahrbuch für Antike und Christentum* 13 (1970), pp. 123–52; and Frederick H. Cramer, "Bookburning and Censorship in Ancient Rome," *Journal of the History of Ideas* 6 (1945), pp. 157–96.
7. Cf. Henry Charles Lee, *A History of the Inquisition of the Middle Ages,* vol. 1 (New York: Russell and Russell, 1958), p. 555.
8. Cf. Robert Shackleton, *Censure and Censorship: Impediments to Free Publication in the Age of Enlightenment* (Austin: University of Texas Press, 1975), p. 19.
9. Cf. Leon Poliakov, *The History of Anti-Semitism,* trans. Richard Howard (New York: Vanguard Press, 1965), pp. 222–23.
10. Cf. Edwin O. Reischauer, John K. Fairbanks, and Albert M. Craig, *East Asia: Tradition and Transformation* (Boston: Houghton Mifflin, 1973), p. 88. Cf. also K. S. Latourette, *The Chinese: Their History and Culture* (New York: Macmillan, 1934), pp. 91–97.
11. Cf. Victor Wolfgang von Hagen, *The Aztec and Maya Papermakers* (New York: J. J. Augustin, 1944), pp. 31–33.
12. Cf. Henry Kamen, *The Spanish Inquisition* (London: White Lion, 1965), p. 98.
13. Quoted in Karl Dietrich Bracher, *Die Deutsche Diktatur: Entstehung, Struktur, Folgen des Nationalsozialismus* (Cologne: Kiepenheuer & Witsch, 1969), p. 281.
14. Günter Steiger. *Aufbruch, Urburschenschaft und Wartburgfest* (Leipzig: Urania Verlag, 1967), pp. 115–16.
15. Jorge Luis Borges, *Labyrinths* (New York: New Directions, 1964), p. 186.
16. Speyer, pp. 128–29.
17. Cf. Elke Fröhlich, "Die kulturpolitische Konferenz des Reichspropagandaministeriums," *Vierteljahrshefte für Zeitgeschichte* 22 (1974), p. 368.
18. Cf. George L. Mosse, *The Nationalization of the Masses: Political Symbolism and Mass Movements in Germany from the Napoleonic Wars through the Third Reich* (New York: H. Fertig, 1975), p. 41 and passim.
19. Quoted by Hildegard Brenner, in *Die Kunstpolitik des Nationalsozialismus* (Reinbek bei Hamburg: Rowohlt, 1963), pp. 47–48.

20. Ray Bradbury, *Fahrenheit 451* (New York: Ballentine Books, 1953), p. 3.
21. Ibid., p. 47.
22. Ibid., pp. 54–55.
23. Paul F. Grendler, *The Roman Inquisition and the Venetian Press, 1540–1605* (Princeton, N.J.: Princeton University Press, 1977), pp. 119–20.
24. Speyer, p. 127.
25. Kamen, p. 99.
26. Compare Kamen.
27. Quoted in Roy A. Medvedev, *Let History Judge: The Origins and Consequences of Stalinism* (New York: Knopf, 1971), p. 560.
28. Cf. Medvedev, p. 524.
29. Leo Löwenthal, "Terror's Atomization of Man. The Second Article in a Series on the Crisis of the Individual," *Commentary* I (1946): pp. 1–8.
30. Quoted in Steiger, p. 111.
31. Johann Wolfgang von Goethe, *Werke,* vol. 23 (Zürich: Kanzler von Müller, 1950), p. 24.
32. G. W. F. Hegel, *Grundlinien der Philosophie des Rechts: Vorrede* (Leipzig: F. Meiner, 1921), pp. 8–9.
33. See note 32.
34. Goethe to Zelter, December 16, 1817, *Werke* 21, p. 254.
35. Quoted by Joseph Wulf, *Literatur und Dichtung im Dritten Reich. Eine Dokumentation* (Gutersloh: S. Mohn, 1963), pp. 59–60.
36. Bradbury, p. 146.
37. Tacitus, *The Annals of Imperial Rome* (New York: Penguin, 1956), p. 175.

12

Sociology of Literature in Retrospect (1981)

For more than a half century I have primarily concerned myself with the sociology of literature and the problem of mass culture. With financial support from the Institute of Social Research at the University of Frankfurt, I began in 1926 with studies on German writers in the nineteenth century.[1] Discernible in these studies is the socially critical spirit that motivated this group of then still young scholars to reject conventional research methods and to seek a new and bolder mode of analyzing material in the social and human sciences—in short, to dare to break through the walls of the academic ivory tower, where specialists pursued their professional interests without any social or moral consciousness. I had the privilege of being one of the first members of this group, which I joined in 1926 at the invitation of Max Horkheimer and Friedrich Pollock.

The years of my academic training were devoted to the study of sociology and literature. Later, in my first independent work, I attempted to apply what I had learned from Marx, Freud, and the great philosophical tradition of Europe to a new appraisal of European literature since the Renaissance. Like many other intellectuals in my circles of that time, I was convinced of the decadence of Western society. All of us felt Hitler's threatening advance, and the rest of the so-called civilized world we considered to be impaired. We strove, each according to his own knowledge and inclination, to interpret historical and contemporary problems in such a way as to reveal their socially regressive or progressive character. We rejected the concept of a "value-free science" as an unpardonable renunciation of the moral responsibility of those who, amid the general misery of average people, had the good fortune to lead the life of an intellectual. If some of the formulations in what follows appear partisan or even angry, I offer no apologies. On the contrary, I would be pleased by such accusations. There was reason enough for anger—in the scientific enterprise as well as in public life.

110

Since my school days I have been attracted to literature, and it is certainly no coincidence that I spent several years as a German teacher at a *Gymnasium* in Frankfurt before joining the Institute. I suspect that from the outset I tended toward literary criticism, for as a high school student and young teacher I had experienced the utterly banal approach to the teaching of literature practiced by most instructors and supported by the officially approved textbooks. More than anything, however, I was irritated by the utterly conventional choice of literary texts. Because I lived through the years after World War I as a politically rebellious, if not out-and-out revolutionary, young man, it seemed to me quite natural to apply the practical experience gained in school and in politics to my theoretical endeavors within the academy.

I soon discovered that I was quite isolated in my attempts to pursue the sociology of literature. In any case, it was almost impossible to find allies in approaching this task from the perspective of a critical theory of society. To be sure, there were Franz Mehring's articles, which I read with interest and profit; but despite the admirable decency and the uncompromising political radicalism of the author, his writings hardly went beyond the limits of a socialist journalist writing in essentially the same style about literature as about politics and the economy. Georg Lukács hadn't yet published his impressive series of essays on Marxist aesthetics and literary interpretation. Of course, I was deeply touched and influenced by his fine little book *The Theory of the Novel* (1920), which I learned practically by heart. Besides Levin Schücking's small volume on the sociology of literary taste, the only other major influence I can recall was Georg Brandes's monumental work on the literary currents of the nineteenth century.

Nonetheless, I had the courage, or even the hubris, to plan an ambitious, socially critical series on French, English, Spanish, and German literature, the beginning of which was to consist of the above-mentioned studies. My attention was especially focused on the writers and literary schools that the German literary establishment either punished by total silence (''Young Germany'' and Friedrich Spielhagen, for example), raised up into the clouds of idealistic babble (Goethe and the Romantics), or relegated to quasi-folklore anthropology (C. F. Meyer and Gottfried Keller).

In these studies, I limited myself to the narrative forms of literature; for reasons I hold to be sociologically and artistically valid, I believe that novels and stories represent the most significant aspect of German literature in the nineteenth century. While I am in no way ashamed of these documents of my youth, I am conscious of their weaknesses. If I were to write them over again, I would certainly be less sure of some of the direct connections I drew between literature and writers on the one hand, and between literature and the social infrastructure on the other. In later publications I attempted to analyze with greater circumspection the mediation between substructure and superstructure, between social currents and ideologies; but my views on the social world and the necessity to combine social theory and literary analysis have not changed in any essential way. In the last decades the sociology of literature has become progressively more fashionable. The writings of my contemporaries have often amazed me because some—frequently in unnecessarily complicated and esoteric language—are so concerned with "mediation" that the connections between social being and social consciousness become almost obscured.

I

The first issue of the *Zeitschrift für Sozialforschung*—the only one we managed to publish in Germany before the Hitler-night descended—gives an indication of what Critical Theory means: namely, a perspective, based on a shared critical fundamental attitude, that applies to all cultural phenomena without ever claiming to be a system. It includes critical analysis of philosophy, economics, psychology, music, and literature.

Critical Theory—a term, by the way, that we began to use only in the late 1930s—should not, then, be understood as anything more than this collective "common denominator." As the only survivor of the founding years in the 1920s, I feel almost ill at ease. . . . Why should I survive and not the others, who in 1926 invited me to join an intellectual alliance they had created in an institutionalized form two years earlier? We did not speak of "Critical Theory" at that time, and the thought of a "school" was certainly far from us. We were and remained "Nay-sayers," in the tradition of Hegel's particular form of negation; each one of us tried to express what was wrong in his particular field and, therefore, in our society. We were consciously on the periphery of established power. Even now, as you will see, this position on the periphery, this marginality, remains for me in my work, and perhaps even in my own perception of life, the most important category. What I have tried to do in the last fifty years is guided by my unbroken commitment to the European literary heritage and simultaneously to the critique of the production of commodities and words for a manipulated and manipulable mass market. I shall now try to sketch my critical approach.

II

First, the most important thing to stress is that art and consumer goods must be held strictly apart. I cannot accept any of the current radical attempts, either in Germany or in the United States, to do away with this distinction. To be sure, the consumption of high art can also turn into mass culture and play its part in manipulating society. I need only remind you of Wagner's role during the Hitler years, about which Adorno has written extensively. More peculiar examples are found in the history of theater direction, for example, when bourgeois common sense trivializes the socially inherent tragedy of marriage and love. Here I am thinking of an eighteenth-century English production of *Othello* in which the Moor did not kill Desdemona in the final scene but rather realized his own mistake and asked her forgiveness so that they could be eternally happy on earth; or, for another example, when in a turn-of-the-century staging of Ibsen's *Doll's House* in Munich, Nora, at the end of the play, closed the door not from the outside but from within and returned to her boring husband—for, after all, a woman's place is in the home. These are certainly examples that reflect the social climate. In contrast, certain materials, originally produced as articles of consumption, can sometimes—if seldom—pass into the realm of folk art, or rather of folkloric mythology. But those are borderline cases. And I must not neglect to point out certain differences between the American and the European scene. In the United States the sociology of literature is more or less limited to content analysis and the study of the effects of mass culture, with particular emphasis on commercial and political propaganda. The model used in these studies is behavioristic, that is, unhistorical; sociology of literature in the sense of an analysis of art remains suspect. I sense today in Europe an inclination to perceive a work of art merely as a manifestation of ideology, which strips it of its specific integrity, that is, its historically conditioned, but also rationally creative and cognitive, role. To put it in a more provocative form: Marxist literary criticism is not merely totally adequate, it is indispensable in the analysis of mass culture. It must, however, be applied with utter caution to art itself and must, as a critique of social illusions, limit itself to the residues that are unequivocally ideological in nature.

To put it in even stronger terms: art teaches, and mass culture is learned; therefore, a sociological analysis of art must be cautious, supplementary, and selective, whereas a sociological analysis of mass culture must be all-inclusive, for its products are nothing more than the phenomena and symptoms of the process of the individual's self-resignation in a wholly administered society.

III

I would like to speak first of the sociology of literature as art. Adorno once said, "Works of art . . . have their greatness only insofar as they let speak what ideology conceals. They transcend, whether they want to or not, false consciousness." Literature is not ideology. We are not engaged in research on ideology; rather, we have to focus our attention on the special truth, the specifically cognitive aspect, that the literary work imparts. This does not mean "new criticism"; on the contrary, it implies studying the social history of art and its reception, as suggested in Marx's comments on Greek tragedy and the novels of Balzac. At this point I would like to identify the great themes of literature as I perceive them from a sociologically critical perspective. To begin with the most general: literature is the only dependable source for human consciousness and self-consciousness, for the individual's relationship to the world as experience. The process of socialization—that is, the social ambience of the private, the intimate, and the individual—is raised to consciousness by the artist, not only for his time but also for our time, and thereby functions as a constant corrective to our false consciousness. Awareness of this aspect of art has come to be an important issue on the intellectual agenda only in the past fifty years, when the Western world entered into a severe crisis with the rise of totalitarianism. The sociology of art is indeed one of Minerva's owls. The sociology of literature, rightly understood, should interpret what seems furthest removed from society as the most valid key to understanding society, especially its defects. Psychoanalysis, by the way, in revealing the social dimension of the most intimate aspects of body and psyche, is a good model for what I am attempting to express. Of particular importance to me is the role of a critical sociology of literature in the analysis of the social ambience of the intimate and the private, the revealing of the sociological determination of such phenomena as love, friendship, the human being's relationship to nature, self-image, and the like. This approach does not mean reductionism, however. Literature is no mere site to be plundered. I reject all attempts to regard literature as a tool for learning facts about such institutions as the economy, the state, and the legal system. Social scientists and social historians should be forbidden from regarding literature as a source for raw materials. Literature teaches us to understand the success or failure of the socialization of individuals in concrete historical moments and situations. The novels of Stendhal, for instance—in particular, *Lucien Leuwen*—would be a perfect source for studying the transitions of forms of experience from a feudal to an aristocratic to a bourgeois type of individual.

If what I have said thus far seems too formalistic, let me assure you that a critical perspective is absolutely necessary. When I speak of the history of the individual's socialization, I also speak of the history of his sufferings, and of his passions. The literature I am familiar with, that of Western Europe since 1600, is the history of human passion in our everpresent crisis, the long-endured story of tension, promises, betrayal, and death. The literature of bourgeois society makes the permanent crisis of the individual apparent. A criterion of literature as art demands assessing whether and to what extent the crisis is manifested as being permanent. And thus we enter the precarious realm of the fringe, or marginality.

The most extreme form of the marginal existence, that is, the conscious or unconscious critique of society, is expressed in the emphatic utterances of those characters who know humanity's death sentence to be already sealed before we enter the so-called fullness of social life. Stendhal had one figure, with whom he identified, say in *The Charterhouse of Parma* "I can see nothing other than a death sentence which characterizes a real human being . . . . Everything else can be bought." And a half century later, Walter Pater assured us in his *The Renaissance: Studies in Art and Poetry:*

> Well, we are all *condamnés,* as Victor Hugo says: we are all under a sentence of death but with a sort of indefinite reprieve—*les hommes sont tous condamnés à mort avec des sursis indéfinis:* we have an interval, and then our place knows us no more. Some spend this interval in listlessness, some in high passions, the wisest, at least among "the children of this world," in art and song.[2]

This means, in the language of a neo-Romantic, that art alone communicates what is truly good in human life and experience; it is a promise of happiness that remains unfulfilled.

Here I come to the most significant aspect of marginality, namely, the sociology of the artist himself. He has a skewed view of the world. By looking at the world obliquely, he sees it correctly, for it is indeed distorted. The artist is no Cartesian but rather a dialectician focusing on the idiosyncratic, on that which does not fit into the system. In short, he is concerned with human costs and thus becomes an ally of Critical Theory, of the critical perspective that is itself a part of critical praxis.

The marginal in the work of art is represented by groups, situations, and protagonists.

First, from the perspective of Critical Theory, the literary artist becomes our ally as the spokesman for the *collective of outcasts,* of the poor, the beggars, the criminals, the insane, in short, of all those who bear the burden of society. Here, however, the true dialectic of art is immediately apparent, making it meaningless to interpret it, in the sense of Adorno's remark cited above, as mere ideology. In the writer's representation— which comes nearer to reality than unmediated reality itself—the collectivity of those excluded from profits and privileges is shown to be the true first nature of humankind. In the collectivity of misery, the possibility of true humanity is revealed not as distortion, but as an immanent indictment. It is a dialectical irony that those who least correspond to a trivial bourgeois-ideological concept of the individual bear the mark of liberated, autonomous humaneness.

Here I may perhaps refer to my analysis of the works of Cervantes as an example of social groups on the periphery:

> There are two, not mutually exclusive, ways of looking at the marginal figures of Cervantes; they are the refuse of a society that has cast them aside, and they are, by virtue of their own right, moralists. . . .
>
> All these marginal creatures, the beggars, the crooks, the gypsies, the insane, constitute "overheads" of society, to which they are either unwilling to belong or from which they are forcibly excluded. But while they are accused, indicted, and confined, they themselves in turn are accusers. Their very existence denounces a world they never made and which wants no part of them. The artist, in giving these people a voice, may seek to inspire uneasiness on the part of those who have profited by the prevailing order. The author's voice is the voice of the losers. The other aspect in which the marginal figures may be viewed leads us back to the concept of the utopian. The marginal figures not only serve the negative function of indicting the social order; they also positively demonstrate the true idea of man. They all serve to show the possibilities of Utopia, where everyone has the freedom to be his own deviant case—with the result that the very phenomenon of deviation disappears. The outcast society of robbers and thieves who are plying their trade on the fringes of Seville, and the society of gypsies encamped on the outskirts of Madrid, are grotesque utopian prototypes: everybody works according to his own talents, and everything is shared by everybody. . . .
>
> The meaning of Cervantes' critical idealism is even clearer in *The Little Gypsy*. . . . The tribal chief says, "We observe inviolably the law of friendship; no one solicits the object of another man's affection; we live free from the bitter curse of jealousy. . . ." Thus at the threshold of the new society Cervantes describes the law by which it operates and confronts it with its professed measure: the autonomous and morally responsible individual. And this responsible and independent man is to be found only at the margin of society, which at once produces and expels him.[3]

The most extreme case in which a critical perspective attempts to highlight the cognitive character of peripheral groups portrayed by literature is that of woman. Ever since the Renaissance, the literary artist has made female protagonists the true revolutionary critics of a defective society. Ibsen once said, "Modern society is not a human society; it is merely a society of males." However, this disenfranchisement of woman has not only negative but also positive consequences.

Ibsen's men never practice what they preach, and the only principle by which they live—the materialism of personal gain—they never admit. The women, too, are materialistic, but their materialism is clearly of a different nature, and it is, above all, openly articulated. It is a conscious dramatic irony that morality is preached by the egotists, whereas egotism is preached by the moralists.

Second, *situation-marginality* and group-marginality are very closely related. Significant examples are found in Shakespeare's plays, especially in *The Tempest, King Lear,* and *Timon of Athens,* where the characters are driven out into the wilderness of unsocialized nature. Here nature is not perceived as raw material to be abused and exploited by a class society's lust for power—an exploitation that parallels that of the marginal groups of society of which I just spoke. When in these plays nature emphatically appears in the form of the untamed elements, it heralds at the same time a reconciliation of nature and man. Outraged nature forms an alliance with outraged man in order to indict an evil society. In *The Tempest* this is made very clear, as unmastered nature leads the human being's second nature, his reified and socialized mask, back to his true nature. The marginal situation of absolute poverty (not to be confused with Robinson Crusoe's situation), which initially besets Prospero, Lear, and Timon, eventually turns into a blessing and thus represents the anticipation of utopia. Implicitly or explicitly (and this I can only boldly assert without proof), utopia—the reconciliation of human nature and nature—remains the fundamental theme of authentic literature.

Third, where the *protagonist* himself appears as a peripheral figure, the synthesis between marginal groups and marginal situations has been reached, or at least anticipated, all the way from Rabelais's Pantagruel to, if you will, Günter Grass's *The Tin Drum,* and into the present—here, the identity of the average person in class society and that of the protagonist are totally incompatible. Don Quixote is symbolic of a critique of bourgeois society, of its manipulated conformism from its late feudal forms around 1600 up to the present day. He is the ahistorical symbol of a genuine historical materialism. In every situation he is insane—that is, he is sane; in every encounter he is irrational—that is, he is rational. He is the only one who is really happy, nearly fulfilled—precisely because he sees society from an oblique critical perspective and "straightens it out" by his fantastic deeds. By converting his critical idealism into practice, he represents the fulfillment of the potential of every individual. Although he is destroyed and finally dies, he still stands for the premonition of what life could be. His fantasies anticipate what remains invisible in this damaged world. To quote Hegel:

> We find in Don Quixote a noble nature in whose adventure chivalry goes mad, the substance of such adventures being placed at the center of a stable and well-

defined state of things whose external character is copied with exactness from nature. . . . In all the madness of his mind and his enterprise he is a completely consistent soul, or rather his madness lies in this, that he is and remains securely rooted in himself and his enterprise.[4]

In short, in him, through him, the identity of theory and practice is realized.

Before I turn briefly to the topic of mass culture, I would like, as a transition, to refer once more to Stendhal, who to my mind is the master analyst of the experience of socialization, and who, if in a now dated way, anticipates a social climate in which genuine experience becomes completely overpowered by conformism. And this is indeed the essential characteristic of mass culture. When, in *Lucien Leuwen,* Lucien can endure the decadent restoration society as little as the *juste-milieu* of the new bourgeois world, he toys—as does the hero of *Wilhelm Meister's Travels*—with the idea of emigrating to America. This quotation speaks for itself:

All Lucien's sensations had been so dreary since he came to Nancy that for want of anything better to do, he let this republican epistle absorb his attention. "The best thing to do would be for them all to sail to America. . . . And would I sail with them? I am not quite such an imbecile! . . . I should be bored in America among men who are, it is true, perfectly just and reasonable, but coarse, and who think of nothing but dollars."[5]

Boredom is indeed the key word; it is the form of experience in which nineteenth-century artists express the perspective of Critical Theory in relation to the emerging manifestations of modern life.

IV

When I think about my own works on the analysis of mass culture, it is easy for me to appreciate the term "boredom," because this term offers access to the most significant factor: the crippling of imagination that obstructs artistic experience and gives free rein to the forces of manipulation. The extent to which the "administration," or suppression, of the imagination is part of the business of mass culture can be made clear in a few examples. In the United States, as well as in Germany, book clubs are a big business. One enterprise, called "Time Books," offers a "Time Reading Program." For a modest sum, three or four books are delivered each month and, with them, participation in a "planned approach" to reading, which guarantees that "though your time may be limited, you will be reading widely and profitably . . . many books that are truly timeless in style and significance." The reliability of selection is beyond doubt: "This plan draws its strength from the fact that the editors spent thousands of hours finding the answers to questions that you, too, must have asked yourself many times. . . . It is part of their job to single out the few books that tower over all others." Significance, quality, and relevance of the publications are assured: "In each case, the editors will write special introductions to underline what is unique in the book, what impact it has had or will have, what place it has earned in literature and contemporary thought." In addition, a kind of religious sanction is bestowed upon the wrappings: "The books will be bound in durable, flexible covers similar to those used for binding fine Bibles and Missals."

Another example: the Literary Guild, one of the most successful American book clubs, recently offered inexpensive special editions of *Anna Karenina, Madame Bovary,* and Dumas's *Camille.* The advertisement reads about as follows:

> These three classical novels, which are now published together in an attractively bound set, tell the story of a trio of tragic and unforgettable ladies who risked their lives for love and thereby lost everything. Tolstoy's Anna Karenina, a woman who gives up her aristocratic society for the cause of an insuperable passion; Dumas's Camille, a lady who makes the highest sacrifice for the man she loves; and Flaubert's Madame Bovary, a tender dreamer whose romantic longing leads to an act of violence.

These descriptions illustrate how art is degraded into commodities of mass culture. After all, the triumphs and tragedies in love experienced by Faust's Gretchen or Anna Karenina are not eternally valid statements about the nature of woman; they are, rather, to be seen as specific perceptions about women in certain circumstances. It would not be such an outrageous act of manipulated mass culture if, instead of tossing such books cheaply onto the mass market, the experts were to proclaim that these ladies are all neurotics and would certainly be better off today after psychoanalytic treatment! In short, the organization and "administration" of the imagination is taken over by agencies of social control, and here reductionism, including that of the behavioral sciences, is a justifiable method, indeed the only appropriate method.

Mass culture reinforces and signals the instructions in the late-capitalist world that promote a false collective. In this sense, I have always regarded my studies as political. Two examples in particular come to mind, which appear to me symptomatic of the shattered bourgeois self-consciousness and the insurmountable impotence that characterized the mood of wide strata of the middle classes. One of the examples is related to literary reception, the other to genre, both of which are closely related.

One of my studies had as its subject the reception of Dostoevsky in Germany at the turn of the century, as documented in a voluminous corpus of books, as well as in articles, journals, and newspapers. It soon became clear to me that the massive reception of Dostoevsky's works was not necessarily a function of their aesthetic quality but rather of deeper social-psychological needs. With the probable exception of Goethe, Dostoevsky was the most written about literary figure at that time. The analysis of the material revealed that the reception of Dostoevsky's works illuminated significant idiosyncrasies of German society in a time of total crisis: infatuation with the so-called irrationalism of the artist; the alleged mystery in the life of the individual; the wallowing in the "dark regions of the soul," the glorification of criminal behavior—in short, indispensable elements that were later incorporated in the psychological transfiguration of violence by National Socialism.

That studies on reception can have social-political significance was confirmed years later when I took a closer look at the reviews of the writer I had predicted—years before the event—would be a Nazi-sympathizer: Knut Hamsun. A history of the reception of Hamsun's works can reflect the development of political consciousness all the way from liberalism to the slogans of the authoritarian state. Indeed, bourgeois literary criticism was not nearly as surprising as the Social Democratic responses. The observations on Hamsun that appeared in *Neue Zeit,* the leading theoretical journal of German Social Democracy, reveal as early as the 1890s a clear political stance: Hamsun's novels are to be rejected; they do not portray living human beings but rather vague attitudes that have nothing to do with tendencies directed toward positive change.

The volumes of *Neue Zeit* from the early years of World War I and the immediate postwar years, however, contain glowing descriptions of the same writer who twenty years before had been so unambiguously rejected. What was previously judged as "empty atmosphere" and "mere nervous stimulus" was now perceived as "gripping depictions of life and soul in which the most vivid reality with all its lights and shadows is transposed into the allegory of innermost life." The author who impressed the earlier critics as an "amorous exclamation point in a melancholy easy chair" had now grown to such "solitary greatness" that one might not compare him with others without doing him an injustice; what had in his novels previously been seen as "ephemeral as the atmosphere" suddenly became "a parable of the eternal." After World War I, this hymn of praise was joined by the liberal spokesmen of the bourgeoisie, as well as those of the proletariat that Hamsun so despised. Conventional bourgeois criticism and *Neue Zeit* criticism both belong to the same constellation: that of political resignation and a susceptibility to ideological seduction within broad social strata in Central Europe.

My studies on genre examined the biographical fashion. I attempted to analyze, in two different societies, popular biographies as an illuminating criterion for significant transformations in political and social structure. The first study was carried out in Germany before 1933. It is difficult today to imagine the flood of popular biographies that inundated Europe and Germany at that time. Already by 1918, the popular biography was the classic example of German bourgeois escapist literature. Biography is both the continuation and the inversion of the novel. In the bourgeois novel, documentation functions as raw material. In the popular biography, on the contrary, the various kinds of documentation—that huge pageant of fixed data, events, names, letters, and so on—come to take the place of social relationships, which have become the individual's fetters; the individual is, so to speak, nothing more than a typographic element, a column heading that winds its way through the book's plot, a mere excuse to attractively arrange a certain body of material. The heroes of the popular biography have no individual destinies; they are nothing but functions of the historic. Latent relativism, although rarely the manifest credo of this literature, is always present. Conscious cynicism of the masters is completely absent, but what remains is the need to cloak the helplessness of the losers. The aestheticism of the 1890s, the *fin de siècle,* could be called the very epitome of activity when compared to the fatigue and weakness emanating from the writers of popular biographies. In these testimonies to the immortality of mortality, in this maze of superlatives and uniquenesses through which reason can never guide us, the writers are every bit as lost as their readers.

Popular biographies in the United States operated in a different social context. I attempted to show in my work on the triumph of mass idols in several American high-circulation magazines the structural change in the treatment of popular biographies in the period of transition from liberal capitalism to manipulated collectivism. I called it the transition from the idols of production to the idols of consumption. Whereas around the turn of the century the so-called heroes were the representatives of production, at the end of the 1930s and the beginning of the 1940s these "heroes" were increasingly replaced by athletes and entertainers, especially those of the cinema, who appeared to be "newsworthy" because of their private affairs rather than their productive functions. The identification offered to the reader was no longer with entrepreneurial success but rather with the imitation of consumption. Ultimately, the German and the American phenomena share certain identical characteristics, although in different political contexts. As I put it then:

The distance between what an average individual may do and the forces and powers that determine his/her life and death has become so unbridgeable that identification with normalcy, even with philistine boredom, becomes a readily grasped empire of refuge and escape. It is some comfort for the average person who has been robbed of the Horatio Alger-dream and who despairs of penetrating the thicket of grand strategy in politics and business, to see his heroes as a bunch of guys who like or dislike highballs, cigarets, tomato juice, golf and social gatherings . . . just like he himself. He knows how to converse in this sphere of consumption and here he can make no mistakes. By narrowing his focus of attention he can experience the gratification of being confirmed in his own pleasures and discomforts by participating in the pleasure and discomforts of the great. The large confusing issues in the political and the economic realm and the antagonisms and controversies in the social sphere are all submerged in the experience of being at one with the lofty and powerful in the sphere of consumption.[6]

V

With the power of a seemingly prophetic insight, Shakespeare, in act 3, scene 2, of *Hamlet,* suggests the threat to the autonomy of the individual through social manipulation, although he certainly could not have guessed that finally, nearly four hundred years later, the Guildensterns would defeat the Hamlets.

Hamlet: Will you play upon this pipe?

Guildenstern: My lord, I cannot.

Hamlet: I pray you.

Guildenstern: Believe me, I cannot.

Hamlet: I do beseech you.

Guildenstern: I know no touch of it, my lord.

Hamlet: 'Tis as easy as lying; govern these ventages with your finger and thumb, give it breath with your mouth, and it will discourse most eloquent music. Look you, these are the stops.

Guildenstern: But these cannot I command to any utterance of harmony; I have not the skill.

Hamlet: Why, look you now, how unworthy a thing you make of me. You would play upon me; you would seem to know my stops; you would pluck out the heart of my mystery; you would sound me from my lowest note to the top of my compass; and there is much music, excellent voice, in this little organ, yet cannot you make it speak. 'Sblood! do you think I am easier to be played on than a pipe? Call me what instrument you will, though you can fret me, you cannot play upon me.

Guildenstern represents, if you will, mass culture, which mediates social domination, which tries to force the individual to obedience and plays with him as on a passive, but well-prepared, instrument.

What finally happened is clearly expressed in the words of the American poet, Randall Jarrell, who has the following to say in his book *Poetry and the Age:*

> The poet lives in a world whose newspapers and magazines and books and motion pictures and radio stations and television stations have destroyed, in a great many people, even the capacity for understanding real poetry, real art of any kind. . . . the average article in our magazines gives any subject whatsoever the same coat of easy, automatic, "human" interest.[7]

Jarrell contrasts Goethe, who stated, "The author whom a lexicon can keep up with is worth nothing," with Somerset Maugham, who once said, "The finest compliment he ever received was a letter in which one of his readers said: 'I read your novel without having to look up a single word in the dictionary.' " And Jarrell closes with the observation that "popular writing has left nothing to the imagination for so long now that imagination too has begun to atrophy." In short, the wasting away, the end of imagination, is the end of freedom.

I cannot say anything definitive about the possibility of genuine artistic experience in the present day. Although the acquaintance with great art is certainly growing, an acquaintance without genuine experience, rooted in critical openness, only serves to support the system. Acquaintance and experience are mutually exclusive. I am very concerned about the dwindling possibility of the aesthetic experience as experience of freedom in today's world. I can say no more. What I have tried to convey here was perhaps not so much a summary of my work in the sociology of literature as a chapter of a perhaps too presumptuous intellectual autobiography, an autobiography, however, that—and I will not be falsely modest—does not lose sight of the marginality of the field. As an intellectual, one certainly can, and possibly ought to, live on the margins. And for me, sociology of literature has served me in that respect quite adroitly.

Notes

1. Cf. Leo Lowenthal, "Studies on the German Novel in the Nineteenth Century," in *Literature and the Image of Man*, vol. 2 of *Communication in Society* (New Brunswick, N.J.: Transaction Books, 1986), pp. 221ff.
2. Walter Pater, *The Renaissance: Studies in Art and Poetry* (London, 1912), p. 238.
3. Leo Lowenthal, *Literature and the Image of Man*, pp. 43–46. (Translation emended.)

4. G. W. F. Hegel, *The Philosophy of Fine Art*, trans. F. P. B. Osmaston (London, 1920), vol. 2, pp. 374–75.
5. Stendhal, *Lucien Leuwen*, trans. Louis Varèse (New York, 1950), vol. 1, p.35.
6. Leo Lowenthal, "The Triumph of Mass Idols"; first published as "Biographies in Popular Magazines," in *Radio Research, 1942–1943,* ed. Paul F. Lazarsfeld and Frank N. Stanton (New York, 1944); later published in *Literature and Mass Communication,* vol. 1 of *Communication in Society* (New Brunswick, N.J., 1985), pp. 203–35.
7. Randall Jarrell, *Poetry and the Age* (New York, 1953), p. 18.

PART III

Correspondence

13

Correspondence
of
Leo Lowenthal with Theodor W. Adorno

The essay on Husserl referred to in this letter was originally planned as a contribution to the Zeitschrift für Sozialforschung. *When it was finished, the manuscript far exceeded the scope of an article and first appeared thirty years later in book form.[1] The reviews mentioned refer to books by Ernst Cassirer, Ernst Krenek and Siegfried Kracauer.*

September 14, 1937

Dear Teddie,

I have a bad conscience for not having already acknowledged the various items you sent me in the mail. I hope you will excuse the delay, partly due to Horkheimer's stay in Europe—involving, of course, more than a few letters—and partly due to the truly overwhelming burden of obligations that awaited me in the office after my two-month absence. You saw during your own stay in New York that this last remark is no mere phrase.

So, once again with sincere apologies, I want to acknowledge your letters of August 19th and September 5th, the Husserl manuscript and the reviews of Cassirer, Krenek and Kracauer. I've not yet managed to read them carefully, but will get to the reviews in the next few days and then write you about them in detail. I read the article once, but must read it again more carefully to give you my precise appraisal. A more comprehensive exchange will probably be fruitful only after Horkheimer has studied the manuscript and the three of us discuss it together in New York.

Once again, all the best to you and your wife on your marriage—and Golde joins me most heartily in my wishes. At the Institute we didn't

127

know exactly where the wedding took place, so I don't know if you received our "Apporta" telegram on time.

My heartfelt greetings to both of you, from Golde too,

[Leo]

This letter conveys an impression of the conflict-ridden relations, between Adorno and the research group in the Bureau of Applied Social Research, under the direction of Paul Lazarsfeld, at Columbia University. The conflicts had methodological as well as psychological aspects. The letter documents Lowenthal's attempt to mediate in this difficult situation. The review by George Simpson appeared in the last issue of Studies in Philosophy and Social Science *(1941). Robert Lynd is the author of the classic sociological study,* Middletown in Transition. *The paragraph concerning contributions to Selfhelp alludes to the Institute's diverse efforts to help emigre intellectuals. The Benjamin festschrift was a small memorial collection which appeared in a limited mimeographed edition. It was originally planned as a special issue of* Studies in Philosophy and Social Science, *but the journal meanwhile ceased publication.*

429 West 117th Street
New York City

April 17, 1942

Dear Teddie,

Many thanks for your letter of April 13th.

I understand how Lazarsfeld's memorandum upsets you. I agree that the remark concerning your lack of generosity is rather crude. On the other hand, I would ask you to consider Lazarsfeld's relative loyalty in sending a copy of the note to Lynd to you and Simpson. It's Simpson who gets a slap in the face, in that Lazarsfeld clearly affirms to him that he hasn't contributed a single new thought and has produced a work that one might expect from a capable secretary without particular scientific training. The leitmotiv of the memorandum is the sentence: "I don't think Dr. Simpson has a justified complaint." That seems to me a very decent statement. And I find it consistent with the long telephone conversation between Lazarsfeld and Lynd of which I was an involuntary witness and which I already mentioned to you. Lazarsfeld clearly underscored your scientific competence and responsibility for the parts concerning music (not only the parts you signed), and he strongly indicted the ridiculousness and neurotic distortions contained in Simpson's demands. Lazarsfeld makes it clear in the memorandum to Lynd that he, Lazarsfeld, is only willing to lift a finger for Mr. Simpson on Lynd's formal order to do so—and "lifting a finger" consists then in no more than a trifle, so that he, Lazarsfeld, gets rid of the gripers and Lynd can assure himself that he's once again done something for the underdog.

That Lazarsfeld considers your style difficult to understand and that, for this reason, he and his research underlings doctored around on your manuscripts while you were working with him is a simple fact about which one can't turn indignant at this time. Moreover, I see no offense in the confirmation that the American public has difficulties in understanding us and that there remains something for us to learn along this line. You can't deny that you worked with Simpson on formally friendly terms for months and that he gave you tips concerning "understandability." I see no insult in that.

To begin a quarrel with Lazarsfeld now—which would necessarily consist in my declaring that the whole Institute feels insulted—I don't consider the wisest thing to do. Till now he's done nothing improper to us. On the contrary, looked at objectively, he's helped us in a number of matters. Among these is his agreement to employ you before he knew you. Now he's our strongest personal tie to the [Sociology] Department and is going to some trouble (among his connections) to make something of it, both for you and for me. I don't know whether he will succeed. But I don't think it right to spoil this relationship unnecessarily.

My advice is as follows: write him a letter in which you thank him (1) for the application to [the] Carnegie [Corporation] which, as I had already reported to you, he is presently submitting and (2) for his loyalty in forwarding to you a copy of his file memorandum to Lynd. On the latter, you would only want to comment that it's peculiar to reproach someone for lacking generosity who goes so far as to give credit even to the secretary, as you had done with Miss Cooper. If generosity had been lacking, then certainly because of a mutual decision. It would therefore simply be fair and right for him to inform Lynd that he'd forgotten himself that you and he undertook the task of formulating the acknowledgment together. By the way, it's best to remember here that Lazarsfeld accepted complete responsibility in his note, just in case there should appear to be some impropriety.

You can believe me when I say that I declined your request to intervene in this case only after careful consideration. You know that, as a rule, I have always tried to get what you have wanted from Lazarsfeld without delay. To check my judgment, I sent Lazarsfeld's note on to Pollock without giving him the slightest hint what my opinion was. He characterized the note as a particularly loyal document. I wouldn't go that far, but as far as consequences are concerned, I agree: I think it would be a serious mistake to turn this affair into a casus belli.

I would also ask that Horkheimer's desire to remove Simpson's review be reconsidered. He was assigned the review at a time *after* we had already quarrelled with him once and, indeed, with the conscious intention, which we had discussed, of not allowing any smouldering enmity to develop. When he called me a couple of months ago and asked if he should deliver his review, I responded positively. I already knew at the time of the phone conversation that Simpson believed he received too little credit; Lazarsfeld's memorandum is not in any way the result of any new steps on Simpson's part, but a long postponed response to this incident, which was unpleasant for Lazarsfeld. I suggest that we be the generous ones and go ahead and publish this little review—especially since it concerns a Columbia professor—and not give Simpson any new grounds to inspire in Lynd the impression that we're petty and vindictive.

Yesterday Wild wrote to Marcuse concerning the Selfhelp contributions. Unfortunately, Selfhelp cannot provide any regular payments to refugees living in America. It's forbidden in its statutes. The American committees should step in instead. I did arrange today with Tillich to grant [Ernst] Bloch, if at all possible, a one-time donation from the Selfhelp funds. I propose that you and Marcuse send Selfhelp about $1.00 a month, and Horkheimer about $3.00, preferably on a quarterly basis. It's a certain question of prestige, if not a terribly important one, that we remain contributing members.

I haven't forgotten your reviews. But they are so extensive that they would cause considerable added expense. I don't think we should do that just now considering that a few of Marcuse's reviews are already type-set and the fact that I didn't print a single one of his reviews in the second issue and only one in the first. I think you should show your generosity here, since you certainly are a distinguished and much-published author of the *Studies [in Philosophy and Social Science]*.

Before the Benjamin festschrift is finally finished, please read through the enclosed prefatory remarks which you wrote on Benjamin's aphorisms. Should they really remain as they are? They made good sense in a fat, extensive book, in which the aphorisms were in danger of being nearly physically overwhelmed. Here, at the beginning of a much thinner volume, these explanatory lines don't seem to me understandable anymore. Please think it over and let me know your and Horkheimer's opinion immediately. Didn't you suggest that we replace the present title ("On the Concept of History") with another stemming from Benjamin that I've forgotten?

I visited your parents. They are charming people. My modest advice to you is that you write them more regularly and more cheerfully.

My opinion that continuously energetic steps would be taken in Washington to prevent harm coming to bonafide refugees has been thoroughly confirmed. Much is being done; I hope with favorable results very soon. I judge the danger of evacuation to be practically zero. I spoke at length about this with a number of people who understand something of the matter and have themselves taken part in the negotiations.

Cordial greetings, from my wife as well, to you and Gretel,

[Leo]

Adorno's commentary concerning work on magazine biographies refers to Lowenthal's study, "Biographies in Popular Magazines."[2]

[Santa Monica, Calif.]

November 25, 1942

Dear Leo,

Meanwhile I've read your paper on magazine biographies, and I like it very much. In research terms, it certainly expresses as much of the truth as the constraints of a "methodological" straitjacket allow. I seem to remember that your original draft contained much more theoretical material, which probably fell victim to some kind of censorship mechanism in Lazarsfield's office. I know the problem which you confront here all too well: on the one side to represent our theoretical interest, and, on the other, to handle the material in such a way that it has a good chance pragmatically and that Lazarsfeld can swallow it. All the same, I think it can only strengthen your position in relation to him if you insist on a small theoretical section (10 to 15 typewritten pages), in which something fundamental is said concerning the function of biographies in the current social phase and in the set-up of mass culture. At bottom, the problem is that the concept of life itself, as a unity that makes sense and unfolds out of itself, possesses no more reality whatever—just as little as the concept of the individual—and that the ideological function of biographies is to demonstrate to people through some kind of models that something like a life, possessed of all the emphatic categories of life, still exists, and, indeed, precisely in an empirical context which those who have no more life can reclaim for themselves without any effort. Life itself, in a very abstract form, has become ideology, and precisely this abstraction, which distinguishes it from the older, more fulfilled concepts of life, makes it possible for this to happen (the vitalist and existentialist concepts of life are already steps along this path.)

And now a request. As you know, Scholem places great value on the memorial volume for Benjamin. Professor Spiegel has just written me that he can take a copy to Palestine and, moreover, would like to have one for himself. With Horkheimer's consent, I would like to ask you to allow him to have two of the Benjamin volumes, one for him to keep and one with the request that he get it to Scholem. He would also like to have one copy for the Jewish Institute of Religion, but we think it more appropriate to present him with only one private copy, aside from the one for Scholem. My warmest thanks for taking this on, although you are under pressure yourself and are probably, with justice, irritated by Jewish institutions. But Scholem truly deserves the volume, and the copy for Spiegel is, so to speak, the carrier's fee.

Loving greetings to you and Golde, from Gretel, too,

Yours,
Teddie

The gesture of support for Lowenthal mentioned at the beginning of this letter refers to a political-methodological dispute that he had with two colleagues at the Institute, Arkadii R. Gurland and Paul Massing. In their Labor Study *evaluations they tended to apply orthodox materialist principles. The* Labor Study *refers to a comprehensive investigation of the spread of anti-Semitism among American workers conducted by the Institute in the years beginning in 1944. The study was published only in part. Lowenthal's contribution, "Stereotypes; Anti-Semitism Among American Workers," is contained in his* Schriften.[3] *This letter was originally written in English.*

October 13, 1944

Dear Teddie,

It was very lovely of you to write me a note of sympathy. In the last analysis the rationalistic lecture which I had been taught with regard to the fundamentals of class society betrays an irrationalistic vitalism: the gentlemen are in a way objects of the sociology of Pareto by really believing the myth of the spontaneous and creative forces of the exploited. They have apparently and masochistically forgotten the teachings of Marx that the class *an sich* has to be transformed in the class *für sich* and that the role of the theoretician is not to imitate ideologically the illusions and distortions which society has produced in the lower strata to a much higher degree than in the ruling groups, but to destroy class-bound imitations as such. If they had really understood that the image as well as the fate of the Jew is the living, or better, the dying witness of nefarious imitation and of all attempts to destroy it, they would realize the shock-like effect which can emerge by focusing theoretical and practical endeavors around the Jewish problem.

It is a rather contradictory attitude (or as our President would say, talking out of both ends of one's mouth at the same time) to apply the attitude of tender protection to the German masses as if they were the epitome of sacred humanitarianism and to neglect the nearly total absence of practiced humanitarianism and rebellion in the name of genuine liberation. There is not much difference between that kind of intolerance, which simply is not on speaking terms with anybody or anything that does not adore the stereotype of the underdog, and the intolerance which fascism has practiced.

I do not quite share your outright condemnation as far as the persons are concerned. As a matter of fact I like them and I prefer working with them quite considerably to working with some of the gentlemen who at present are not on our payroll. What really excites me is the stagnation of theoretical and political thinking even among people who have lived for so long in our atmosphere.

Thank you again for the spontaneous expression of your solidarity. With kindest regards for Gretel and you,

Very cordially yours,
[Leo]

The first paragraph refers to the study of the authoritarian character.[4] *Lowenthal's prospectus mentioned in the second paragraph is a suggestion for the organization of* The Dialectic of Enlightenment. *Daniel is Lowenthal's son. This letter was originally written in English.*

October 31, 1944

Dear Teddie,

First of all, I would like to congratulate you on your diplomatic success. I think you did a very good job at Berkeley, and I am very eager to hear how the actual work goes on and especially about your own share in cooperating with Sanford.

I enclose a copy of the prospectus I have drafted for the "Fragments," which I think is not too good but may serve as a basis for a good one. Horkheimer would be very grateful to you if you would go through this little manuscript as soon as you can and return it to me either with your suggestions or—as I would considerably prefer—in a revised version. As far as your version is concerned, you needn't bother about 100% perfect

English as we can take care of that in New York. You can imagine that I am very happy about Horkheimer's being in New York, although I would prefer much more to be together with all of you on the west coast—and to see him too—and also work on much more decisive issues than we have to do at present. But never mind, one never knows what it is good for.

We continue to have very good news from Daniel. Golde is all right and sends her kindest regards to both of you. I hope that Gretel is feeling well and that your own attacks of migraine are gone.

Very cordially yours,
Leo

The letter deals mainly with problems of editorial organization for the Labor Study. *It was Lowenthal's intention to structure the study topically for eventual publication, according to its political, economic, and sociological aspects. The substance of Adorno's suggestions concerning evaluation in the* Labor Study *is treated in his content analyses of the American agitator Thomas.[5] This letter was originally written in English.*

Dr. T. W. Adorno
3016 So. Kenter Avenue
Los Angeles 24, California

November 22, 1944

Dear Teddie,

Thank you very much for your letter of November 8, the draft of the Prospectus, and the copy of your notes on Qualitative Evaluation.

I agree with your idea that the abstract of the content of the book should be much shorter than I had planned it. I am sending you enclosed a copy of the version as it stands now. As you will see, it follows closely your suggestion with minor stylistic changes. Be good enough to go over it once more, and if you propose more changes, return it to me by marking them.

Congratulations on your Memo on Evaluation. I have read it, but not studied it. My impression is that it will be extremely helpful in our work. Whether we can elaborate or even mention all of the points you make is a matter of time, and should the final tentative product not contain all of the points you make, it is certainly not because of disagreement. I guess that your memo should not be interpreted as a schedule for the organization of the write-up, but more or less as comprehensive suggestions on crucial problems and tentative results mainly on the psychological aspects.

The organization of the evaluation is still a big headache. I first thought I could undertake it alone, but it is beyond my capacity to do that with about 700 interviews in the short time which is at our disposal. We have come to the conclusion that the most efficient way of processing our material is that we all concentrate now on the interviews, and only after finishing with the qualitative as well as quantitative work to tackle the so-called expert reports, and all the other things, such as description of procedure and methods, which should be incorporated in the reports.

The distribution of the various assignments is not an easy job, and I should be extremely grateful to have your advice. There are two schools of thought: one which thinks that each of the people available here (Gurland, Massing, and I) should get one-third of the interviews, and evaluate them on the basis of a catalogue of questions and on which one would have to agree tentatively, and which could be changed as the work goes on. The other opinion is that such a split-up of material is completely mechanical, because there is no clear-cut criterion for the division of the interviews, because the catalogue of questions with which each interview could be studied is a mechanical administrative procedure, since theory is formed while busy with the material and not beforehand. Furthermore, because each of the analysts, due to his training and predilections, will produce a completely different study, which to marry with each other would be a giant job, it is proposed that each collaborator treat special aspects for the whole material. To give you an example—one could study the ideas of the worker about the shop and the Jewish co-worker; another one the ideas of private life and consumption; and the third one the ideological aspects. The totality of the interviews cannot get lost because each aspect has to be viewed in its relationship to all answers given.

My letter makes quite clear that I consider the second way the only possible one, and I am struggling hard to attain a reasonable division of labor. Pollock (and he alone) adheres to the first school because he thinks that my way will consume endless months. I do not want to bother you with a whole catalogue of arguments and counter arguments, but imagine for yourself how difficult it would be to unite the Thomas and the Phelps study into one manuscript. After all, our ideas, yours and mine, go exactly in the same direction, we are as close to each other theoretically and personally as one could wish, and still, what a job would have to be done! This is the best illustration that I can give for my resistance against the mechanics of assigning three different piles of interviews.

I should be very thankful for your thinking over this complex situation, and if you accept my point of view, to contribute an idea or principle about the three or four different assignments or aspects for evaluation. If you do so, please take into consideration that the time at our disposal is relatively short, and the program should contain the "Must" but not all "Desirables".

Kracauer's address is: 56 West 75th Street; of Arnheim: c/o New School of Social Research, 66 West 12th Street, New York, City. I do not have his private address.

I hope you will send me a copy of your paper on Art and Religion. We continue to have very good news from Daniel. With kindest regards to both of you, also from Golde.

Very cordially,
[Leo]

The following letter also refers largely to the Labor Study, *especially to the parts Lowenthal worked on. Lowenthal is reacting to Adorno's concern that insufficient attention would be given to the relationship between qualitative and quantitative analysis.*

January 18, 1945

Dear Teddie,

The work on the *Labor Study* is going rather well—not as quickly, not as well, and not as smoothly as I would like, but we have to make do as best we can with the capacities available and with due respect for the objective difficulties presented by such an immense amount of material.

As for all of your suggestions in the two big memoranda and the letters to Pollock, I can only say that I agree with all the major points and with nearly all of the details, insofar as I've seen them.

I am only concerned that your wishes are in part too extravagant for what I have to accomplish under enormous pressure. A thorough discussion of the relationship between quantitative and qualitative interpretations of the results of the interviews or of the relationship between the experts' reports (which, by the way, are not expert) and the interviews would mean a delay which is impossible to estimate. Certainly, there can be no doubt that rudiments of all these problems must be included in the study. I'm afraid, incidentally, that the [American Jewish Labor] Committee, for which the report is intended, would discourage a really responsible discussion of these theoretical problems, even if we had the people and the time to undertake it. Once you are here—and I'm already very much looking forward to your arrival—we can probably agree easily on a plan of how we can make up, for purposes of publication, what's been partially neglected.

To give you an idea of how the qualitative analysis is organized, I'm sending you a classification scheme that we will hold to in general, if, admittedly, not precisely. Section IV dealing with types still has problems as sketched there, and I'll probably work on a typology with Herta

Lazarsfeld that will be significantly simpler and correspond very closely to your suggestions in your first memorandum.

I'm also sending a breakdown of my own chapter. I'm thinking of completing it with a presentation of a few case studies and a discussion of especially characteristic consistencies or inconsistencies, once again wholly in keeping with your own impressions.

I am still busy myself with the formulation, which goes slowly in the beginning, but then, as you know, generally picks up speed very quickly.

Horkheimer is very overworked and doesn't look well. I'm worried about him.

I hope things are going more or less well with you. I see from a remark in a letter to Pollock that once again Gretel is not entirely up to par. I only hope that meanwhile she's doing better.

Our kindest regards to both of you.

[Leo]

This letter refers exclusively to the manuscript of Horkheimer's later work, Eclipse of Reason[6] *which demanded extraordinarily thorough editing.*

May 25, 1945

Dear Teddie,

Here you have the new version of the proposed text. I hope you like it better than the previous one. First a word about the story of the text: the first version was produced at a time when, because of the *Labor Study*, I could contribute almost nothing. All that [Norbert] Guterman did was advise Miss Anderson on the passages she felt she didn't understand. In fact, Miss A. was not at all competent to edit a philosophical text, not to mention taking on incisive reorganizations. Now, after I've worked for a few weeks with Guterman, I feel confirmed in my old judgment: that he (aside from [Benjamin] Nelson, who, unfortunately, is unavailable for other reasons) is, among our acquaintances, the most competent and refined philosophical editor.

I would say that, on the whole, the manuscript is ready for publication in its present form. Obviously, it does not appear to be a document which Max, together with you, spent a year working on. It consists, after all, of lectures, which were not themselves produced under the most favorable of conditions, and sections from a few essays, which, from the perspective of the present state of theory, would probably look somewhat different here and there. I agree with Max, that one shouldn't conceal the origin of the text, namely, that it was originally based on lectures. You will find an appropriate reference in the Foreword by Guterman. Naturally, the Foreword cannot remain as it is, but I'm enclosing it anyway as a starting point.

Now, as concerns your suggestions, they were, as I've already told you, of immeasurable value. As you read the text, you will see that they made a difference in most of the cases. Either we held fairly precisely to what you suggested, or we made changes, insertions, transpositions or cuts in which we think your legitimate doubts were heeded. Where we didn't follow your suggestions, it was either because we weren't entirely convinced that there wasn't perhaps some misunderstanding or because we didn't feel up to the expansion you desired. The leading principle was in each case to get down an understandable and responsible text.

As you go through the manuscript now, we ask that you not put your ideas for changes in the form of suggestions, but that you go ahead and add or change it immediately as you find best. It is not necessary that you do this in English. On the contrary, wherever you would like to add one or a few sentences, please formulate them in German. It turns out that this makes editing easier, rather than harder.

On the organization of the whole: the second chapter, which you saw, was, of course, completely unacceptable. We've made mention of tradition and the majority principle in the first chapter and we've combined the real theme to which the second chapter, that is, the second lecture, was devoted with the third, to which it is most closely related. In the second lecture, it was really only the last pages that applied to the genuine subject at hand (from page 18 on in the old text). Using appendices is not such a good idea for such a small book; one would have very great difficulties with a publisher. You will probably find as well that the use which is made of the essay on social class in the present fourth chapter no longer causes any serious problems. A reader not versed in philosophy might have some difficulties with the section on positivism, but not decisive ones. In the context of the whole, this section fulfills two functions: it exposes several opposing positions, and, via the polemic itself, clarifies the fundamental concepts, namely the attributes of formal reason. In my opinion, the first and fourth chapters pose practically no more problems at all. In the third chapter, there may remain here and there a noticable hitch in the development of the thoughts, although I would not now know how to specify them clearly, since I'm somewhat too close to it. On the second chapter, I have already commented. The last chapter could stand a few more additions from the author, but it's not absolutely necessary.

A few technical misunderstandings: the manuscript of the first version was not shorter, but longer than the lecture text. It's a question here of an optical illusion resulting from different typewriters and margin settings. The same is true again with the present manuscript, in which the secretary got a bit more on each page. I couldn't use older versions or preliminary work for the lectures, since they're not here and Max could do nothing to get them to me. A German version of the section on positivism, to which you refer a few times, has never existed. It was written originally in English. As concerns the theory of class and rackets, it is not an interpolation of two manuscripts patched together, as you assume; only the essay on class relations, again written originally in English, was used. Incidentally, it turned out to be more helpful for the presentation not to make use of the racket concept.

You can imagine that I'm anxious to get your reaction. I think Max would also be very relieved to know whether you think we now have a usable text.

I'm truly sorry to hear that you still don't feel well. I hope the last news I got on this is already outdated. I'm confident that the doctor in San Francisco found nothing serious.

With my warmest regards for Gretel and you, also from Golde,

[Leo]

This letter refers to preparations, reports, reviews and annotations concerning the authoritarian personality study. The letter documents how closely members of the Institute cooperated with each other, even after they were no longer working in the same place. This letter was originally written in English

New York, N.Y.

Spetember 26, 1945

My dear Teddie,

Thank you very kindly for your letter of September 14th. I am very glad to hear that Gretel's state of health has taken such a wonderful turn. I can see from Max's reports on Alexander [a physician] that one could not have any better medical advice. I hope that your own difficulties have been alleviated in the meantime.

Your complaint that I did not write to you about your two books is legitimate. During the month of August I have done nothing whatsoever because I was completely exhausted. Until Max's arrival the month of September was almost completely taken up by *Betrieb*. Now I start again the existence of an intellectual and I am eagerly looking forward to studying your manuscripts under psychologically favorable conditions.

Only two days ago I received the various studies concerning the Berkeley project: (1) the report of 98 pp. which was shown to me by Miss Jahoda, (2) an abstract of this paper called "Berkeley Report Final Draft" and (3) your paper "Psychological Types of Anti-Semites." I have studied all three manuscripts responsibly and send you enclosed my notes on all three of them. I am certain you will understand and forgive my sometimes rude and outspoken formulations which probably have to be explained by sheer envy of the wealth of ideas and material incorporated in these studies.

Seriously: the Berkeley study sounds very good. Many of the results have been reached by admirable imagination and the corroborating figures and correlations bear out many of the wide-reaching theoretical aspects. As you will see my main worries go in the direction of the formulation for public consumption what the methodological aim of the project is. I do not think that this is brought out clearly enough and I feel that some drastic reconversion work is necessary clearing up the complex directness–indirectness.

I like the typology very much. You will see from my notes that there is hardly a point where we differ basically. My main objection here is on the stylistic side. Your effort to sketch therapeutic measures for each of your types is truly heroic. But I can feel (and I think the average reader, although for other reasons, may also feel) that rightly you do not believe that certain educational or psychiatric measures are the answer to a situation which drives mankind closer and closer to barbarism. I would, therefore, be much more reluctant in recommendations and even make question marks wherever positive recommendations have been made. I trust that you will find a few suggestions in this direction incorporated in my notes.

I am sending copy of this letter and the notes to Pollock by the same mail. Kindest regards from both of us to you and Gretel,

Very cordially yours,
[Leo]

This letter refers to Lazarsfeld's suggestion of a literature review on the application of qualitative methods in research on mass culture. Adorno proposed categories for Lowenthal, on which the latter based his overview. However, this "bibliographie raisonnée" never reached the stage of publication. "Fragments on mass culture" became the "Culture Industry" chapter in the later Dialectic of Enlightenment. *"Max's essay on*

Adler" refers to Horkeimer's essay, "Art and Mass Culture" in Studies in Philosophy and Social Science *(1941).*

February 23, 1948

Dear Teddie,

Excuse me for my delay in thanking you for sending me the advance proofs. I assume that you no longer need this copy and that I can cut it up if necessary. Please let me know if I'm wrong.

Once more I have a big request. As you know, I plan to write a chapter on so-called qualitative studies in the area of mass media for a book on communications research that will be prepared by Lazarsfeld's office. To put it briefly, it will concern everything that's been written about mass culture in English, German, or French. Naturally, it is impossible to be comprehensive, but at least the most important works should be identified. In case you have any ideas about the selection of literature, I would be very grateful for some bibliographical notes. Of course, everything from our own circles should be included, as well as Kracauer, Orwell, contributions to *Politics*, and *Partisan Review*. Nevertheless, I'm certain that I'll end up overlooking something important, if only because it's so obvious. For that reason, I'd be especially grateful for your free associations. But that's still nothing at all. Now comes the so-called main request. What is essential for my paper is that I organize the material in categories which make it possible for the average American intellectual to come to terms with it, that is, to understand what's actually going on in the speculative sphere, and to build himself a bridge from there to the accustomed model of empirical research. Put in "official" terminology, I would have to establish the specific contributions of qualitative media studies, i.e., whether they originate in other traditions, above all, intellectual history, and what that means, and whether there exist connections between qualitative conceptualization and empirical research and what the empirical researcher can learn from qualitative material. Whatever thoughts you have—and it is enough if you formulate it as if you were simply talking with me while we're waiting for Max—about how to organize something like this would help me immeasurably. Do you still remember your extemporaneous reflections when we drove down Sunset Boulevard on a Sunday in a thick fog and you conjectured how you would organize a lecture on the sociology of literature? That's exactly the model I have in mind for my present study.

I've made a mistake. That wasn't yet the main request. It comes now, assuming that you're even still reading and not already drenching me in a torrent of curses. You can imagine that I would like to use this chapter to emphasize the work of our group especially strongly. Of works to be treated I think first of all of the Fragments on Mass Culture [the Benjamin memorial], then of your work on popular music, and of Max's essay on Adler. What I'd like to have from you are notes that explain what the main results of the various studies are—especially, of course, those on mass culture—and what specific methods, that is, fundamental theoretical concepts are applied. If I may dramatize an example to let you know what I have in mind: please assume you want to explain to well-meaning people like Peck or Miss Reinheimer what is actually supposed to be said in the works and how it's said and why—that's exactly what I need. A special aspect, about which you might have a Machiavellian thought, is whether the methods used are learnable.

I dare express all these wishes because I know that writing, fortunately, does not subject you to the same inner costs as it does me and because you are, after all, the author or coauthor of the works concerned here. Besides, we all have a common interest in my study being solid and not requiring all too much time. I already spoke with Kracauer and he sent me a manuscript on his film book, of which I can make very good use.

Let me hear soon how you react to my shameless demands. Kindest regards to you and Gretel,

[Leo]

Adorno wrote this letter to Lowenthal shortly after his first post-war visit in Frankfurt. He refers to Lowenthal's book, Prophets of Deceit, *which had just appeared (Harper, 1949). The "Berkeley book" mentioned is* The Authoritarian Personality *(Harper, 1950).*

Frankfurt a.m.
Liebigstrasse 19 III, bei Irmer

January 3, 1949

Mon très cher,

Many thanks for *Prophets,* which gives me great pleasure. I've read much of it and I think that you have succeeded in setting the proportions and achieving a tone which reveals the deadly without falling into the kind of gesticulations that are scarcely to be avoided with topics so inexpressibly emotion-laden as this one. Against the nonsense that is blossoming under the title "content analysis," in which quantitative methods themselves proceed ad absurdum, it is a highly effective antidote.

If it were possible for you to persuade the publisher or the Jews [meaning the American Jewish Committee] to send me a couple of free copies, I would be glad to see that they get into the right hands here and would supply the seminar with one as well. But only if it's not too much trouble. I could understand it all too well if you don't want to ask the Jews for anything. That they say nothing of the Institute on the jacket, where they speak of you, but then refer to Guterman, is really quite something. Flowerman is quite a scoundrel. You probably already know that they [the Scientific Department of the A.J.C.] also cheated us out of a reference to the Institute with the Berkeley book. It's a case of *l'art pour l'art,* pure pleasure in wickedness—they really don't even get anything out of it.

If I could bother you with yet another request, it would be that you arrange to have sent to me a pre-publication copy of the Berkeley book as soon as possible. Then I could use it, as I would like to, in my lectures, where I am now dealing in part with empirical research. I do have all the proofs here, but they are too unwieldy to handle.

It's very hard in a few words to formulate anything reasonable or even somewhat coherent about my impressions. Of course, it makes a big difference whether one comes here as a detached observer in the *function* of a detached observer, or whether one, in the midst of work, is plunged into a European context. Naturally, one's experience is more positive in the latter case—while just a few days of vacation suffices to establish distance. I cannot keep secret from you the fact that I was happily overwhelmed by the European experience from the first moment in Brittany and that working with students excels everything you would expect—even the time before 1933—in intensity and rapport. And the contention that the quality of the students has sunk, that they are ignorant or pragmatically oriented, is mere nonsense. Instead, much suggests that, in isolation and estranged from politics, they had plunged into intellectual matters with an unequaled fanaticism. The decisively negative factor that is everywhere in evidence derives from the fact that the Germans (and all Europe, in fact) are no longer political subjects, nor do they feel themselves to be; hence a ghostlike, unreal quality pervades their spirit. My seminar is like a Talmud school—I wrote to Los Angeles that it is as if the spirits of the murdered Jewish intellectuals had descended into the German students. Quite uncanny. But for that very reason it is at the same time infinitely canny in the authentic Freudian sense.

Personally and in terms of health, I'm better than I've been for a long time. I'm three times as vigorous and productive as I was over there and haven't had headaches even for a minute. Only the separation is painful, and the only problem is getting to work on the essential things, which until now I've scarcely approached because of the teaching load.

Do write me a letter. I hope things are going well for you. Warm greetings to Golde, and especially to Daniel. Do you plan to show up here again?

All the best, your
Teddie

This letter deals with the study, Die Biographische Mode, *which appeared in German in a festschrift for Max Horkheimer's 60th birthday.*[7] *The work was finished in the 1930s and intended for inclusion in the* Zeitschrift für Sozialforschung. *It was not published at that time because of its cutting analysis of Jewish writers.*

Institute for Social Research
Johann Wolfgang Goethe University

Frankfurt/M
Senckenburg-Anlage 26
December 2, 1954

Dear Leo,

Many thanks for your letter of November 19th.

I'm taking care of copying your dissertation—I will have it done on stencils so we get some more copies. But, of course, it will take a little while. I sent you the microfilm only to avoid any delay.

As for the Institute output, I arranged immediately for a proper package to be prepared and sent to you. Among other things, there is now the big, four-volume *Imago-Studie* about the German image of France, which contains quite a lot of material. I will definitely have a copy of the Darmstadt monographs sent to you as well. By the way, they are in fact a product of the Institute, much more so than one can recognize from the paltry "acknowledgments" by the people whom we helped out of a mess. If I hadn't taken the whole matter in hand, it would have fallen completely to pieces.

Concerning the study on biography, I am of the firm opinion that it should be published. Not only because I think it is necessary that you make an *acte de présence* in the first issue, but also because I believe that the topic has the same relevance today as it did before. The genre is unexterminable, the love of the German people for Stefan Zweig and Emil Ludwig has undoubtedly survived the Jews, and the biographical essays that inundate illustrated magazines (often still featuring Nazi celebrities) derive in large measure from this kind of writing, the dregs of the dregs.

Your arguments are so striking that we shouldn't do without it. And your work has methodological significance as well, insofar as it represents a very legitimate parody of the official practice of content analysis. To enumerate sentences of the sort, "Never before has a woman loved like . . . ," is quantification rightly conceived. Finally, I would like to say that I fundamentally do not adhere to the conviction that our works will become outdated for external or thematic reasons a couple of years after they are written; for the emphasis of what we are doing lies, I would think, in a theory of society and not in ephemeral material. We, at least, should not pursue the kind of modernity that consists in making abstract chronology the standard for relevance and that thus represents the exact opposite of the truly progressive. In this context, perhaps you may wish to read the piece "Consecutio temporum" in *Minima Moralia*. In brief, my vote is unequivocal: publish! Of course I would have liked it much better had you acted as your own copyeditor, but you didn't have the time for it. Nevertheless, should you decide in the next couple of days *still* to deal with it yourself, then the essay probably could be included, since the appearance of the issue, or volume, continues (for reasons you can easily guess) to be delayed. I must only ask that you get busy with it soon and energetically.

By the way, my major paper on [Stefan] George in the Benjamin memorial will probably not appear in the first volume, but instead a new piece, which you don't yet know, on the relation between psychology and sociology. I have to do some more thorough work on it, since it turned out we had too little time to do what we'd originally planned—namely that Max and I would work on it together, which would have been very good but would have meant a matter of months (it's a pretty extensive piece).

All the best to you and Marjorie, from Gretel too,

Your Teddie

This and the following letters once again concern the Horkheimer festschrift. The double issue of the journal mentioned at the letter's opening shows that the group planned a continuation of the Zeitschrift für Sozialforschung *immediately upon its return to Frankfurt. This idea was then given up in favor of the book series,* Frankfurter Beiträge zur Soziologie, *Frankfurt/M, 1955ff. The planned volume on mass culture did not materialize.*

Institute for Social Research
Johann Wolfgang Goethe University
Dr. Leo Lowenthal
Apt. 5A
90 Morningside Drive
New York 27, N.Y.

Frankfurt a.M
December 8, 1954
Senckenberg-Anlage 2

Dear Leo,

The idea has arisen to bring out the double issue of the journal as a dedication for Max on his 60th birthday and I would like to ask you to agree to have your biography essay appear in this issue. Please let me know quickly—one probably gets three guesses what you'll decide.

The Institute is now planning a publication which is supposed to include the Institute's mass culture studies. A German version of your essay on [American] magazine biographies would fit there very well. It would not be appropriate for the journal because the latter is not supposed to contain translations of work that have already appeared in other languages. Of course, it would be best if you prepared the German version yourself and took current phenomena into account. I'm saying this already now so we don't get pressed for time, since the manuscript is supposed to be ready not later than the end of May. The volume is also supposed to contain: "Art and Mass Culture" by Max; the reproduction study by Benjamin that's appeared only in French; a revision of my astrology study and an empirical study of astrology by [Ludwig von] Friedeburg; perhaps something from the local radio investigations; a contribution by [Alexander] Mitscherlich about the psychological foundation of mass culture; perhaps something by [Arnold] Hauser on its historical preconditions; and maybe also something from my American music pieces—for which, incidently, I'm in urgent need of the old Damrosch study and the manuscript "Social Critique on Radio Music" which are at the Bureau of Applied Social Research. I would integrate all the contributions and gear them to one another so that what would result would not be a conventional anthology but something somewhat more systematic.

Naturally, something decisive is lacking, namely a theoretical-economic analysis of the foundation of mass culture. But who could do something like that?

All the best to you and Marjorie, from Gretel too.

Yours,
Teddie

December 13, 1954

Dear Teddie,

Many thanks for your letter of December 8th.

I must confess that I'm not at all unhappy with the transformation of the journal into a book series. As a matter of fact, Max will recall that I've been a very enthusiastic advocate of a series and have expressed the most spirited reservations about the journal. I don't see why a festschrift for Max isn't a very good idea. He wrote me himself about this plan and also asked whether other contributors might perhaps be brought into it. In my opinion you should at least ask Paul Massing—but also Charles Wright Mills (Columbia), considering his fine essay in *Saturday Review*—whether they couldn't deliver a contribution in time. Marcuse, with whom I discussed the question, thought that perhaps Jakob Taube would be a good idea. Max must make up his own mind whether [Adolph] Loewe and [Paul] Tillich should be asked. They would probably be offended if they weren't, but since the book must surely represent Max above all, he'll have to decide himself. My opinion is that the letters asking these people or others in America to contribute should be sent from Frankfurt over your signature. And here you have my "permission," probably not unexpected, to use the piece on biographies as you find best.

It would be appropriate if you wrote to Lazarsfeld soon about his contribution; he did originally count on the journal coming out by the end of the year.

The mass culture book sounds good. I'm very much in favor of my American biography study appearing there, but whether I can translate it myself, I don't know. It seems to me somewhat uncertain how I could manage that in Berkeley. Perhaps one of the younger co-workers in Frankfurt could do a draft translation that I could then revise and supplement. In one matter I know that I completely agree with Marcuse: we couldn't very well publish a volume on mass culture that didn't contain a statement of our position in principle. Given how busy we all are at the moment, I don't see at all how that could be done—unless Max could retreat for a while to devote himself entirely to this task, which is, I suppose, quite utopian. I'll give it some more thought.

All the best from both of us to both of you.

[Leo]

This letter was originally written in English.

90 Morningside Drive
New York 27, New York
Professor T. W. Adorno
Institut für Sozialforschung
Senckenberg Anlage 26
Frankfurt am Main, Germany

December 29, 1954

Dear Teddie:

Thank you very much for your telegram of December 20th which, for good measure, arrived twice.

After having thought through the matter, and after having, in addition, talked to Lowe, Tillich, Mills, and Massing as prospective authors and after having discussed again the issue with Herbert Marcuse, it has become quite clear to me that we face a completely impossible situation. None of these authors have, or pretend to have, any unpublished manuscripts immediately available. There is no doubt that all of them are willing to contribute papers, but this will take a minimum of five weeks (as, for instance, in the case of Mills) and an unforeseeable maximum for such slow and compulsive authors as Lowe and Massing. I believe that we have made a terrible mistake not to think of preparing a festschrift at least a year ago. To get papers and to wait until they are ready for publication takes, in my experience, all about four months and it takes at least another half a year until one can produce a book.

On the other hand, the first volume of the Institute must come out under all circumstances and I believe, therefore, that necessity will turn virtue and the volume will perhaps in the last analysis be more an intrinsic gift for Max than might have been a collection of essays, many authors of which have polite personal, but certainly not theoretical affinities to our friend.

I have never seen a complete table of contents of the originally projected double issue of the periodical. I believe, however, from various communications of yours that the majority of papers will come from our own group and this is, after all, as it should be. Even Lazarsfeld's article, while certainly not "Geist von unserem Geiste" [entirely of our spirit] is at least a documentation of a personal tradition. (I shall see him on December 30th and shall inform him about the change of format; he wrote me that he had received galley proofs.)

Perhaps the article of [Otto] Kirchheimer (which I mailed to you yesterday) might be a suitable addition to what you have collected anyway and if one of the papers which Taubes prepares should come in time, that might also be a congenial contribution.

My main concern now is that the volume comes out quickly so that the

Institute delivers an impressive calling card and so that Max has a birthday gift in time. If for unforeseeable reasons you can still accept papers for publication in this volume at a date late in January or during February, please let me know so that I can try again. The only firm commitment which I have is from Mills, who said that he would be willing to either enlarge his article in the *Saturday Review of Literature* or write a condensed version of his book on elites, which he now prepares and have an English copy ready by February 1st. But this would require that I write to him within a very short time. In this case, you would have to cable me, but I would feel ambivalent about the cable because it would indicate that the volume can only appear with great delay.

The question is now whether one should plan a kind of a second volume with contributions of such friends and acquaintances to which one should also add Kracauer and (perhaps) Nanda [Anshen] (in order to avoid hurt feelings). I am doubtful whether Max would like this idea very much, but he would have to decide that.

Be certain, dear Teddie, that I acted within minutes after your cables came and you may be certain that my advice to drop the idea originates in very responsible considerations.

My apologies for writing in English, and for rushing off this letter, but I am presently in the impossible situation of having no regular secretarial help and facing a mountain of work for the next three weeks with regard to Berkeley and pending New York affairs. That does in no way mean that I will not follow through any suggestion or decision which you convey to me.

Happy New Year!   Cordially,

Leo

Notes

1. Zur Metakritik der Erkenntnistheorie. Studien über Husserl und die phänomenologischen Antinomien. *Frankfurt/M, 1956; as well as* Gesammelte Schriften, *Bd. 5, Frankfurt/M, 1971.*
2. *Originally in Paul F. Lazarsfeld, Frank Stanton, eds., Radio Research, New York, 1944; now in* Literature and Mass Culture, *Transaction Books, New Brunswick, NJ, 1984, pp. 203ff.*
3. *Bd. 3, Frankfurt/M, 1982, S. 175ff.*
4. *First published as T. W. Adorno, Else Frenkel-Brunswik, Daniel J. Levinson, Nevitt Sanford et al.,* The Authoritarian Personality. Studies in Prejudice, *vol. 1, New York, 1950.*
5. "The Psychological Technique of Martin Luther Thomas' Radio Addresses," *in Th. W. Adorno,* Gesammelte Schriften Bd. 9.2, S. 7ff.
6. Zur Kritik der Instrumentellen Vernunft, *Frankfurt/M, 1967.*
7. Sociologica, Aufsätze, *Frankfurt/M, 1955, the first volume of a book series published by the newly established* Institut für Sozialforschung; *and later in Leo Lowenthal,* Schriften, *Bd. 1, Frankfurt/M, 1980, S. 231ff.*

14

Correspondence of
Leo Lowenthal with Max Horkheimer

This letter was addressed to Max Horkheimer shortly before the entire Institute emigrated to New York, where Horkheimer was investigating work opportunities for the group. "P" is the abbreviation for Friedrich Pollock, "J" stands for the Journal of Social Research *and "H. R." for Heinrich Regius, the pseudonym under which Horkheimer published his collection of aphorisms,* Dämmerung, *in 1934.[8] The reference to the "work on the family" concerns the* Studien über Autorität und Familie, *Paris, 1936. "M" stands for Herbert Marcuse. Kundig was the name of a bookstore in Geneva.*

Geneva
June 21, 1934

[Dear Horkheimer]

I was very pleased with your letter of June 11th. I believe I may infer from it, especially given your cable, that your health has significantly improved and, beyond that, that you are very much inclined to assess our chances of working there quite favorably. Both of these circumstances cause me great pleasure—though at the moment the pleasure is clouded by thoughts of the genuine distress that your dear wife is going through. I had already warned her back then that one has to be extraordinarily careful with tonsilitis, which she no doubt was. But in such cases and even with the best doctors it is often impossible to avoid ensuing difficulties. I hope she is already far enough along by now that the doctor has no more acute symptoms to treat, but remains concerned only with strengthening her general condition. Enclosed is another list of proposed books from

Kundig but it might not add much of anything new to my long list of a few days ago.

As concerns the details of your letter, you know that you couldn't give me any greater pleasure than by directing me to come over very soon. I can truly say that my readiness to come harbors no wish for change, especially since my and our living conditions in the moment are indeed thoroughly satisfactory. It involves much more the most spirited of needs to resume personal and scientific contact with you just as soon as possible—in short, it means continuing my real life. I have the impression that I have rather composed myself internally in the last while. The essay is ready, and, while constantly toying with my "aesthetic" interests, I am pursuing, with some elan, the work on the family, so that you will be pleased once we are together again. And there is altogether *un tas de choses* on my Horkheimer program.

P has probably already informed you that I value most highly my readiness to make the journey over any time, but that he is what's holding me back. I can easily accept a delay in my departure until about the middle of July, for I must get myself intensively into the spirit of the "Family" in the next two weeks. As for the J, I have the reviews for the third issue already fundamentally together, and they could be completed just as well from there as here—in any case without any difficulties worth mentioning. Moreover, this argument has a strange dialectic: it has already proved valid for the second issue—it is now technically completely finished, and one can indeed continually reproduce this argument. There comes then in addition for P the financial consideration. That is made up of imponderables; it is difficult for me to judge the relation between real and psychological factors. In itself a joint stay at your holiday resort could certainly be made valuable scientifically as well, above all for fundamental questions; and Marcuse's presence could only raise the value of the discussions. As for the families, it is surely correct to arrange for their arrival there only in September. My wife and certainly Mrs. M agree completely, although it causes me some uneasiness that they will have to handle everything alone with the children. I write you this not because any tension has arisen here—on the contrary, in this whole matter P displays the true loyalty of friendship. But I don't want to miss any chance to clarify as exactly as possible my stance on these questions.

To my great satisfaction, I assume from your handwritten postscript that you were very pleased with H. R. For the bulk of the printing that remains, a cosmetic problem could be remedied by the insertion of a blank page between the title page and the table of contents. I agree completely with you concerning publicity: we've sent out over 200 copies and in the next few days I'll forward you a list so you can inform us here of whom you would like to add. The J is not going well—this is my single big disagree-ment with P: I'm of the opinion that in June and perhaps the beginning of July I should go to Paris and maybe a few other places to arrange for reviews. The written attempts we've made have not so far been very successful. But P is opposed. I don't know if you are prepared to take a position on this question from over there.

Concerning your book wishes, I've done everything necessary to ar-range for M to appear—not on a reef in Bermuda—but on the pier in New York with a small crate of logic.

Excuse the typing errors. Since I didn't want to dictate the letter to anyone and, on the other hand, cannot make of you a martyr to my handwriting, I've resorted with a groan to the typewriter.

As for the general situation, I have nothing to add to P's report and your supplemental telegram.

All the best to you and your dear wife!

[Leo Lowenthal]

Horkheimer wrote this letter to Lowenthal immediately before the latter's emigration to New York.

July 7, 1934

[Dear Lowenthal!]

You will probably arrive here when I'm in the country. Since Fromm, Marcuse, and Gumperz are away, the problem of having you picked up at the pier is not easy to solve. But it is easy to solve after all. My secretary, who is typing this letter, Miss Alice Heumann, knows you not merely from our correspondence and my flattering description of your person, but from some photographs as well. She will pick you up at the pier and help you get off immediately along your way to the resort. A mistake is next to impossible, since your steward will inform you that your luggage will be delivered to the pier under the letter "L" in the tourist class. You must wait there until the large and small luggage arrives from the ship, so it can pass through customs. If we assume that the ship is full—which I can hardly believe, since almost all passenger travel in these months goes from America to Europe and not vice versa—then there would still be barely a dozen people with the initial "L" traveling in your class. Probably it will be even fewer. Miss H, who in my experience is in no way stricken with blindness, will definitely find you among the ladies and bearded men with names beginning with "L". Aside from this, and in the interest of further certainty, I would ask that you cable me your cabin number as soon as you know it. Then Miss H will recognize you from your luggage as well.

Incidentally, Marcuse said that his trip in tourist class thoroughly satisfied him. His experience is that, for a little tip, one can always obtain a private cabin in the ship, even when the travel agent has no more to offer. I must add that the food consists of only a couple of rolls and water for breakfast, a kind of oatmeal porridge for lunch, and in the evenings a torte for the female passengers and a sour bonbon for the male. My wife, however, will request from the line you are travelling on that they serve you a portion of cauliflower with each meal, for a modest increase in price. If you cable me personally, I'll see that you get caramel pudding.

[Max Horkheimer]

This is one of Lowenthal's last letters from Geneva before he emigrated to New York. It mainly concerns Lowenthal's collaboration on the Studien über Autorität und Familie *and its publication. "D-studies" means Lowenthal's essay, "Die Auffassung Dostojewkijs im Vorkriegsdeutschland,"* ["The Reception of Dostoevsky in Pre-war Germany"] *which had already reached Horkheimer in manuscript. This essay was first published in 1935 in the* Zeitschrift für Sozialforschung.[9] *Maurette, who is mentioned in the letter, was an editor at the Félix Alcan publishing house in Paris.*

Geneva
July 14–15, 1934

[Dear Horkheimer!]

You cannot imagine how glad I was to receive the telegram in which you requested my speedy departure. It's a pity that P's departure today delayed mine somewhat—which is pleasant for neither of us. On the other hand, I must admit that there in fact remains much to be done if I'm to order affairs in the office here completely and carefully before I depart. It's not as if they were all first order matters, yet I haven't felt justified in opposing P's urgent desire to leave on the 2nd. Still, I'm very happy that there is now a firm date in the not too distant future when I will see you again.

Above all I would like to thank you sincerely for having done everything exactly as you proposed to me here to enable me to leave as quickly as possible. This includes the detail, which could in certain circumstances be very important, of having arranged for me to be able still to take advantage of the English visa. Unfortunately, the schedule will not allow me to see Paris again, but at least I'll take with me an impression of London. That

I'm able to leave the family in relatively pleasant conditions is, of course, an agreeable thought for me. I hope that circumstances don't force too long a separation—if I judge things reasonably correctly, the families will follow in the course of September, unless the impossibility of extending the Marcuses' visa past its expiration on August 30 dictates an earlier date.

And I thank you for your serious and humorous travel tips and forecasts. They could stand correction only on one point: cauliflower isn't the vegetable that portends the end of a friendship; it's boiled cabbage. But that can probably be taken care of on the ship! Must one actually play a demonstration rubber of Colbertson bridge for the immigration official? I'd be afraid then, especially given my only rudimentary knowledge of the language, that I wouldn't be allowed in. But I hope that your dear wife (who, incidentally, will receive the books she desired directly from Kundig) will take care of me in these as in other more intimate vital questions, in her usual friendly manner.

You didn't mention my Dostoevsky manuscript, but I hope nevertheless that it came into your possession as registered mail a few days before Marcuse arrived. Should that not be the case, please let us know in Geneva so we can complain at the post office.

I hope that you've both gotten well started with your relaxation and are practically bursting with health by the time I arrive. We will certainly have a great deal to discuss—you can well imagine that I ponder all the affairs of our Institute very intensively. With P I've also had relatively probing conversations about all the questions. (Your prediction concerning this point has been fully confirmed, if, as well, and especially in light of the not altogether uncomplicated situation in general, occasional tensions and grumbles are not to be avoided.)

Since it occupies me greatly, might I already say a word about the work on the family? I hadn't discussed this with you before your departure more than to welcome very much your decision to get me involved in it after the D-study was pretty well finished. I continue very much to welcome it, especially since I may assume from your letter of the 6th that your plans for this work would entail my close collaborations with you. I knew nothing more detailed about your particular intentions for the organization of the first publication, nor did I come to know anything from P. He welcomed my proposal that I be provided first with an overview of what is being considered and then make an organizational proposal concerning a certain coordination of the materials at hand and a very vague disposition of the planned work. I have to confess to being the author (essentially) of this plan and of the schema which you so decidedly rejected. To be sure, I have to add that I didn't regard as right the large space already allotted to the survey studies. On this I'm now wavering somewhat: (a) for reasons

I'll mention in a moment; and (b) because after the last two days I have the impression that Mrs. Leichter will be able to produce a very representable final report on the survey of Swiss youth.

Don't be unfair! Of course, such a plan as the one presented to you is anything but scientific in the sense of what is suitable to you and how such things must be according to very strict standards. P and Marcuse are doubtless able to confirm to you that I am personally very conscious of how problematic the matter is. Moreover, I had to guide myself into this new land in a very short time without, so to speak, a leader. But a plan, after all, doesn't hurt anything, even when one then gives it up completely. And—here is the main thing for me—if in the foreseeable future we, as the Institute, bring out a thick volume that contains very abundant literature reviews, indirectly or directly collected primary data, and then hypotheses as well, we will have accomplished, circumstances permitting, something which might legitimize our scholarly endeavors, or at least, in this context, can present a "weighty" document. If, finally, you do not withhold your approval of the plan in principle—a refusal, of course, I could accept with the most conscientious parts of my scientific mind—then perhaps something would result that carried, indeed, all the signs of concession in itself, but that would allow us to breathe more easily. And, besides, it goes without saying that the work (compare above all the first and last planned chapters) should be blood of our blood. In this context, I also think that it would be conceivable and not inappropriate to our purpose to take a look at the entire complex of the family, at least for the literature review. It is perhaps in part merely a stylistic problem (which doesn't appear to me impossible to overcome) that over and over, especially in the pedagogical, legal and socio-political reports, the plan begins with a more general point of departure but then the explanations proceed to the problem of authority, which, for theoretical reasons, must constantly reappear as a central point. I was of the opinion that such a plan would meet half-way the American need for facts, facts, facts and do so in a fashion that would show us to be people who knew how to value the scientific virtues of both continents. Now, after P's visit to Maurette, about which he has surely reported to you, it appears to me that such a "bold" undertaking (certainly in the bad sense as well) could possess significance for us in Europe too.

It is easy for me to see how you might condemn the whole standpoint (excuse the dreadful image!) that I suggested; that is, that you regard it as insufficiently grounded. But I cannot refrain from at least mentioning it to you, because the thought that the whole of what we pursued here suggests merely bad formulations from bad impressions makes me feel terrible. As for me, I felt obliged toward you in every way to rack my brains as intensively and as hastily as possible over the collective work. Admittedly, that doesn't mean it's not still nonsense.

As you requested, I will pack the material together and bring it with me. Aside from my two or three suitcases, the typewriter and such, I will probably arrive with two or three boxes of books. But I assume I'll be able to leave these somehow in N.Y., since there's probably no purpose in having them shipped to the resort right away. Probably, your secretary (to whom I send my regards and, as you suggested, will cable my cabin number) will instruct me on what to do about that. I suspect that I'll not be able to bring my typewriter (on which I'm constantly writing you so zealously). My wife will take care of that.

My wife asked me to enclose the little picture with her most heartfelt greetings to you and your wife. It was made during a visit from Mrs. Jacot and her children in our garden. I take particular pleasure, by the way, in Daniel, who is developing very well. Things are mixed for my wife—I'm a little worried in particular about her knee pains. But I think that she will arrive there in fine shape, since her living conditions here are good. I'm already eager to see how it all looks over there.

In any case I'm very much looking forward to the trip, to seeing both of you again, and to our collective work in various areas. Because of the delay in my departure, it's probably still possible that you will convey to me one or another request or bit of advice.

[Leo Lowenthal]

This letter is addressed to Max Horkheimer, who was traveling at the time in Europe. It provides insight into the conditions under which the journal was produced. Oppenheimer is the former economist and sociologist Franz Oppenheimer from Frankfurt/M. Mrs. Sommerfeld is the wife of Professor Sommerfeld, a former Germanist at the University of Frankfurt.

New York
November 22, 1935

[Dear Horkheimer!]

As I'm writing this letter, that is, at 4:30 European time, you are perhaps already sitting in a train for Paris, and in any case have already caught sight of the coast of France. I hope you and your dear wife had a pleasant crossing. I assume the horrible storm, which evidently caused your wife to suffer right at the beginning of the voyage, let up as you left American waters. I hope you were left unbothered by unwarranted demands from your internal organs.

Yesterday evening the proofs of your essay arrived. We, that is, Marcuse, Maier, and I, are reading them today, and I'm sending you a galley in the same post, where you will find the corrections that have already been made. I estimate that it will easily take a good two weeks until all the proofs are collected and it is possible for me to make the page proofs, so it will be quite sufficient if you let me know in New York what changes and corrections you still wish to have made. Should there be a delay for some reason, your further corrections could (reluctantly!) be made according to your instructions in the Paris Office; that means they would be entered in the page proofs that are to be expected from New York. The essay itself reads truly magnificently; I've read through about two-thirds now and have scarcely the slightest change to suggest. Incidentally, it is significantly more poorly set than has been the case till now; evidently, on account of the work on the book, Mr. Lisbonne, that is, the press, did not use the same employees as on the composition till now of the third issue.

Yesterday afternoon I was at a lecture by Oppenheimer to which Pollock went on Monday. O set forth his economic theory so miserably he inspired pity. It was so boring even the largely American public could hardly endure it. This obstinate liberalism, which was always brave only where it wasn't too costly (as measured against the dominant tendencies), can't even gather laurels anymore. Not only those like [Meyer] Schapiro, but even less sophisticated people left the lecture hall during the talk.

We invited the Tillichs over yesterday evening and it was, so to speak, a *succés*. Aside from the personal, one notes in every word he speaks how much he falls under the Institute's influence—that is, yours—and, since he is, after all, an honest fellow and in spite of his love, anchored in inclination and character, for the New School of Social Research, how much he feels that it is we who take up the better cause. Unfortunately, he somehow has assumed the mission of sponsoring a close discussion between those people and us anyway. As long as you're away and insofar as I can do anything one way or the other, I will treat these attempts to bring about a discussion dilatorily.

By the way, I met Mrs. Sommerfeld at Oppenheimer's lecture. She had evidently long forgotten that it was your turn to call and had a bad conscience because she hadn't called you again. Apparently, the sensation of a bad conscience here is transferred from one thing to another.

I think my own work is moving right along. I will spend the rest of November primarily studying the materials, and hope to begin writing in the first week of December.

At home things are just fine. Unfortunately, my wife had another very serious attack of migraine for two days after you were gone, from which she's still not completely recovered.

I hope the two of you are *physiquement* and *moralement* in the best of shape.

Since P told me that you'd like to have all the copies of letters sent to Europe, I'm enclosing the carbon.

Tillich also brought his "self-portrait" with him yesterday. It will probably appear in an English edition of essays by him. There's a small, not so apt, mention of us in it (about which one should probably speak with him) as follows;

"One can understand Marxism as a method of unveiling and in this compare it with psychoanalysis (see the works of my friends from the Institute of Social Research, formerly of Frankfurt/M, now at Columbia University in New York, above all their *Journal of Social Research*)."

I know how fond you are of just that word, "unveiling"! A misguided favor if ever there was one.

[Leo Lowenthal]

––––––––––

Meyer Schapiro, named in the paragraph numbered 2, is an important historian of art who taught at the time at Columbia University. The book referred to in the remark in the paragraph numbered 5 is the Studien über Autorität and Familie. *The Korsch mentioned in the postscript is Karl Korsch; Weber is Alfred Weber.*

New York
December 11, 1935

[Dear Horkheimer!]

1. Your decision in regard to the third issue pleased me very much. This way it will be among the best of the issues we've brought out. I reread your essay and I'm extraordinarily impressed all over again. One can say that in a certain sense all of the themes of your previous articles have been taken up again in this essay and appear, insofar as we can even talk about such a thing, as a "system," precisely as moments of an open-ended dialectic. As for the technical aspects of getting the issue ready, it was easy on the basis of the existing page proofs to take the ten pages by which Fromm's essay exceeded Weiß's from the review section. The psychology section in the reviews is bad this time, since the better pieces, which had been newly set, couldn't be used anymore; but that's probably acceptable because there's a psychological essay in the issue itself. The newly set pieces would also have made the section on "Social Movement" more

comprehensive. But I think these shortcomings are of less harm than getting the page proofs to the printer after Christmas would have been, that is, practically speaking, next year. Besides, the issue gains as a whole through the addition of the impressive annual register. I would like to propose that you give the enclosed copy of my letter to the Paris Office, including the table of contents which has already been sent, and the annual register to Mrs. Favez, so she can eliminate the excluded reviews altogether and take care of the changes in the table of contents for articles in both the index and the annual register. That way, she'll have a faultless basis from which to proof the revisions.

2. Recently in the history students' club (where you should give a lecture sometime) Schapiro spoke about the relationship between art history and social history. The man is extraordinarily gifted; he speaks excellently with no manuscript whatsoever, as quickly as I've heard anyone speak, and without losing his train of thought or muddling his sentence structure. On the other hand, the talk was revealing of the American mentality. One would assume, after all, that if Schapiro is going to speak about such a topic, he would treat it dialectically—the very formulation of the topic cries for it. Instead, he delivered an analysis of the exchange value of artistic versus historical documents and mounted a polemic against an abstract view of aesthetics. He proceeded approximately on this level: idealism and positivism alone won't do, one has to regard the things more cynically and precisely. There was no more to it than that. And I don't think he can do any more either, unless he's addressing a specific problem in his narrower area of expertise.

3. Meanwhile, I've gone to the Van Gogh exhibit, which you probably didn't manage to see. At first I didn't really want to go—and had never gone to the Metropolitan Museum—because I have the feeling that the same things look different here as in Europe. I have to say, though, that I was able to abstract from all that at the Van Gogh exhibit, even if I regretted being able to understand English, since the viewers were all babbling dreadful nonsense. But the revelation of the unavoidable grief of the individual in this society, tied directly into the constitutive elements of suffering on the part of human beings altogether, receives such authentic expression at the hands of this artist as one can only imagine from critical art of the present or from art of other times devoted to specific themes. Despite all the material that I've read or reread for my essay, and although I'm not at all qualified to speak on the visual arts, here was where I learned what was crucial for my plans for the essay.

4. If you get one, please don't miss the chance to see the film *Crime et Chàtiment*. It is excellent. I know scarcely a single film that remains so true to the literary work of art as this one. Indeed, since it was made by

the French, it might even surpass Dostoevsky to include a good bit of Flaubert. Harry Baur is an excellent actor. He played the investigating judge, but all the other roles are cast with great sensibility as well.

5. I was very pleased and moved to hear yesterday from P that you've received the first copies of our book. I congratulate all of us, but especially you, on having it now—and, if one thinks about everything involved, in such a relatively short time. From final planning to delivery, it took barely a year; and that, even under more normal conditions, would have been very fast. By the end of 1935, we'll have four years' of complete volumes of the journal and this work of 1,000 pages to show, and God knows have no reason to be embarrassed by questions as to what the Institute does.

6. My wife is not doing well. Her attacks of migraine follow in extremely short order of late and all of Dr. Lichtwitz' shots and medicines have no effect whatever. It's a terrible condition, and we have no idea what we should do. You have to imagine that during one of these attacks you're so plagued by headache and nausea—for days—that life is unbearable, and when it passes you're terrified and already waiting for the next one. Pleasant it's not.

7. We haven't yet had any direct news from you, and P, as you know, is somewhat stingy with information. But I definitely assume that your health and your wife's has been good so far. That Paris and Geneva were so irritating was to be predicted, but I'm sympathetic anyway. I hope you've also had good days and pleasant experiences.

[Leo Lowenthal]

P.S. Korsch wrote, among other things, that he couldn't take on the Weber, sociology of culture. Should you happen to meet our historical collaborator in Geneva, August Siemsen, please consider whether we can give it to him. Apparently, the book is miserable. Incidentally, Paris just sent a pile of French reviews. They're mostly too long and many are also unimportant. Everything seems to go through Mr. [Raymond] Aron. None of the books that are truly important and that we've complained about getting for the last year is there: *Annales sociologiques,* Bouglé, *Bilan de la sociologie,* the new Levy-Bruhl; *A la lumière du marxisme.* I'm writing nothing about this to the Paris Office.

This letter gives a detailed impression of Lowenthal's editorial work on the journal, especially of his efforts to get important intellectuals to contribute reviews. The essay discussed in the second paragraph is a work on naturalism that was not published in its original form. It was replaced by the essay on Ibsen that appeared in the Journal for Social Research *in*

1937.[10] *The letter documents the Institute's resolve to continue the journal's publication in Europe, that is, by Alcan in Paris. P.O. refers to the Institute's Paris Office.*

New York
January 24, 1936

[Dear Horkheimer!]

We weren't exactly pleased to hear that your stay in Europe will now be somewhat longer than you originally assumed. I hope, at least, that that means you won't have to spend the last weeks so hectically as I've heard was so far the case. Your remark that your health, aside from a few relatively minor problems, has remained good made me especially happy. We hope that your wife's flu is altogether gone now and finds no successors.

My essay was finished yesterday, and I'm sending you a copy enclosed. The title is a bit dull; but I couldn't think of anything else, especially since the kind of literary titles that are in themselves more appropriate for the subject (like "The Self-Judgment of Liberalism" or something similar) aren't really acceptable to us. As my own self-judgment, I anticipate the following: a number of things that in themselves ought to have been pursued are only suggested—for example, the relationship of art and practice, the role of sexuality in private reification phenomena, the relation of *l'art pour l'art* (including Flaubert) to naturalism, ultimately the affinity between art and death; moreover, P, who could read only five pages, had the impression that sentences were often too long for a foreigner to understand, even if they were thoroughly understandable for people like us. But this defect (if it is one) can be relatively easily eliminated. To my own surprise, the attempt at an analysis of naturalism, especially of Ibsen, became largely a critique; but things have gone so far by now that one who measures even such progressive phenomena as naturalism against theory [Critical Theory] is forced to genuinely negative conclusions.

The issue is so far advanced that the whole manuscript can be sent on March 31 on the "Europe" to Paris. I think it right to send you now a copy of a few reviews containing certain problems, so that you can have a look at them and instruct the P.O. on appropriate changes or cuts to be made in the original manuscript to be sent on the 31st. Concerned are:

1. *[Paul] Tillich's review of the [Kurt] Goldstein book.* In itself it was kind of T to write the review at all; I think it's the first he's ever written. The review is very long and very positive. In respect to the length, he's expressly authorized me to make it shorter. Marcuse and I propose to cut the parts that I've marked on the enclosed copy in brackets. If you agree

with them, please pass it on to the P.O., since I'm not marking cuts on the original.

2: *[Kurt] Goldstein's review of [Friedrich] Alverdes.* This review is also somewhat long. But G maintains you and he agreed on an extensive critique and that he has your approval for this review to appear under a pseudonym. I have no material reservations.

3. *Honegger's review of [Helmut] Plessner.* The original version, as you have already indicated, was completely unacceptable. We've thoroughly marked up the manuscript and in the present form one could perhaps publish it if need be. A pleasure it's not. In any case, I would be grateful if you'd like to make a decision on it. The manuscript will come with the packet on the 31st.

4. *[Siegfried] Marck's review of [Kurt] Breysig.* There are probably no reservations to be had here. It's only that M, unfortunately, has written that he'd rather write an essay than a review for us, because the books in his area are so outstandingly reviewed by Marcuse.

5. *[Karl] Löwith's group review.* On account of this review he started a horribly fussy, long correspondence with me and finally reviewed seven books on not less than seventeen large typewritten pages. Marcuse shortened the manuscript and edited it, but it's still long. On the book by Heyse, L writes: "With the best intentions the review of Hans Heyse could not be made shorter. Since the book is so representative and the single more important publication since Heidegger and Jaspers, I ask that in this case you make an exception to the usual length limitations." Marcuse says he's in fact correct in his opinion of Heyse, but we were able to make a few cuts there anyway

The technical part of the reviewing apparatus is now so refined in New York and apparently also in Geneva, that I believe I can repeat my promise that in the future gross errors will be completely avoided. As far as I can tell, I bear hardly any responsibility for the mess in France; my lists of proposed books were never worked through—apparently, never even read—up until the resulting intervention now. That will probably not happen again. The main problem appears to me to be that the P.O. doesn't simply send us the books whose titles we give them, but checks whether the books are worth reviewing. With minor exceptions, I agree completely with Pollock's remarks on the last packet of French manuscripts. Among Bouglé's suggestions was, incidentally, a book that we could hardly review. It was the text (which came out simultaneously in America) by that half-crazy doctor and Nobel Prize winner, [Alexis] Carrel, about the unknown man.

On the reviews for the next issue it just occurred to me that we could probably publish the group review by Asters, while I propose holding back the Jaspers review for the moment, and maybe having Marcuse write it anew. He, incidentally, is preparing the reviews of the books we discussed in the Italian restaurant on East 13th St. for the next issue.

I was enormously pleased with the authority book. In all good faith I can't bring myself—on account of the certainly significant technical deficiencies, including a few unpleasant typographical errors—to forget how inestimably positive this volume is for the Institute, and maybe not just for the Institute. It's actual weight is a materialization of the weightiness of its arguments! Moreover, we are much too much specialists in publications and tend to get upset over things that a non-specialist doesn't even notice or even things (as, for example, the type of paper) that make a positive rather than negative impression.

P informed me that you have decided for the present to have the journal continue to come out in Europe and even to keep it at Alcan. That pleased me very much too; in one of my last letters I probably hinted at the troubles that I think could arise for us should we move the organization to America.

I'm enclosing copies of a few letters.

[Leo Lowenthal]

This letter offers insight into the relationships within the Institute's circle of collaborators. Beyond that, it documents the Institute's relations with contemporary Marxist groups in the U.S. Robert Lynd and Robert McIver were the best-known chaired professors in the Sociology Department at Columbia University. Benjamin Nelson later became world famous as a historian at the New School in New York, similar to Finkelstein (alias, M. I. Finley), who later became one of the leading classicists in the anglo-saxon world. Sidney Hook was at the time a well-known Marxist intellectual; he is now a prominent neoconservative.

September 14, 1937

[Dear Horkheimer!]

I was very pleased with your letter of September 5th, which arrived today. I can imagine how many demands are made on you over there. A card from your dear wife tells us that at least she gets to see you when everyone is asleep. It's truly a paradox that Europe means more activity for you now than America. But then the unparadoxical is altogether rarely our lot anyway.

The lectures [at Columbia University] are a real headache. To begin with, it's been established that we absolutely have to remain with Tuesdays. Monday Lynd has his main seminar; Wednesday evening McIver has his, and Thursday his assistant Innes. Friday is, as always, termed impossible by all the experts in these matters.

My mainstays as prospective participants are Nelson and Finkelstein. They are fairly certain they'll be able to provide enough people. I'm once again not so sure. The majority of the students hasn't arrived here yet, so the man-to-man discussions, that is, discussions between us and the students, can only begin next week. Schapiro is still out of town; [Bernard] Stern, with whom I was to have had a lunch date today, is ill. By chance I met Louis Hacker today (Nelson introduced us)—he's the one [Franz] Neumann wanted to speak to. He's the embodiment of *ressentiment,* and one doesn't really know if he calls himself a Marxist out of *ressentiment* or holds *ressentiment* to be the virtue of Marxists. After he conversed for twenty minutes in his version of a friendly manner (not without mentioning three times that the *Marxist Quarterly* needs money) he had ultimately to stammer out after all that we should finally formally invite him and his like-minded friends. It is out of the question that this kind of person can do anything for us. Compared to him, Mr. Hook seems a great personality.

Meanwhile, we've drawn up a kind of overview of the seminar, which I'm sending to you enclosed. I think the text is not too candid and rather interest inspiring. In any case I'll take it upon myself to see that the text doesn't get into all that many hands once it's been copied.

I had a conversation today with Lazarsfeld and that, together with what I read between Brill's lines, forces me to say that I'm amply irritated with Teddie. Obviously, he followed none of our advice concerning his appearance [. . .]. That he explained in front of a large group of positivists that you traveled to Europe to be present at his wedding belongs in the realm of the comic. But that he—in response to a question from [Rudolf] Carnap, whether he represented all of his anti-positivist formulations as personal views or as those of Horkheimer and the Institute—ultimately affirmed the latter, and then added that you discussed every sentence of your postivism essay with him, is less humorous. I believe it would be just as good for his own self-confidence, as for our security, if he appealed more to the voice of his own intellect and less to big brother.

Marcuse and I, at Pollock's request, have let you know what we think of the essay [by Adorno] on Husserl. It is hard for me to comprehend how Teddie sees this as his greatest accomplishment. For the rest, he's sent three interminable reviews of Cassirer, [Ernst] Krenek, and Kracauer, which, with touching modesty, he characterized in the accompanying letter as model reviews. It is simply tragic, what a blockage of inner and outer activity threatens this high intellect.

The English translations are progressing approximately in accord with the program I described in my last letter. Your essay and Marcuse's will be completely ready this week and mine begun tomorrow. Lazarsfeld still hopes to be able to complete the manuscript in September.

I've begun the reading for my new piece. I think you have picked an excellent topic; we only hope that I can get "a handle" on it too.

Personally things are going just fine—even if Marcuse's definition of the family turned out true for the three of us [Marcuse, in jest, had once defined the family as a group of at least three people of different gender and age, of whom at least one is always ill]. Only Daniel is still ill with his gland infection. You see, in geophysical terms, New York has it's constants.

With the warmest regards from both of us to you and your dear wife,

[Leo Lowenthal]

Among other things, this letter provides a view of Lowenthal's participation in the Institute's endowment and funding policies. Karsen (or "K") is Fritz Karsen, the former director of the Karl Marx Gymnasium in Berlin. Hans Meyer is the journalist and well-known historian of literature. Angelica Balabanoff was a famous Russion communist and companion of Lenin.

June 24, 1938

[Dear Horkheimer!]

Many thanks for your letter of the 21st. Your trip seems to be going not only pleasantly and interestingly, as was to be expected, but to be exceeding expectations. We're happy about that.

Meanwhile, the recovery has broken loose in America. I don't really believe in it, but the stock market is recovering for the time being. I have to pay you the compliment of once again having had a much better instinct for judging the situation than I. I recall that you counted on us approaching 140. That's exactly how it looks now. I've given up our purchase—too expensive at the time we purchased them—for approximately the purchase price and sold short. Both were wrong. We won't indeed lose anything, but we do forfeit profits. The last three days seem to me as if they've cost me three years. It's not all bad, if one thinks in absolute numbers. But it is damned irritating—to avoid a much more precise and stronger expression—when everything goes differently than one expected when one does believe to have considered it carefully. Among all our direct and distant advisers, S proved himself the most able. Had I had his skill or he my courage, much would have gone differently. I did indeed learn a lot from the affair, but unfortunately I can make use of my knowledge only on the next swing. Originally, I called the current swing a rally for the dumb people; in the moment, I'm the dumb one.

Pollock asked me to write you my opinion on the Karsen matter. I read the file memo, which he is sending you, about his visit to Rockefeller. In distinction to Pollock and Neumann, I don't find it dangerous to deliver an explanation that says: We have the intention of appointing Karsen for the next three years as corresponds to the Foundation's proposals. It is known to Rockefeller (see the file memo) that we are in difficulty; furthermore that K has been a collaborator of ours for years. The fact that a scientific institute receives money for one of its collaborators from various committees indeed already proves that its situation is not overly brilliant. That doesn't yet mean, however, that the institute closes down, releases all its collaborators and refuses all proposals for future scientific projects along with the accompanying tentative appointments *a limine*. If we don't send the letter, then Karsen cartainly won't receive the money from the Duggan Committee; nor will be receive it from Rockefeller if we write a completely lukewarm letter and if we don't say at least something about our intention. I simply don't believe that such a relatively trifling sum as we hold out in prospect for the next years, but don't firmly promise, blocks our plan to apply for amounts for our scientific aims that really do come into question. I almost want to say, to the contrary. By appointing K we document our interest in an area of social research that rings particularly nicely in American ears, namely, education. That, put extremely, the assurance of one year's existence for Karsen simultaneously means putting our own security in jeopardy is something that doesn't seem to me correct. I'm anxious to see what you decide.

We can't publish the article on Georg Büchner by Hans Meyer. I already wrote him on May 4th that though the article was very nice, etc., it was doubtful that we could publish an article so monographically oriented. Marcuse judged the work very positively, as the enclosed opinion shows. I find the work less satisfying, since it deals only in wholly general literary categories and simply cites you and other authors for the journal now and again in a byzantine manner. It claims, for example, that Büchner occupied the transitional point between traditional and critical theory! It's my opinion that one should tell him that the journal is already more than full for the current year anyway and that for us to publish the work, in itself not specifically appropriate but otherwise qualitatively satisfactory, would cause difficulties.

As was to be expected, Mrs. Wendriner's literary historical undertaking is also inappropriate for us. One could only summarize and cut the nineteen page work into a notice, but the result would not be satisfactory.

My opinion is that we should keep it, as we did her last contribution, and even pay an honorarium, but for the moment pass over the question of publication with a refined silence. At my request, Marcuse has also summarized his impression of the article in a brief memo.

At your request, I met Mrs. Balabanoff and remain in contact. I find her an extraordinarily pleasant woman. We are being helpful to her in a whole series of matters.

As I read through you letter once again, I see that you wrote the same thing that I just said to Pollock on the telephone: that the world is out of joint. If my remark referred only to the market climbing ever more furiously into the heights, then the fright that overtakes me there, more for reasons of chance, belongs to the general horror that subjects us all, but more than us, the others, the ones closest to us, to the most terrible of contingencies.

[Leo Lowenthal]

Alongside atmospheric insights into the difficulties of editorial work on the journal and the administration of the Institute's funds, this letter reflects concern over a law that was planned at the time but then left unpassed which would have threatened the security of emigrants in the U.S.

Woods Hole (Mass.)
P.O.B. 504

July 30, 1939

[Dear Horkheimer!]

As I prepared to sit down and write you about all kinds of things I was interrupted by the arrival of the newspapers, which are rather alarming. Unfortunately, the New York papers that are available here don't contain the original text of the law that's just gone to the Senate where, in my opinion, it will face no big battle. The extent to which the progressive liberals are already allowing themselves to be terrorized can't be imagined. If I read it correctly, this law is an instrument by which practically every foreign resident can be expelled. The only thing really missing now is a traffic offense as grounds for deportation. If I get Atropin from the pharmacist, for which I needed a prescription, and that is known to me, then I'm already an unwelcome foreigner, because I've transgressed a state narcotics law; if my son is in the possession of a knife which a judge regards as a weapon, then the same is true. That of which a resolute group in Congress is capable is something one can easily calculate, but perhaps also something one cannot yet dream at all. [. . .] Incidentally, one more problem concerning the law that I don't understand from the texts known to me thus far: if someone belonged to an undesirable organization twenty years earlier for eight days, can he still be expelled even though he immigrated much, much later? [. . .]

I'm also enclosing the correspondence with [Henryk] Grossmann. He's making a modest attempt to place his essay in the next issue. I hope you agree with my reply.

And the article is enclosed with the letter. I'm grateful that you sent it to me. It is really splendid. Incidentally, it is astounding and one of the highest praises of your style that occurs to me that a friend can quote your article "out of context" so that what's essential comes directly to light, while in the mouth of an enemy the same sentences would be a truly powerless and for certain experts scarcely persuasive weapon. [. . .]

Once again on the third dividing page: I had asked B at the time to make up the sheets so that only the title of the authority book and not the table of contents appeared, and have the reviews, which were previously on the third page, come immediately after the title information. I would like to withdraw my proposal to print an index for this issue instead of this review, and think it better if our respectability remains documented somewhere in the journal by the former reviews. Please let me know your decision in time so we don't lose any time for the page proofs.

Meanwhile, I've received the [Julian] Gumperz and [Felix] Weil reviews, which I am returning to Mrs. Bloch in the same post. In the enclosure you'll find a list of the changes I think are necessary. I sent the original of my remarks to P, because, after all, he exercises a kind of protectorate over the economic review section. But I will ask for your decision in those cases where he doesn't agree with me. Your opposition to the printing of Guillebaud took a load off my mind. I told P when I first looked into it that I can't regard this tedious and boring bit of pedantry as a gain for the journal.

Since I know your aversion for long letters, I want to postpone some of the questions that I must still ask you about the journal till tomorrow or the next day and address only one more matter. A few days ago Pollock sent me a receipt for my countersignature in which the trust fund thanked SIRES [Société Internationale des Recherches Sociales] for the transfer of $50,000. Now I recall very precisely a conversation before the founding in which you explained to me that the SIRES had absolutely no right to make such bequests—or whatever they are. I, in fact, aired the question whether we couldn't simply take the money over from the SIRES. It came thus from the ROBEMA company at the time and for that the gentlemen's agreement to lend $50,000 to Ryelake was regarded in more or less obligatory form as invalidated. What's changed about that now? I don't feel very good about it. You and P are directors of SIRES. P pays money to a fund which he administers with a 50 percent vote and whose sole beneficiary is you. And we explain to third parties (F[elix Weil]), who have contracts with the SIRES, that we have almost exhausted our funds. Perhaps I've overlooked something in my presentation of the issue, or there's an important fact which should be adduced here that I don't know about. But if that's not the case, then the procedure isn't exactly possessed of the circumspection that we normally observe in such transactions, and I don't understand why the second installment can't be transferred in the same manner as the first. In case P should say that it has to do with the fact that the foundation's tax exempt status has meanwhile been recognized, I couldn't accept that as valid because he explained to me at the time of the Dutch check that it was questionable to what extent this donation from out of the country could remain tax-free if the charitable or educational purpose of the foundation wasn't recognized.

Here—as I said, out of consideration for your reading patience—I would like to close. You haven't, I hope, forgotten that I'm happy to come to New York immediately, any time at all you might wish it. But that so approaches personal matters that the letter would get too long after all. So I don't want to touch any further on the matter that, along side my wife's and my well-being, causes me so much concern. It's just this: please, count on me always.

[Leo Lowenthal]

After the occupation of Paris by German troops, the publication and printing of the journal had to be transferred to New York. The first paragraph of the letter reflects the move.

The paragraph numbered 2 concerns an extensive research project about Nazi Germany, for which resources were to be applied for from the Rockefeller Foundation. The project was never realized.

Mirra Komarovsky was a sociologist at Columbia University who occasionally worked with the Institute. Hans Fried was an attorney with an interest in sociology and, incidentally, a nephew of Hans Kelsen. David Glass, a famous sociologist and economist, taught later at the London School of Economics.

429 West 117th Street
New York City

July 24, 1940

[Dear Horkheimer!]

You can imagine that your letter of the 21st and your congratulations-advance telegram of the 23rd pleased me more than a little. I hope that you and your dear wife have recovered the energies and wind in Estes Park that I anticipated must have been lost to you in the prairie. I still recall in great detail a post card the Schachtels once sent me from Estes Park years ago and assume that the landscape is a very fine one. But Colorado Springs is not ugly either.

The work here is going according to program and we are very busy. Since you've been away I've been stricken, as I might say out of the modesty that suits me so well, with a regular epidemic of diligence, under which, as she informed me, Miss von Mendelssohn suffers. It's atrocious for her to say so after I not only, as usual, drive her home (now without any competition from you), but also bring her to work every morning. But unfair accusations are evidently my fate.

As for "business", I have the following to report:

1. *Journal*. The page proofs are not yet there, because the printers made a mistake; but I expect them in the course of the afternoon and believe I can promise that the journal will be shipped, that is, the shipping completed, at the latest on August 2nd. The necessary letters to the book review editors of the important journals, to the publishers and to the subscribers have already been drafted. For the letters to prominent people I have conferred with Teddie, as you requested, and called upon Neumann to give me suggestions as to what requires special attention in the case of one or the other. Mr. Glass will help me too.

I ask myself whether it's correct to send out many rather long letters. By now we've corresponded quite a lot with prominent professors—when the Advisory Committee was founded, and when the projects were shipped off, and when the letterhead was made. It could perhaps make a somewhat obtrusive impression to send out a lengthy letter once again. It's my opinion that it is better to write briefly, especially since the reasons for founding the new organ will be clear from your foreword.

2. *German Project*. I sent you Neumann's statements first off without commentary. I don't agree with them. A duplication of our previous projects for the time period from 1933 to 1940 lacks theoretical justification. The chapters on philosophy, literature and music would be more collections of jokes than contributions to enlightenment. Insofar as these areas are important, I think they belong in a chapter on propaganda. I would find it much more correct if Neumann—who has all the material at his disposal for his book anyway—wrote a tentative outline under the headings economy, politics, and working class. There must then be added an outline on propaganda, which could perhaps be based on Kracauer's manuscript. Newmann's idea, to bring [Alfred] Vagts in on the project, I think to be a happy one. As you see from the copy of my file memo for Pollock, I would like to suggest that he inquire of Vagts whether he would be prepared to

contribute a study of National Socialist military policy and the relation between the army and the party. I think, for substantive reasons as well as for reasons concerning the division of labor, it would be quite practical if you assisted Neumann in understanding the hint in your letter somewhat more distinctly and in getting busy on a draft outline. I may add that I've discussed this whole set of questions with Teddie, with whom I thoroughly agree.

3. *New School.* I don't consider it terribly adroit to begin dealing somehow officially with the New School just now. Since Teddie and I are quite well acquainted with [Jacob] Marschak, we thought of a luncheon that's now supposed to take place at Teddie's with the ladies, and there we want first to hear a bit more about what's really going on there. Since, according to everything I heard from Halasi and also according to what Teddie managed to get from Fried, there's no real clarity at the New School in the moment about what they really ought to be doing, I consider it much better if we try to work something out that conveys, relatively, a united impression. Anyway, only you or Pollock should speak to Askoli; September seems to me an appropriate date for that.

4. *Komarovsky.* Since I was downtown yesterday on account of the blunders at the printer, I couldn't write you myself about the Komarovsky foreword. Lazarsfeld attaches great significance to the inclusion of the acknowledgements in the foreword. I have no reservations whatever, but, of course, I didn't want to give my okay to a text signed by you before you knew about it. I let Miss Komarovsky know (she is out of town) that the foreword may not be printed before I've gotten your authorization.

5. *Fried.* F handed in a dreadful research project on civil rights under National Socialism and claimed on the telephone: a) that you said that Dr. Glass should work through it; and b) that he understood that you were prepared to submit it to a foundation—indeed, as he thought, to Earle in Princeton. Glass took a look at the project and says that it is completely unusable in its present form and that he would have to completely rewrite it. I think, though, that it has nothing to do with us and that we have no cause to spend money on it. I told Fried that I couldn't imagine that you had the intention of submitting it for him during the holidays, which, after all, apply to the foundations as well. I said that it was probably your intention to decide at the beginning of the semester which projects of the Institute or of individual members or individual associates ought to be submitted and where. Since I promised F I would inform you of his conversation with me, please make a comment to me concerning this point. [. . .]

7. *Glass.* That Miss Orent was away for the weekend when we needed someone to go over an important letter turned out to be a real stroke of

luck (I get the credit once again—it was I who thought of Glass). He works absolutely excellently and, indeed, for the present for next to no pay— namely, $20.00 for the last three weeks! Naturally, I call on him as little as possible. What's important to me in this context, though, is the following: Teddie diligently writes the letters with which you have entrusted him. The results are not always very happy. Most of the time Pollock's and my persuasive skills help, but not always. The products of Teddie plus Pollock and Lowenthal aren't good either, and Glass is the only one who really knows how to write a good letter to an American professor. You would do me a very great service if, as soon as possible, you remarked in a letter to Teddie that you've established repeatedly how ably Glass edits letters and that you would propose that he regard Glass as a kind of higher instance whenever an agreement as to content has been reached between Glass, Pollock, and me. Otherwise, please believe me that the collaboration with Teddie is going quite well, even if it means for all of us a lot of frayed nerves, time, and worn out telephone ears.

Cordial regards to both of you.

Yours,
Leo Lowenthal

This letter to Max Horkheimer illustrates the manifold scientific, editorial, and personal activities of the Institute for Social Research at the start of the 1940s. Charles Beard was a significant American economic historian; Alfred Vagts, his son-in-law, a well-known military historian. Kurt Pinthus was one of the most important expressionist writers. Karl Landauer, a former Frankfurt psychoanalyst, died in Buchenwald concentration camp. Kander was a personal friend of Horkheimer.

429 West 117th Street
New York City

August 2, 1940

[Dear Horkheimer!]

Forgive me that I haven't written yet this week, but made do with a telegram to Albuquerque instead. I was in a constant rush between the office and the printer's, the office and the refugee organizations, and then the same over again. Now I'm taking care of what's been neglected.

1. *Journal.* It seems to be an internationally valid law of the species that printers don't keep their promises. In France one is deceived by weeks and months; in this country at least it's only days. I hoped that the journal, which was firmly promised for August 1st, would be delivered Monday at

the latest. Now it will be Tuesday. You will receive the first copy (at great expense) by air mail, and, unless I hear otherwise from you, further copies as normal printed matter. I'm enclosing in this letter a publisher's blurb that goes primarily in the copies meant for the editorial board. We're sending you ten more copies with the same post as regular printed matter. For further publicity, the prospectus is important. I've implored Pollock not to return without prefatory remarks from Lynd and Beard and also not to leave here without having tried to get MacIver committed to a few lines. As I imagine it, these remarks will appear on the first page of the prospectus; on page three comes the table of contents for the issue just appearing; the fourth serves for the announcement of the next two issues and of articles otherwise planned as well as for the order blank. I need your help for the second page, which should probably contain a short history of the journal. Enclosed you will find a draft text for this second page, and I would be very grateful if you would return it soon with your comments so the prospectus can definitely be ready before the end of August.

2. *German Project*. Your letter to Neumann came straight from my heart. Already when you wrote him from New York I had the feeling it would be right to suggest to him a quick return. You've done an injustice to your present letter; in terms of content and style it was appropriate to its goal, and, moreover, I considered it advisable to let the additional pressure of your own handwriting work on him. In case Neumann does come, I imagine putting Karsen in contact with him to outline a chapter on education under National Socialism. Unfortunately, till now he's left us painfully in the lurch, nor did he deliver anything in the previous period. I'll probably have to take him to task (naturally, in your name). If Pollock gets a promise in principle from Vagts, I can imagine the thing turning out very nicely.

3. *German Project Abstract*. Pollock reported to me about your objections and Teddie and I will work on them this afternoon. Unfortunately, Glass is out of town for the weekend, so the new version can't be finished until the middle of next week.

4. *Anti-Semitism Project*. Teddie told me that his first outline is finished and will be written now by Gretel [Adorno]. So I will get busy on it sometime next week and discuss the whole thing thoroughly with Teddie. I hope Neumann will be there too so that we can pick up a little speed. As we learned from Pinthus, a woman by the name of Dr. Edelheim, who used to work at the Association [Central Association of German Citizens of the Jewish Faith (Zentralverein deutscher Staatsbürger jüdischen Glaubens)] in Berlin, wrote a book-length manuscript on Hitler's law on the Jews for the Jewish Committee. The Committee doesn't want to print it

because it thinks it would only serve to disseminate anti-Semitism. Teddie got in contact with the woman, but in a quite reserved manner in keeping with your instructions to Neumann that no one on the Committee find out right away what we're working on. Fried will visit the Committee and take a look at the manuscript.

5. *Visit from the Police.* On Tuesday, July 30th at 1:30, two officials of the local police, Mr. Schultheiss and Mr. Zuckermann, appeared—one Christian and one Jew, as they said themselves with a chuckle, to allay mistrust wherever they visited. They came at a time when only Miss von M was there, and returned two hours later and then spoke with me for three-quarters of an hour. In a fashion extremely friendly, extremely amiable, and a little bit embarrassed, they explained that the visit had to do simply with a general surveillance of foreign institutions and that there was in no way any investigation in process. During the long conversation, they informed themselves precisely as to the individual members, how long each had been there, who is American, and they also took down home and vacation addresses. The letter head, our pamphlet, the book by Rusche and Kirchheimer, the title and table of contents of the new journal and the combination of "Social Studies" and "Philosophy" in the title all made a deep impression. To Mr. Schultheiss, who was the more intelligent of the two, I promised a new issue of the journal. They also wanted to know exactly why we'd left Frankfurt, and when they heard the Jewish names, they didn't inquire any further at all. Of course I said that certainly every cultivated person and every new citizen of this country is only grateful that such investigations are undertaken, for it is nothing but our most personal interest to have undesirable elements recognized right away and rendered harmless. I don't believe that we have reason to worry about this visit, especially since, God knows, we've got nothing to reproach ourselves for. Besides, it's in the papers nearly everyday that the authorities are concerning themselves with immigrants from the last few years.

6. *Landauer.* Pollock already told you about Mrs. Favez' telegram. Meanwhile, I've had a visit from Landauer's friend, Dr. Wadler, a doctor and artist, whom you probably still remember from Geneva. He wants to try to free frozen German and Turkish assets for Landauer's benefit. Miss van Leer, whom we telegraphed, is also prepared to use the $1000 that she originally thought of as traveling money for his subsistence in Holland. First of all, however, she hadn't gotten it approved at all and, second, I don't know whether it wouldn't be a big mistake, in case the American government does release the money, to encourage her to use the amount for Holland instead of for the trip. In one of her last letters, Mrs. Favez wrote of a mysterious sum of 440 Swiss francs which she could send Landauer. I don't know at all, however, what that had to do with. Are you

agreed then that, aside from a ticket for his passage, Institute money should go to Holland? One could, of course, say that one was using the ticket money for Holland, since it is Miss van Leer who wants to make available the large sum for the trip. That has only one catch: that it's more than doubtful that the money will be released. Please let me know your position on this.

7. Enclosed you will find the sponsorship affidavit Pollock mentioned for Benjamin. It is probably appropriate to keep it somewhat general and also to omit any reference to a contractual relationship between him and the Institute. In his affidavit Pollock will furnish a statement guaranteeing $80.00 per month. How far the Committee has gotten till now, I'll find out in half an hour. I've made a lunch date with [Kurt] Rosenfeld, [Former Social Democratic Minister of Justice in Prussia] who evidently knows precisely what's going on. By the way, Pollock's opinion that the original effort came to nothing isn't right. I just heard from Mrs. Staudinger that the first family has crossed the Spanish border as a result of the action undertaken by the unofficial representative of the State Department in France. [. . .] One expects further news to arrive. Perhaps we'll be lucky and yet hear about Benjamin because of this action. Of course, we may not on that account suspend the other efforts, that is, the other two, namely, the one through Razovsky and the one through the Warren Committee, for which your affidavit is necessary. Please return both copies; I will make efforts to see that (via [Otto] Nathan's mediation) the Warren Committee gives its recommendation.

8. *Johnson Action*. Pollock informed you of our controversy over the appropriateness of listing Landauer. Please decide. Information about what kind of points of view the committee works with comes from Mrs. Staudinger. In the telephone conversation mentioned above, she told me that Gustav Meyer had already been turned down because he was too old. Nevertheless, in my opinion one must continue trying. And if one receives a very strong recommendation from, for example, Beard, then I don't think it impossible that the Committee would do something after all out of shame.

9. *Kander*. The only place till now that has given larger sums for overseas travel is HIAS [Hebrew Immigration Aid Society] (Selfhelp always gives only very small contributions, up to $20.00.) HIAS, however, isn't doing anything more at all in Europe, because it has no office there anymore and can't process the applications. I spoke with Dr. Strauss, which is something one can do. A small chance is that one writes Kander that half of the sum is available here and that he should try to get the Berlin Hilfsverein [Jewish Selfhelp Organizaton] to agree, via the donation of large sums of German marks out of Kander's pocket, to raise the other

half. This procedure, as I, by the way, already knew, has been carried out successfully in a number of cases. One could, of course, advise K to travel by himself—but better not. He wouldn't leave his wife alone now and, besides, he's a sick man. Please let me know whether I should write K, what you are prepared to do for him and, for the rest, what advice we have to offer. I've arranged with Strauss for him to inform me as soon as he's scouted out something new.

10. *Fellowship for [Ernst] Bloch.* You probably already know from P that Oberlander agreed to $1000, if not in an entirely legally binding way. Are you agreed that I should now apply to the American Philosophical Society for the same sum? Maximilian Beck and Hallgarten both had luck there when they applied. Moreover, I'd like to say that if this doesn't work, I don't have such terribly big reservations about working out a similar arrangement as in Beck's case through Teddie or myself. And if it becomes known? I can't imagine that Thomas would be seriously irritated if one found a way to secure the existence of a writer through a small trick that satisfied the formal requirements of his foundation.

I will write you personally over the weekend. Everything is much too hectic for that in the moment.

And how are things going for your wife? Unfortunately, we've still received neither notes nor snapshots from her.

[Leo Lowenthal]

P.S. I just had lunch with Rosenfeld. It was important insofar as he could give me the text that was written by the new committee (evidently in association with the State Department). Nathan, who signed the same document for Gumbel, says that Warren recommended writing the sponsorship letter on the most impressive letter head possible. Nathan, of course, wrote on New York University stationary. I haven't the slightest reservation about you providing the sponsorship affidavit on the Institute's new paper. In case you don't want that, however, I'm sending you the same affidavit again on legal paper. Naturally, right now I'm not sending you my draft text at all.

In the following letter "German Project" refers to the research plans on Nazi Germany mentioned in previous letters. The "Anti-Semitism Project" discussed in the fourth paragraph was published in the last issue of Studies in Philosophy and Social Science *under the title, "Research Project on Anti-Semitism." It was the nucleus of all later research works originating in the Institute's circle.*

The last paragraphs of the letter convey an impression of the Institute's

aid activities for emigre intellectuals, which consumed a significant por-
tion of Institute resources in the early 1940s. Mrs. Favez was the secretary
of the Institute's branch office in Geneva.

765 Riverside Drive
New York City

August 13, 1940

[Dear Horkheimer!]

I thank you most heartily for your letters of the 7th and the 10th. The hotel engraved on the envelope looks so magnificent that it really shouldn't have to bear the name, if in mangled form, of the preacher of poverty.

Please let me think through the problem of your travel plans exactly. I will give my opinion, as you requested, sometime tomorrow morning.

Enclosed you will find a copy of a long letter to Pollock. Unfortunately, the copy is not terribly good, because the letter was written at home. But please read it anyway. The first part verifies, not indifferently, the liberality that is still very vital here; the second part contains my opinion on the organization of resources for the German Project. I was completely dejected by Neumann's reaction and was and am very sceptical about Pollock's aims, which, however, no doubt derive from the best of intentions. If it is done as I am proposing—namely, that Pollock edit the first and Teddie the last parts, and then, in barely a week, a final editing is done with Neumann—it can turn out very nicely.

Now comes a technical problem about which I need your opinion, that is to say, decision. Teddie is pressuring me terribly about the English translation of the Anti-Semitism Project. My opinion, which I've also told him, is as follows: just now Gretel is typing the draft that Teddie produced on the basis of suggestions from me. This draft should then go to all involved, including you. It should really be translated only after you have looked through the manuscript—if only superficially—and supplied comments on the basis of which further changes are to be made. I am absolutely decidedly against getting the translation started in a rush right now and then having a second and third draft translated. Better to spend somewhat more money one time, but then for something that makes sense. Should you agree with me, I would be grateful for a few lines to Teddie indicating that he might want to send you the manuscript in the draft he regards as final before the translation, and should then wait for your word. [. . .]

Now comes another matter in which I require your decision. Lazarsfeld would like me, together with his wife, to write an essay for the next issue about the family programs on the radio. Evidently, they play a gigantic role, second only to music in significance. The material is so vast that Lazarsfeld himself said I would need at least two months to work through it and the help of his staff to get the thing done at all. If I don't do it, he would just get someone else. But since he's always been very fond of my academic work, that is, of the literary interpretations—he would really like to have me. I answered him evasively, and said that that, to begin with, I would have to take a look at the material and, besides, that I couldn't commit my working time for a few months without having gotten your agreement. As the matter rests now, I can't do anything on it during August. Current business and, above all, looking after the French interests and other emergency cases are so demanding that I'm glad when I have the time to do something on the projects, with and without Teddie, and to do some publicity for the journal. What September means you know yourself—especially should I go away. And here's the difficulty. Ultimately, I can get this work done if I'm in New York the whole winter, that that, after all, is doubtful (to formulate it cautiously), means it would not be fair to Lazarsfeld, that is, would endanger the journal, if I give my assent. So what should I do? Today I've been on the lookout to speak to Mrs. Lazarsfeld, because to begin with I have to see what you think about the whole matter.

I'm extremely unsettled about Benjamin, because we've heard nothing of whether he's gone to Marseille. And Mrs. Favez has been silent about B in her cables for a week now. [. . .] Mrs. Favez has received word from Landauer again; he thinks the General Consulate in Rotterdam is functioning again and asks for a certificate to the Frankfurt Institute. Evidently then, he didn't yet receive the document you sent to Mrs. Favez just before your departure. I find the behavior of Miss van L marvelous.

Our role in the aid activities for Europe seems to me extremely important. Everyone is in need of our counsel. Today, for example, a letter came from Jacob Wasserman's widow, who would like for us to procure affadavits for herself and her children. That Wittfogel shirks his cases off onto us goes without saying. [. . .]

[Leo Lowenthal]

This excerpt from a letter to Horkheimer refers to Lowenthal's parents' difficulties leaving Nazi Germany.

429 West 117th Street
New York City

May 9, 1941

[Dear Horkheimer!]

Today it's not your parents but my parents about whom I must write you, because I'm very worried. You probably remember that my parents were to leave Germany on May 6th and board an American ship in Lisbon on the 16th. On the night of the 6th, I received a telegram from Frankfurt that goes as follows:

"Due to [delay of] Portugal visa Lowenthal parents May 6th ship impossible. [Please] Attempt to rebook possibly on Spanish line.

Jewish Travellers' Care" [Jewish Selfhelp organization] Unfortunately, the plan suggested in the cable cannot be carried out. One can't book Spanish ships from here and, besides, they're sold out, and, furthermore, they're not even sailing at all. The last ship left the Bilbao harbor on April 17th, but, for reasons unknown, never got out of Spanish waters. Why the Portuguese visa didn't work out is hard to say. I suspect that is has to do with a racket whereby the visa is blocked in the last minute and such desirable places as those my parents had on the ship are passed on to others against fantastic advances.

The situation this creates for my parents is probably catastrophic. I assume they have neither an apartment nor furnishings nor money, since everything must be given away before the Germans let anyone leave. The only thing left to try is the Portuguese visa. Here I would like to appeal to your aid, primarily in the form of your great imagination. Do you know anyone in Los Angeles who could get me in to see the Portuguese envoys or who himself has good contacts in Lisbon? Could you possibly obtain a letter for me through Mrs. Dieterle [the wife of the film director William Dieterle] to someone in Washington whom I could seek out with the reliable prospect of thereby gaining contact to the Portuguese authorities, whether in Washington or Lisbon? For any hint, even the slightest, I would be eternally grateful, for I'm as anxious as I can be.

[Leo Lowenthal]

This letter refers once again to the problem of continuing Institute business in New York after the group gave up the facilities belonging to Columbia University. The Marshall mentioned in reference to Adorno is John Marshall, who was director of the Social Science Division of the Rockefeller Foundation.

429 West 117th Street
New York City

June 18, 1941

[Dear Horkheimer!]

I hope you've been able meanwhile to celebrate your reunion with your books. I assume that the exertions, not wholly unpleasant, after all, of arranging everything are over and you are enjoying your justified pride in possessions. I'm very anxious to see how everything turned out and I hope that you and your dear wife will soon afford us a preview by way of some pictures.

You will have understood why I sent my letter of the 15th under protection of a few precautionary measures. Your precise address is still not entirely clear to me and, besides, I wanted to make sure that the letter landed only in your hands, especially at a time when I suspect that one or another member of the Institute is lending a helping hand around your house.

Early this morning I had the following idea. Pollock has concocted a plan whereby, should it be decided to maintain the business here, an apartment could be rented that includes administration. It would bring down expenses by some $2000. I have the following points against this idea: first, the prestige of any scientific organization suffers whenever it occupies the same space as a business; second, that our specific prestige would decline once we were no longer located in a university building; third, that the activity in such an apartment would exceed by far that in our institute at present, and then it would be almost impossible to create a situation in which one could work scientifically at least two hours a day undisturbed; and fourth, that these three disadvantages are so large that the considerable but not overwhelming savings are hardly worth it.

Now, it must also be considered whether a share of the house couldn't be sold to Lazarsfeld. I don't think he would buy it, because he doesn't really need it and also has no extra money (but, as before, I do believe we could interest him financially in the journal). One could for a moment consider turning the tables and seeing if it's possible to get some space in Lazarsfeld's office. The top floor, where I am right now, consists of a tiny room, a big entrance hall and my work room. It all looks rather ugly, but could be made prettier by a painter and the addition of some of our Institute furniture and a small library. The space would suffice for one main worker, a younger assistant and a secretary; and we would have a Columbia address. With such an arrangement—admittedly a poor solution—we would save considerably, and it wouldn't be a gigantic deal if we disappeared from the place after a year was up. I don't think this solution is in any way ideal; but it would have a certain pragmatic significance. Please add it to the list of issues I began on Sunday and want to continue in the next few days.

Unfortunately, Teddie didn't get his grant from Rockefeller. Marshall, apparently, received him most kindly and buried him in compliments. He also promised every possible thing, among others, to think over how Teddie can get the recognition and status that by rights are due him, and that he would also speak about it with Virgil Thomson, the editor of the *Herald Tribune* who made the excerpts from Teddie's essay (with which I was sincerely pleased). But: Rockefeller had no money, and, besides, they only wanted to give fellowships to applicants for whose areas they had specialists at the Rockefeller Foundation, and nobody there knew anything about music. This last argument is, of course, a specious excuse; with our project and also Lazarsfeld's, the word was always that the Rockefeller Foundation didn't at all think of itself as a board of experts who had to judge the merits of a case, but exclusively as an administrative authority. Lazarsfeld, who is naturally sad about it too, wants to think over in the next two days whether it's not possible to find some way to get something out of it after all. He, incidentally, is of the opinion (Marshall himself evidently hinted at this too) that the opposition comes not from Marshall, for whom the rejection seems to have been very unpleasant, but from other members or from trustees of the Foundation. Perhaps we'll figure it out yet, especially since Lazarsfeld is interested in it too.

It is now high time we made up our minds about the final shape of the new issue. The article section should probably be put together as follows:

1 *Pollock*. There's nothing to say about this now, since you already have two thirds of the manuscript yourself so you can form an opinion.

Incidentally, please pass this as all the other contributions on to David as soon as possible so he can get them in order one after the other.

2 *Gurland*, who is writing about the economic and political economic institutions of National Socialism;

3 *Kirchheimer*, who is treating the legal and administrative side of the problem from the point of view of class compromise;

4 *Adorno*, whose Spengler essay David has been holdng on to for two and a half weeks.

The review section is composed essentially of three big group reviews: by *Massing* (about American agricultural problems, from the perspective of the technical revolution in agriculture); by *Soudek* (about bureaucracy); and by *Felix Weil* (about the U.S. Senate's monopoly literature). Then there comes one or another review that we either already have or have yet to receive.

In principle we could also publish in the article section the work ordered from [David] Glass on population policy under fascism or one of the chapters (admittedly, rather popular) from Neumann's book, whether on National Socialist imperialism or on National Socialist minority policy. The issue would then have a yet more unified character and would probably do Pollock especially good. On the other hand, Teddie's essay, the use of which would mean excluding Glass or Neumann, would without doubt raise the level of the issue, and beyond that, my nerves aren't up to a battle against this author. In principle, an article by Neumann in this as in the next issue wouldn't be unpleasant to me for reasons of Institute politics, because we should give him, even more than Kirchheimer and Gurland (for whom, however, the same applies), the chance to improve his academic chances by way of publications in English.

I would be very grateful to you if you would let me know what you think about the structure of this issue soon.

As I've already told you, we're giving up our apartment at the end of June. I arranged with Mr. Stern to leave it open whether this means a move within the city or resettling in California, which would then take place under the same conditions as with you. We would have had to give up the apartment anyway, since, given Daniel's growth, it has already become too small. I would have to thank you sincerely, should it be at all possible for you to let me know in the second half of July what you've decided about where I should live. If I remain in New York, I would like to look at the end of July for an apartment for September 1st, for which I would surely receive a month's concession, [Due to the surplus of apartments at the time, the renter usually received a month or two free rent upon signing a rental contract.] which would cover the cost of moving. Then, if at all possible, I would try to relax in August. Obviously, I don't want to put the burden of this decision on you alone, but will, as my letter of Sunday suggested, write to you how I feel about it personally.

On Walter Benjamin's legacy, I want by all means to tell you that I ordered it provisionally in the two suitcases that were in your closet. In one suitcase are the books and individual printed pieces and in the other the manuscripts. Evidently, much has been saved; but I don't now feel up to the task of investigating it more closely. In any case, I secured the manuscripts against further ruin by sorting them into strong paper envelopes.

My address starting Monday evening: Holderness Inn, Holderness, N.H.

[Leo Lowenthal]

The excerpt documents the Institute group's practice of making detailed annotations to each of their publications. Lowenthal's remarks refer to the preface with which Horkheimer introduced the first issue of the journal to appear in English, as Studies in Philosophy and Social Science.

August 1, 1941

[Dear Horkheimer!]

Your telegram of July 31 just arrived.

1 *Preface.* My brief remarks should not, of course, replace the usual

detailed commentary. First of all, I would like to repeat that my original impression has been confirmed: the text, which expresses our decisive theoretical themes, not only helps supply Pollock's essay with a needed theoretical and timely framework, but it is composed in many places as a masterfully formulated program. I'm neither bothered by the allowances made for the local situation—which, incidentally, are not so formulated as if internally we had made some compromise—nor have I anything against the discrepancies between the text of the preface and that of the article; they seem to me desired and voluntary. In the following, I will offer a few suggestions.

Page 1, paragraph 1. The last sentence isn't exactly right for an exposition which characterizes the historical movement in the nineteenth century. Also, the sentence before last is already valid, at least for western Europe, in the preceding periods. I think these reservations can be done away by the replacement of the first four words of the preface with the words "until recently". I would have no tactical reservations about that.

Page 1, paragraph 2, line 5. Is the restriction "for increased investment" really valid already in the first stage of monopoly capital, since at first the quantity and quality of the organic composition [of capital] rise beyond all bounds?

Page 1, paragraph 2, lines 5–7. Is this sentence really completely clear? The leaders are first of all peers among themselves, namely, leaders within a nation. Beyond that, they are, of course, peers with the leaders of other nations. That is no different in monopoly capitalism than in feudalism. Think about the relations between Christian and Arabic knights.

Page 2, paragraph 1, line 1. Instead of "dualisms" I would prefer "antagonisms." It fits better with "obscured," with which the sentence ends.

Page 2, paragraph 1, lines 4–5. I raise a substantive doubt. Is it really that every trace of independence disappears? Today, the individual pays more dearly, mostly with his money or his life, wherever he realizes traces of this independence. And I consider you and myself fortunate that it still exists in concept and in reality.

Page 2, paragraph 1, line 5. Must there not be an article before "policy"?

Page 2, insert sheet, lines 2–3. Aren't the leaders reviled also on account of their so-called "generous" social policy? I would really like a reformulation in this sense, because the following sentence (lines 3–4) would lend the contradiction with the [ruling] clique yet stronger expression. On line 5 you could say "such hostilities" instead of "their antagonisms" should you follow my suggestion in reference to line 1 on this page. On line 6, I would say "feudalism" instead of "clergy." Mustn't it be "were" instead of "had" on line 7? On the second to the last line, as I've already indicated, I suggest cutting the third to last word.

Page 3, line 6. Here something has been added in handwriting; I read the 6th word of this insertion as "plain"—which I don't understand.

Page 3, lines 4–5 from the bottom. The words "intelligence service" don't appeal to me because they derive linguistically and institutionally from the western democracies. How about "fifth columnists"? Or "secret police"?

Page 4, line 5 from the bottom. I have something against the word "soul." Couldn't you say "live nerve" or "core" or something similar?

Page 5, line 4. I suggest saying "European society" instead of "world."

Page 6, line 11. The word "attempted" seems to me too weak; the past tense bothers me too. How about "is endeavoring," which gets picked up again 3 lines later anyway?

Page 6, paragragh 2, line 1. I suggest cutting the word "however." [. . .]

[Leo Lowenthal]

The issue discussed in the letter's second paragraph is the last issue of the Studies in Philosophy and Social Science, *that is, the English-language version of the* Zeitschrift für Sozialforschung. *This issue was organized around the theme of mass communications research. The Mead mentioned in the third paragraph is the well-known American anthropologist Margaret Mead. Mr. Fromm is Erich Fromm; the book "of inexpressible boredom" is* Escape from Freedom *(In German,* Die Furcht vor der Freiheit, *Frankfurt/M, 1966). Grossman is Henryk Grossman. Stern is Günther Stern (now Günther Anders).*

429 West 117th Street
New York City

September 13, 1941

[Dear Horkheimer!]

Many thanks for your telegram of the 11th and letter of the 9th. Both arrived yesterday.

I cabled you yesterday evening concerning the issue. It is my conviction, shared by the others, that the issue contains no formulations that could present immediate perils. We can only protect ourselves against that—not against an interpretation of our theoretical views. Aside from the fact that after repeated readings of the issue from beginning to end I feel sure enough to ask for your imprimatur, I see further protection in the scholarly apparatus of the first three essays and in the difficult text of the last two. In the present situation, I think it completely out of the question that the issue provides occasion for attacks from non-academic circles, where attention is directed along totally different lines. The issue is distinguished from the radical tone which one still finds in many progressive liberal academic publications, books and periodicals, by its comparatively conservative style. Besides, the letter from Peardon, which I am enclosing, as such attests to the academic nature of this publication. And it comes from a Columbia professor, however inclined to our way of thinking he might be.

I will make an agreement as you wished with Mead, that is, that I order the essay for the 1942 spring issue. The two will then definitely not begin working on it before the end of the year, and by then we will have a clear picture about whether the public opinion issue will appear at all. The question of the third issue, which absolutely has to be turned in in December, becomes important now. If I understand you correctly, your plan for a philosophical issue has become more definite, and you're thinking of contributions from yourself, Teddie, Marcuse, and Stern. It would be good if it could be arranged for the manuscripts to be available on November 15. One must then make November 1 the final deadline from the outset. The issue itself could potentially be somewhat thinner. Once we reach 500 pages total for the whole year, it probably suffices.

Aside from our lunch together, I've not yet spoken with Pollock. He looks splendid, and I have the feeling that he's returned refreshed in every way. He wanted to get together yesterday evening, but yesterday the boat arrived with my parents. If you'd like to know what a swimming hell is, please read the report in today's *New York Times*. In reality, it's all much worse. To round everything out, they took my parents to Ellis Island, without allowing me to see them, because my mother had a slight fever. They didn't let my father out, because there exists this wonderful principle in both public and private American administration that families mustn't be separated. Evidently, the 76-year-old man in the men's dorm was supposed to watch out that my mother, in the hospital on Ellis Island, didn't fall victim to the white slave trade. When we talk, I'll have to report on the extremely complicated feelings I have in this matter; they have nothing to do with love, but much to do with a mixture of compassion and hate.

Meanwhile, I've spent a few hours talking to Grossman. He makes a somewhat calmer impression. There were no outbursts whatsoever, and even the invectives against Pollock remained confined to gentle snubs. Admittedly, he impresses one as a person who finds himself in a chronic depression.

Your request passed on by Pollock to obtain Mr. Fromm's book will be fulfilled. It is a work of inexpressible boredom. Despite our requests, we didn't receive a review copy, probably due to the author's own wish. Fromm, incidentally, has now landed where he belongs. The courses he is giving at the secessionist psychoanalytic union have been incorporated in the New School's lecture program. Since you enjoy an outstanding memory, you no doubt recall that a few years ago none of us were capable of besting Mr. Fromm in characterizing that institution negatively.

Since I haven't yet spoken to Pollock, I can't say anything about your plans for the future either. I would, though, like to mention a certain reservation I have about Marcuse's planned trip. I don't doubt [Robert] MacIver's friendly disposition, but I really do doubt his determination to fight for anything for us. If Neumann's information isn't completely false, then discussions with the Committee of Instructions [at Columbia] don't mean very much, since the Committee works exclusively for the Extension, while lecture activities within the Graduate School are governed by the faculty. After the experience of the last years, we can't expect all too much from lectures by a member of the Extension. In the current situation, which includes the high cost of living, the students will be even less willing than before to pay their high fees to listen to lecture courses they're not required to take. Therefore, we don't have much to expect here either in the way of money or prestige.

On the question of closing or reorganizing [the New York office of the Institute]—as I said, after I discuss it with Pollock. But, I believe more and more that we shouldn't hesitate any longer, in case it all comes to nothing with the New York Foundation. As before, I'm sticking with what I said about the vicious circle which you quoted in your letter before last.

Pollock spoke yesterday with Teddie and Gretel, and this morning Gretel talked to me about it for a long time on the phone. Evidently, both are a little troubled, because they have the impression that everything still remains nearly as undecided now as at the beginning of the summer. That can't be right, and I will try to agree on a tactic with Pollock whereby the atmosphere clears up a bit for the two of them.

The first of the page proofs, incidentally, arrived today. I'm sending them to you in the same post. I'll stop here so I can try to do something about my parents on Ellis Island. I think I'll be able to write again extensively on Monday.

[Leo Lowenthal]

On the arrival of Lowenthal's parents in New York, who were able to escape from the Nazis literally in the last moment, compare the letters to Horkheimer of May 9th and September 13th, 1941.

The journal—which was meanwhile renamed Studies in Philosophy and Social Science—*appeared for the last time in the fall of 1941.*
Dagobert Runes was the owner of the "Philosophical Library" press, with which the Institute was negotiating.
Kurt Pinthus became world famous in the 1920s through his editing of the anthology Menschheitsdämmerung [Twilight of Humanity]. *He was supported by the Institute in emigration. Pächter is Henry Paechter.*

429 West 117th Street
New York City

September 16, 1941

[Dear Horkheimer!]
Many thanks for your telegrams of the 13th and the 16th. With them, Pollock's return and the arrival of my parents, I am assailed by so many problems that I really need to talk over with you, that I curse and damn my dependence on writing and telegraphing.

In honor of the old custom, I want to try to play a trick on this profusion and proceed point-by-point. Then I'll at least convince myself for two hours that it's all been discussed.

1. *Parents.* On Monday morning we were called to Ellis Island and got them free immediately. It was quite a pitiable sight, the two of them in a worn-out condition. Admittedly, after a few hours my mother's constitution had already fought its way victoriously through, and now I'm armed with new material to continue our old and ignoble competition about our mothers with some prospect of success. My father, on the other hand, can restore one's belief in humanity. Indeed, on the surface he is suffering a complete collapse, can hardly walk, has severe memory problems, and is totally weakened by diarrhea. Concerning the journey, he said only the following: "It went well for me. I slept at night and had fresh air, since the hatch to the cargo room had been removed. I've eaten almost nothing, because one of my age no longer needs it. Otherwise, I lay on the deck and had nothing to trouble myself with. I'm not interested in externalities anymore." Immediately thereafter, he asked me what I was working on at present and how things were going for Mr. Horkheimer. Then he commenced with a philosophical–political conversation about the insanity of humanity and his literary studies of Alexander von Humboldt. Then he said happily: "Leo is glad to see me again." Afterwards, insofar as he wasn't disturbed by his bowels and his wife, he slept. It will remain as one of the strongest impressions I've yet received of the substance of the liberal Jewish bourgeoisie. If he were alone, I wouldn't hesitate a moment,

even at the greatest sacrifice, to take him in so he could enjoy his last days in peace.

2. *Journal.* The page proofs are now here and complete. Because of my plan to abridge the review section, the issue contains 169 pages, that is, just nine pages more than a normal issue. I congratulate myself for that. I'm sending you the remainder of the page proofs today by special delivery, in case you have any last minute considerations. The only trouble I have now is with Teddie. He inferred from a few of Gurland and Pächter's remarks that the two of them regard the translation as especially poor. For myself, I prefer to skip over this to current business, since I don't believe that the contribution—reworked by David in New York and Los Angeles into a talk and then once again into an essay—betrays serious shortcomings. And I couldn't be responsible for letting this thing cause further delay now. Please have David go through the essay again, perhaps with Marcuse, and let me know extensively by cable if something needs to be changed because of bad English. That's the only concession I want to make. I'm convinced that a third American would probably condemn the translation roundly, as has been the case with all our translations for seven years now. And then the new translation that came out of it would be just as problematic as David's. Please be so kind as to hurry the two fellows on to one last *par force tour,* so that you can cable me Thursday night or Friday morning. Meanwhile, the other parts of the issue can be printed. In your telegram, please make citations to Teddie's article according to the page numbers in the proofs I'm sending you today.
[. . .]

5. *Pinthus.* A burden has been lifted from my shoulders. He did it. Starting October 1st he'll work in the academic reference service in the Library of Congress. I really rubbed it in that he has only us to thank for it. The official sponsor of the fellowship is namely the American University, and the intermediary between the Library of Congress and the president of that university is none other than our old friend Eugene N. Anderson, whom we've told often enough what an outstanding expert the Institute possesses in the person of Mr. Pinthus.

6. *Telegram Trouble.* Your telegram of this morning contains two sentences responsible for throwing the local members of the Institute into a state of profound grief, for they couldn't be understood. One sentence runs: "Please tell Pollock Dieterle needs Ludwig manuscript." Pollock has no idea what that could refer to. Teddie expressed the opinion that it concerned my essay about the German biographies. But I can't believe that. Why would you not then cable me, "Please send manuscripts German biographies"? The second ununderstandable sentence goes: "Please send Simmel pamphlet mass suggestions from my pamphlet." What does that

mean? Do you mean a text by the analyst Simmel concerning mass suggestions? And what do you mean by your pamphlets? Since the gray times of our pre-American history, when it was you who faced my telegram about the newly arrived *"Gesamtpost"* without a clue, such telegram puzzles as today's haven't happened. I already cabled you about the puzzle.

[. . .]

[Leo Lowenthal]

In this letter to Lowenthal, Horkheimer considers the future of the Institute and its collaborators. The letter also alludes to the beginnings of the research and reflections that resulted in the Dialectic of Enlightenment.

13524 D'Este Drive
Pacific Palisades, California

November 29, 1941

[Dear Lowenthal!]

I thank you especially warmly for your letter of November 26th. It helps me gain a better overview of the situation there than I've been capable of in the last couple of weeks. Since I believe I mustn't wait to inform you of my view, I'll do it quickly, even if that means that it is formulated in an abbreviated manner and most of the reasons for it are not expressed. I don't believe, incidentally, that I'm saying anything new. I'm simply drawing a conclusion from old ideas.

Our task in life is theoretical work. Now is the time when the experiences and discussions of the last decade should bear fruit. The content of this future work has more or less been gathered, partly in writing in our earlier works and notes, partly in our heads. Concerning the form, practically nothing has been established. The theme around which the efforts center will probably—not altogether certainly—be anti-Semitism. My conceptions as to the manner of representation, which will depart sharply from that of a standard book, is not yet clear. If a German version admits first of the intended theme, then we would probably have to pursue the English version ourselves, either from the beginning or from relatively early on. Given the complete absence of a routine, I will have to make enormous demands on my own energy. For those who work with me, it won't be much different, if for different reasons. From that which results, the meaning of our earlier work, indeed, our existence, should become clear retroactively for the first time. Given the horrors that reign without and approach within, and given the circumstance that we see no one near us, the responsibility is enormous.

In the years 1939, 1940, and 1941, we've maintained an enterprise that far exceeded our capacities. It's not so much the theoretical work that causes this as the desire to afford a new chance to the many others who depended on us. June 1940 was the very last date on which, according to our own firm conviction, the business had to be closed down. Not entirely free of pressure from interested parties, we decided to undertake new efforts. We went so far as to increase our activities in the last months, at the cost of much money and energy. It was not just immediate resources that all this claimed. It also held back the couple of people who should have concentrated their own resources on doing something more reasonable. I don't want to deny that Institute activity in conjunction with the university offers some stimulation. The damage our exertions around the university caused, by impeding intensive and exclusive work on a matter of mutual concern, is incomparably greater than the relative advantage to be expected from them. A small test of what productive powers mutual deliberation about a real problem can liberate in every respect can be seen in the ridiculous anti-Semitism project, which we outlined back then in a couple of days.

To all this is added my own weakness. Had the question of continuing the Institute through the end of the year and even undertaking new activities been raised seriously at the time of my departure, I would have declared myself incapable of accomplishing anything here. It was clear that concerns over the course of things in New York, in which I remain just as involved as ever, would necessarily have exercised an even more crippling effect than if I had stayed there. I hereby declare solemnly that the continuation of activities in New York completely ties my hands here and paralyzes all work. The reasons for this are so manifold that I'm not at all able to list them briefly. One of them is my great disquiet about the theoretical profile we receive. I neither can nor want to bear responsibility for that.

For you personally, the situation isn't all that different than for me. I don't need to tell you again how much the prudence with which you've promoted things there means to me. I believe that you know that very well. Now, however, I must tell you for your own sake that pursuing the business is ruining us materially and theoretically. It will cause us complete distress in every respect. What transpires if, starting in January, we reduce the Institute to two rooms in which the administration as well as the Los Angeles branch are supported by individual grants, I don't know. It could be that difficult struggles would occur, and there are countless reasons for which we could fail. But that is problematic. If, however, we continue the business with Neumann, Grossmann, Kirchheimer, Gurland, then neither your nor even Marcuse's or Teddie's presence could alter in any way its rapid deterioration. For this eventuality, I predict with absolute certainty that approximately in May, if not much sooner, the Institute will fall to pieces in a violent clash. The confrontations will not take place in the context of a radical reduction brought about by us, but there in the Institute as a going concern. It will become completely confused; I'll have to go there (which, even if it's only four weeks, will set my work back six months). If you're already here, you can accompany me. Your own material and theoretical existence, at the latest after a year (not just after two or three years!), will join our own in a general misfortune. "And misfortune strides quickly," as my compatriot Schiller says. From your proposal to extend Marcuse's stay indefinitely beyond December, as from that of the temporary return of one or both Teddies, I see how generously you judge our situation. One such journey is the equivalent of weeks and months of future happiness—if the inflation doesn't ruin everything.

Here is my proposal. A reduction up to the middle of December will gain nothing. Before he departs, Marcuse goes to MacIver and informs him of the following: he must return to Los Angeles; whether the Institute receives a quite substantial contribution, which has been offered to me here prospectively, depends on our holding a few private seminars in the next three months and conducting a couple of research projects (he can characterize the content of these projects however he likes); we cannot let slip this chance, which is important for us. If the institutional connection with Columbia really comes about, then it goes without saying that we'd be there again in the fall full force. The connection with Columbia is more important for us than anything else. We're even prepared to take part in summer classes.

Then Marcuse departs towards the end of December. If by the middle of January there's still no acceptance, Pollock goes to MacIver and explains that the Los Angeles branch needs important members from the staff of collaborators for at least the next six months. For that reason, we want to reduce activities there and are in the position to place the house, except for two rooms, temporarily at the department's disposal. He requests that we be allowed to keep two rooms (I'm thinking of the fourth floor and perhaps the top floor). It is only Pollock and maybe occasionally an assistant or secretary who should ever use the rooms. An unambiguous settlement will be made with Neumann, and with the others so far as necessary, but the business stops completely. That way the extension lectures or talks that we've scheduled can just go on as before.

Should the connection to Columbia be accomplished before this or should there be a smaller grant, then I'm for the same procedure anyway.

Only then it can be explained explicitly that the whole enterprise will be started up again in the fall. That gives us time to think things over. But, if the university wants to take the lectures back, because we don't carry on a costly and superfluous enterprise like good citizens, then it should just do it. If we spend more and more money out of simple consideration for the connection to the university, then we'll end up the fools. The works, however, for which we would have gotten a smaller grant, would be carried through by the individuals to whom they were entrusted. They would work partially in the library, partially at home, to the extent that the projects are not taken over by the Los Angeles branch, which, given the topic, I think is entirely possible. Common discussions could take place once or twice a week in the two rooms remaining to us.

The contribution that we expect here exists not merely in my imagination, but as a real possibility. Since I always judge outside things negatively—because I know the world—I wouldn't like to express myself in percentages. Up to now, no one can reproach me for thinking that the costly pains taken there were even a jot more realistic than my expectations here. Were I Neumann, then, after what was promised me about a week ago, I would have sent a fairly self-confident report. I'm not so optimistic. Nevertheless, I think it thoroughly representable that P make his trip here for reasons of taking advantage of this chance. His presence here is urgently required, for I can make an appearance neither with Teddie nor with anyone else who can't speak responsibly about financial matters. The costs that his trip occasions are trifling in comparison to our other expenses for publicity; they won't even be a burden on the treasury. If we don't harbor any great hopes among ourselves, then I still think it right, after you and P confer about it, to underline these chances emphatically to everyone else. I'll leave it to the two of you to specify what they are. In any case, the measures we undertake are more than justified by the circumstances. P may go ahead and depart with pride. Institute prospects speak more strongly for the trip than those which were ever pursued for it in Washington or anywhere else.

Up to the time of his return, nothing more will be said about the reduction, unless the department has already reached a negative decision—which I consider completely possible. For the time of P's absence, you remain at your post in every respect and defend our policy energetically whenever necessary. Immediately upon his return, the measures mentioned here will be clearly carried out. They really can stand scrutiny; no responsible person in our position would behave any differently. Should conflicts develop with our people or elsewhere, then it's better that they be fought in the next few months than later. In case some kind of intolerable circumstances arise as early as December or so, then we may have to carry through the steps towards a reduction—indeed, the closing of the New York branch if nothing else is possible—before P's departure. In that case, I'm asking for your information in advance.

I believe these statements will have satisfied your desire for me to make my position known as quickly and clearly as possible. Should anything remain unclear, please inquire about it precisely, and then I will respond immediately. It's a ridiculous circumstance that we're always having to do things for pure reasons of prestige, which ultimately cost us not only prestige but our necks.

I have a little of this feeling even in regard to the third issue. We're forced to do all kinds of things that go against the grain in every respect. The whole English language journal, as it stands, is a concession, and it's not for concessions that the Institute was founded. There are places enough for that. The threat from some of our so-called friends—that without such concessions we will finally go under—might be correct, even if it's not exactly concern for your fate and mine that's standing godfather to their warning. Whether the clumsy steps with which we respond to such warnings change anything seems to me questionable; certain is only that in doing so we invest money, time and energy in a thing which we can't support sincerely. I would very much like to know if the publication of this issue is now completely unavoidable, and, if so, why it is that we absolutely have to publish a costly annual register. Given our plans, the "prestige" of which you write is no reason. I'm sorry that Salloch's business will suffer, for he made a respectable impression on me; but if he's a friend, he should help us get out of this thing with as little trouble as possible. In any case, please pass on to me a reliable calculation of what eight and nine signatures will cost us with and without the register.

As for the contents, I propose that we take, aside from my, Marcuse's and Teddie's essays, the one from Pächter, for which we've evidently paid money. Furthermore, it seems to me as if we had requested an article from Kracauer. In view of our local prospects, we could probably demand ten or fifteen pages as a small reciprocation. Neumann's bibliography could probably be published. If publication of the bibliography, as you write, has no theoretical worth, it's also not worthless, and that already means a lot. Please talk it over with Neumann. I suggest publication if he finds and rates it to be something positive himself. Then there's the question of Korsch. If we publish Neumann's bibliography and Pächter (I place some value on this because I've been devoting myself to language problems for months), then the issue will be strongly centered on National Socialism. If this is the case, please speak to Marcuse so he focuses his article on it too. I'll do the same with mine. If the coming weeks go calmly, I hope by continuous work to complete the first draft of "Reason." I will then translate it with Teddie and David as quickly as possible, and perhaps have as much as eight days left in December for the sociology of art, which is really very easy.

I have the feeling that we fundamentally agree. The impatience of the one far from the fray is greater than that of the immediate participants not only in our case but as a rule. The pressure from me, however, derives much less from psychological as extremely rational considerations. Besides, it has this going for it—that it demands what has already long since been decided over and over again after the most careful consideration.

Most cordially yours,
Max Horkheimer

P.S. I sent a copy of this letter to P, because he receives whatever I have to say about our problems at present.

In this letter Lowenthal comments on a draft of Horkheimer's essay "The Authoritarian State". At the time, the article appeared only in mimeographed form in the Institute's memorial volume for Benjamin.[11]

429 West 117th Street
New York City

February 18, 1942

[Dear Horkheimer!]

Your work belongs in a class of theoretical documents, the last of which appeared ninety-four years ago. On those whose tongues were burning with it back then, but who lacked the words and breath to say what was necessary, your work today would have exercised the same liberating effect as that which once issued from that text. It is the judgment of an epoch, of the same epoch, but one that embodies the experiences of the last three generations. Even as I wrote you seven and a half months ago on how your idea appeared to me, I hadn't anticipated such a text. It is of necessity, and much is worthwhile for its sake.

On the present product of your past exertions and a future, I hope mutual, program, I have scarcely anything to say concerning details. [. . .]

The essay must, of course, be typed on stencil and copied. Only we want to wait until you let us know that you'll make no more changes in the current text or until you get a revised version to us. I am raising the thought of a memorial for Benjamin once again as a proposal—one, I mean, that isn't called a special issue of the journal, but is called what it is. Contributions: your new work, the notes Benjamin left, Teddie's George and Hoffmannstahl and the contribution from Brecht. Such a volume would also have the advantage that we wouldn't have to be all too cautious about giving it to friends.

Might I bring your attention to Aragon's novel, *The Century was Young,* published a few weeks ago in English? The book, which I take to be very significant, has not yet appeared in French, with the exception of a few very small chapters in the *Nouvelle Revue Francaise.* It contains a number of decisive themes, especially ones concerning upbringing, family and love, that bear most closely on your and our intentions. You will understand how delighted I am with the fact that the fate of the hero is guided by his efforts to write a biography—about none other than John Law.

I spoke today with Pollock about a few important practical questions. You will have inferred from intimations in my last letters that I'm urgently in favor of our coming personally to an agreement about the future, for reasons that have to do with both my work and the health and morale of my family. Although it's already been rather a long time for me, I wanted to wait on it until you had finished your work. May I pay you a visit soon? I propose that I leave here the evening of March 5th and arrive Monday, March 9th in Los Angeles. The date derives from seminars that are supposed to take place at the Institute on February 26th and March 5th (on the latter date, with our friend Jacoby), at which I, in accord with Pollock's and my own desires, would like to be present. Please let me know if this date is alright for you. I imagine that I should spend a good two weeks with you and be back in New York at the end of March. It would not subject the production of the journal to any interruption, since I can prepare everything and will by then have edited the review section. I'd like to use April to bring the biography piece more or less to completion and, for the sake of the record, to speak on a few evenings for the Extension lectures. Towards the end of April—at the latest, the beginning of May—my private affairs must be put in order.

Should you agree, you must say a few words about how you'd like me to organize my visit, so I can prepare myself for it in every way.

In any case, I'm very much looking forward to it.

[Leo Lowenthal]

This letter offers a view of the relations of Institute members with their colleagues at Columbia University. The altercation over a guest lecture to the sociology faculty addressed here reflects the scepticism with which the emigres' philosophical–theoretical orientation was received by their American colleagues.

The paragraph numbered 2 refers once again to the last issue of the Studies in Philosophy and Social Science.

429 West 117th Street
New York City

January 20, 1942

[Dear Horkheimer!]

1. *Faculty Lecture*. As we were gathered yesterday at the Faculty Club to bid a tearful farewell to Marcuse, Mssrs. MacIver, Abel, Waller, Page, Stern, Casey, and Lazarsfeld were sitting together at the next table. Afterwards, I drove with the latter to the Office of Radio Research where I finally gave my oft postponed talk (more of which later). As we drove Lazarsfeld told me that this lunch gathering represented a meeting of the department at which, among other things, the Institute's faculty lectures were discussed. MacIver had spoken about them in such a way that everyone sensed that he approached them with very positive thoughts. He reported that the Institute had presented him with a long list of lectures and left it to the department to make a selection itself. Among those gathered there, it was only Page—who, incidentally, is not a permanent member of the department, but a professor at City College and at present only working as a guest of Columbia's Sociology Department—who displayed some opposition, in consideration of the rapid decline in the number of students. When it came to a discussion of names, MacIver read a note from Lynd (who is out of town and therefore couldn't come to the meeting), in which he recommended entrusting Neumann with the lecture, since it was necessary to have someone who could speak about modern historical topics and since philosophical themes were already over-represented in the department's lecture series. Then Waller, who is himself lukewarm about the thing as such, is supposed to have supported Neumann, and MacIver also acknowledged (in his uncommitted and indefinite way) that he was very much in agreement with the suggestion of Neumann. Bernhard Stern brought Marcuse's name into the debate, who, after all, "had written such a good book." But that was immediately rejected out of aversion to theory and philosophy. Lazarsfeld, as he told me, considered carefully whether he should intervene, because, as he said, he would himself most have preferred to have lectures by Adorno and me. But then he remained silent anyway, because he had the impression that the mention of new names, some of them nearly unknown, could have lead the whole thing to collapse.

I told him that I regarded all this as the height of tactlessness. If MacIver said that we turned over the selection to him and that we agreed in principle to delivering the lectures in rotation, then there was no one among us who ever doubted for a moment that MacIver and the department would offer at least the first lecture to Horkheimer. I said that this information had the affect on me of someone beating me on the head with a hammer till I didn't any longer know what's what. At first he didn't take it so seriously and said that, in his experience, one has to wait, time will set things straight, and so on with such phrases.

I discussed the matter thoroughly with Pollock this morning. It is clear that if this thing goes through, that is, if Neumann receives the first lecture not as a private person but as a representative of the Institute, it will create a completely impossible situation. It is intolerable that the director of the Institute—which has been tied to Columbia for eight years—would be neglected in favor of the Institute's newest member, and that the name of the latter would appear in the register of faculty lectures (and, indeed, in the context of representing the Institute) while the name of the director was left connected solely to the nothing Extension. Furthermore, it faces us with the extremely unpleasant situation of Neumann ending up gaining a new means by which he is able to demonstrate his indispensibility. One could, of course, spin the idea out God knows how far, but I'm not as masochistic as that.

Since, despite Teddie, I'm not aware of even a moment in which Lazarsfeld has behaved especially disloyally and, in the end, we don't have anyone else with whom we'd have been able to discuss it in such a way that it could have made a difference, Pollock and I were at Lazarsfeld's this afternoon. He is sick in bed with a severe flu. But, anyway, it was important enough an issue for us to weigh this maximum of disturbance to him against the minimum of danger to us.

To his credit, it must be said that L understood immediately why we were there. He maintained that the whole thing appeared as we judged it only to Europeans, because for Americans the directorial organization of an institute was not such a sacred affair. Naturally, that's all poppycock, and, quite seriously and explicitly, we made it clear to him what an impossible situation it created for us. To that, he said he believed he could set everything right and that, in fact, he wanted to call MacIver tomorrow morning (that is, Wednesday) and ask him to reconsider the matter. He wants to say that he's had a chance to speak with gentlemen from the Institute and that he fears the path chosen by the department would have to lead to considerable difficulties. He would propose, therefore, that Mr. Horkheimer be offered the 1942 winter term and then only in the following spring term Mr. Neumann. P and I told him that we regarded such a solution as the least that could be tolerated.

I persuaded Pollock (who sometimes has strange ideas about how you must be shielded and thought that we shouldn't say anything at all to you for the time being) to call you this evening. It is conceivable that, for good reasons which we may have overlooked, you don't agree with what we've done at Lazarsfeld's and its consequences.

2. *Volume 1941, Issue 3.* I received your telegram of January 16th and have remained silent about it to everyone except Pollock. That means, therefore, that Marcuse knows nothing about it either. You have to know that, because, on the day of his departure, Marcuse asked me repeatedly if I had heard from you and I denied that I had.

Your train of thought, I assume, goes as follows: a 1942 volume will cost money that we, perhaps, don't have to spend; and if we must spend something on a publication in 1942, then it should either be more closely tied to our theoretical interests or the quality of the pieces raised significantly. Should we not publish anything else for a time, then we'll want to produce a volume that demonstrates clearly to everyone who really counts theoretically and, in a certain sense, institutionally in our circle. If we must be silenced, then let's talk seriously the last time before it happens. So far, I'm very much agreed. This line of thought is so important that I, if also with hesitation, want to put aside our reputation as a punctual publisher. For it is completely clear to me that it will be a considerable time yet before we're ready with the volume you are planning. We'll probably send a short note to our subscribers telling them that the volume is not to be expected before such and such a time.

The only contribution that poses no problem is yours; I'm now counting on the German version arriving any day. As before, I still maintain my opposition to Teddie's essay on Veblen; you'll have to deal with it by imperial edict. Admittedly, it wouldn't be hard for Teddie, with your supervision, to produce something less captious in a short time. Pollock's work poses great difficulties, given the plans for the volume. Together with the other articles, this one would have been an article that as such would have been viewed leniently. However, if this contribution has to stand on its own, then, first of all, in the current form it presents largely a repetition of the point of view already expressed in the last essay, and, besides, about 30 percent of the text up until now consists of summaries of the contributions of others. That was all very well and fine in the context of a talk and Pollock's person and tone—but can it stay like that? Probably, for this purpose, the work must be characterized as that which it is, namely, a talk and a summary of a series of talks. But even so, it requires much more work.

As for my own contribution, I can't deliver a complete report on the American material in a short time. It would also exceed the scope of an essay. My proposal is that I write a work consisting of two chapters, each about twenty typed pages, the first dealing with the German biographies (more or less in the framework of the talk on the evening with Dieterle) and the second chapter with fundamental points of view and a few theoretical treats along with nice examples from the American material.

Concerning the second chapter, I now have written approximately twenty pages—certainly a very provisional draft, which I want to sent you in the next few days. The talk at Lazarsfeld was, by the way, a quite successful affair, and, I hope, a source of positive reports for some circles of sociology and psychology graduates and lecturers at the university. I could deliver a responsible German version of these two chapters in about two weeks after you give your agreement—given that there are no great interruptions or psychological disturbances from administrative and related affairs. [. . .]

[Leo Lowenthal]

This letter refers to Lowenthal's study. "Biographies in Popular Magazines."[12]

This letter was originally written in English.

429 West 117th Street
New York City

February 3, 1942

[Dear Horkheimer!]

I am afraid the pages I sent you give a very incomplete picture of the basic idea. It consists in a dialectical concept of the "empirical" findings, namely, the heroes as well as the categories in which they are treated belong decisively to the realm of consumption: this reflects indeed the receptive state of mind of the masses and the unconscious admission that the sphere of production and active transformation does not offer any more opportunities (I can quite neatly prove this point by a comparison of the biographical heroes in the same periodical thirty years ago, when they were industrialists, great bankers, and representatives of real culture); but while on the one hand the collection of biographies represents just one more section of modern mass culture of which all of us have now no doubt a clear picture, this phenomenon also contains the dream of a future mankind who might center its interests around happiness not in the harshness of work and labor but in the enjoyment of sensual goods in the broadest meaning of the term. While, on the one hand, historical information for the masses becomes a cobweb of lies and of ridiculous accumulation of the most insignificant facts and figures, the same masses show by their very occupation with these people and with their ways of "consumption" a longing for a life of innocence. From my own inner life I can deduct more and more how hateful the whole idea of production in the sense of permanent changes, transformations, incessant treatment of man and nature by machines and organizations must become to the unconscious and even conscious life of the majority. In a certain sense, the German biographies which I have studied in former years and this American material belong quite closely together. The first one falsifies history by an enchanting net of profound metaphysical and metapsychological phantasmagories; the second one is just the reverse and instead of taking history too serious, it takes it too funny. But, they both represent distorted utopias of a concept of man to which we stand in an affirmative way, namely, they both imply the unconditioned importance of the real, living, and existing individual: dignity and happiness. I don't want to continue, but I guess you will understand in what direction this all leads.

[Leo Lowenthal]

Lowenthal wrote this letter after his return from California, where he had visited Max Horkheimer.

The Professor Eckhard mentioned taught history at the time at the University of Colorado in Boulder. Hans Rosenhaupt, a childhood friend of Lowenthal's, later became director of the Woodrow Wilson Foundation in Princeton. Motte was the nickname of the former wife of Felix Weil. This letter was originally written in English.

429 West 117th Street
New York City

April 10, 1942

[Dear Horkheimer!]

It is rather hard to get used to letter writing again and not just to drop in and leave the wrong door open or closed. Please spare me to repeat to both of you what these weeks together with you meant to me.

San Francisco was as great an experience for me as I had dreamt of. It is the only place I so far have found on this continent where I could speak of a "cultural landscape": the peculiarities of highly developed technical constructions and of the Californian landscape really form here an unseparable unity.

From San Francisco I went on to Denver and spent an afternoon with Professor Eckhart who is a very kind soul and a model of human dignity. Of course, I had a lovely dinner in his house and the whole situation including the conversations was so touching that the old gentleman and I had tears in our eyes when we separated. Unfortunately, both people have to suffer very much because his wife has cancerous metastases and he is a diabetic. His special interest belongs to the history of German liberalism and, by the way, he speaks the language of that country fluently. He sends you his most cordial greetings and is still sorry that you did not come. As it is the case in all places now, he is very worried about the dropping registrations and looks rather black in the future of his university which is just going along on the fees which the government pays for courses in general education given to Navy personnel. His last words were: write to me, and I certainly shall do so.

I then went to Colorado Springs where I had a very pleasant time with Rosenhaupt and the many charming girls he knows. He insisted on my lecturing to his class and I did so for two hours on the day of my departure and was allowed to stop only ten minutes before my train left. I had the impertinence to talk without the slightest preparation first on Shakespeare and in the other class on Cervantes and the young Goethe. I just received an acknowledging letter which I add here, kindly return it!

I spoke to Motte twice who seems to be in rather bad shape, especially psychologically, and falls from one complaint to the other. I promised her to look after Ursel and her problems and perhaps I can persuade the girl to go to the College in Colorado; this might perhaps solve some of the problems of these rather unfortunate women.

I spoke for some hours to one of the directors of the Art Museum who, among other things, told me that they still can store pictures. If you care you might say that to Mrs. Marcuse who could pass on a word to Mr. Arnsberg. She told me he was worried about storing possibilities in Colorado Springs. There is still plenty so far.

I would like to publish now as soon as possible the next issue and I am therefore very anxious to have the last word first concerning the title of your article (I still think "The End of Reason" is a very good idea) and secondly, about the publication of Marcuse's article, which, by the way, has not yet a title.

You will have seen in the meantime Pollock's and Neumann's reactions which I consider as godsent. I hope that you can talk Marcuse out of the publication by sugaring the pill with your promise that we will publish everything else we have of him in the section of reviews (and that is plenty). On the other hand, I made it quite clear to Pollock that it would be a waste of your time if the price of the omission of this article were to be endless conversations between you and Marcuse.

I did not yet talk with P, who yesterday when I arrived was fully taken up with appointments and who will not be free before tonight. My mind is quite clear about everything we agreed upon but I have the feeling it will be quite a discussion.

I spoke today with Lazarsfeld who is convinced that if Teddie would come to New York and would work for a while on problems like music and

war, problems in which the government is highly interested, he would have
no difficulties in finding a research job. L will also apply to the Carnegie
Foundation for a research grant but he gives only little chances to this plan
because of the folding up policy of the foundations during the emergency.
The Sloane Foundation, for example, has closed already. L was very sweet
and hopes that I get my study on biographies speedily ready for publication. He also has contacted a few government agencies and advised them
about my qualifications. We shall see whether something comes of it.

I spoke to Miss von Mendelssohn who fully appreciates the situation as
it is. We shall proceed in the matter as we have agreed upon.

I shall write you as soon as I have spoken to P. My cold is not yet gone
and the awful snow and rain which we have at present in New York is not
a great help. I am very eager to know how your wife is and also about
your visit to San Francisco.

[Leo Lowenthal]

P.S. I received a review by Günther Stern [Anders] on a book by Karl
Loewith. Are we really obliged to print that? Please ask Marcuse to report
to you about it. I don't see any special wisdom in tearing Loewith's book
to pieces. I shall not give the manuscript to the printers before having your
o.k.

---

*In this letter, Horkheimer gives an extensive statement of his opinions
of a draft of Lowenthal's study. "Biographies in Popular Magazines" (see
Lowenthal's letter to Horkheimer of February 3, 1942). This letter was
originally written in English.*

13524 D'Este Drive
Pacific Palisades, California

October 14, 1942

[Dear Lowenthal!]

[. . .]

I again went through your last child, the "Biographies in Popular
Magazines," and I was as happy with it as the first time. Since I was in the
train, I did not have the energy to do it in a "thorough" way, that means,
making annotations on the margin. I did not find anything essential which
I would like to contradict. In some instances, I found that some most
important points you make should be more elaborated in order to show
their tremendous significance. I think here of statements such as the
omission of social issues from the biographies. You mention this fact, it is

true, at point one on page 26 and you again return to it later but I think you could here emphasize the great law of the pre-stabilized harmony between the mechanisms of the profit-system and its ideological requirements. The social issues are omitted because to mention them would prevent certain groups from buying the books and at the same the omission is a function in the ideological apparatus. Furthermore, the omission of all really decisive issues impoverishes also the issues of which one can speak, in a similar way as we become poor entertainers in a party when we know that certain topics are tabu, even if we did not intend to mention them. Again I noticed that you lay too much stress on activity versus passivity, sphere of production versus sphere of consumption. You say that the life of the reader is scheduled and governed by what he gets, not by what he does. The truth is, however, that doing and getting has become identical in this society. The mechanisms which govern man in his leisure time are absolutely the same than those which govern him when he works. I would go so far as to say that still today the key for the understanding of the behavior patterns in the sphere of consumption is the situation of man in industry, his schedule in the factory, the organization of office and working place. Consumption tends to vanish today, or should I say, eating, drinking, looking, loving, sleeping become "consumption" for consumption already means that man has become a machine, outside as well as inside of the workshop? I again thoroughly enjoyed the analyses on pp. 28–76. All I would have to say would be psychological associations of minor importance and, of course, far reaching theoretical considerations on the problem of mass society. Sometimes the language does not sound very familiar to me, so, when you speak of your own methods in a somewhat fearful and fussy way which, in spite of Lazarsfeld, could perhaps be done in a more superior tone. I don't like it when you say that "something can't be emphasized enough." The paragraph on pp. 66 and 67 which starts so elucidatingly, ends with a somewhat forced analogy. But this can show you that I really have only minor critical remarks.

On p. 40 paragraph 2, you come very close to one of the deepest problems of modern biography in particular, and mass culture in general. You say: "There is always a shortcoming in a biography: by picking just one individual out of the multitude of people and events. . . ." This picking out is often identical with a shortening of the objects. You will remember those terrible scenes in the movies when some years of a hero's life are pictured in a series of shots which take about one or two minutes, just to show how he grew up or old, how a war started and passed by, a.s.o. This trimming of an existence into some futile moments which can be characterized schematically, symbolizes the dissolution of humanity into elements of administration. Mass culture in its different branches reflects the fact the human being is cheated out of his own entity which Bergson so justly called "durée." This is true for the heroes of the biographies as well as for the masses. The events and achievements which the biographies mention in the lives of heroes are the reified features under which, in reality, they suffered and by which they missed their particular happiness. Even the heroes are cheated and unhappy. The countertrend in mass culture is represented in the moments of escape from it. Since man's wakeful state today is regulated in all details, the real escape is sleep or madness, or at least some kind of shortcoming and weakness. The protest against the movies is not found so much in bitter critiques but in the fact that people go in and sleep or make love to each other. Every word they could say against the picture would already be in the language of the cinema. I know that much of what I have just said is already indicated in your text; I just wanted to restate it as I understood it when I was thinking about your problems.

[Max Horkheimer]

In this letter, Lowenthal reacts to Horkheimer's remarks on the study, "Biographies in Popular Magazines". This letter was originally written in English.

New York, October 22, 1942

[Dear Horkheimer!]

I should write a letter full with apologies, first, because I, indeed, forgot to wire your wife and then because I have not yet answered your charming letters (three of them) of October 14th and 17th, and your wire of October 17th. Both omissions belong to the same logical context of the unconscious—betraying the unwillingness to take notice of your having gone away.

1) *Biographies.* I am very grateful for your remarks and I appreciated your thoughtfulness to read my paper on your trip home in spite of your physical exhaustion. In the meantime, my manuscript has been rewritten by an editor in Lazarsfeld's office and I must frankly admit that the lady in charge has done a rather satisfactory job. If Lazarsfeld really publishes it without proposing more cuts, I shall consent. I will wait now for another two weeks and then make clear to him that, if I do not have a binding promise of the when and where of the publication, we shall publish it ourselves in the year book. I will send you the revised version as soon as I have a copy at my disposal.

Your remarks about the montage of a life story in the moving picture is

especially revealing for me because it throws more light on my observation of the isolated and piece meal sequence of hardship and breaks or of childhood and adult life. All this seems to be also tied up with the concept of lovelessness because the criterion of love is continuity and this is just the phenomenon which is never admitted. Mass culture is a total conspiracy against love as well as against sex. I think that you have hit the nail on the head by your observation that the spectators are continuously betrayed and robbed of real pleasure by sadistic tricks. This sadism has the special function to prevent psychologically and physiologically "Vorlust." Take for example, the ballet scenes in Holiday Inn, one of the newest pictures where a couple starts dancing a menuet but as soon as this menuet develops to a more amourous situation and one could very well imagine that the dancing partners will end by kissing each other, the sweet and melodious music is suddenly stopped and replaced by jazz which almost verbally castrates the dancers. This fits very well together with elucidating remarks which Teddie once wrote about the connection of castration and jazz. I, therefore, would say that not the fact that people make love to each other in the Loges and Orchestras of the movie houses is the unbridgeable gulf between the sadistic stupidities and failures on the screen and the kissing and petting of the boys and girls while in former years the screen events could serve as a model or stimulus for some modest sensuous pleasures. Our poor friend Hallgarten once made the correct observations that the film stars of today are not any more and are not supposed to be any more beauties.
[. . .]

[Leo Lowenthal]

This letter conveys birthday greetings from Max Horkheimer to Leo Lowenthal on his forty-third birthday. The book dedicated to Pollock is Dialectic of Enlightenment.

13524 D'Este Drive
Pacific Palisades, California

October 28, 1943

L. L.!
This time I will not forget it. [. . .]
But for you (and me) I wish with all my heart that you realize all your aspirations. Everyday I recognize more clearly that the theoretical and practical expression of that which we are able to recognize because of our

special fate constitutes a task which justifies life, however short of its true limits we fall.

Our last conversations are alive in my memory. I trust that you are pursuing unflinchingly the scientific plans that we outlined here for the next six months. Whatever it is that you set about along these lines will please not only me but above all yourself and will bring us closer to a satisfying arrangement of our affairs.

I look forward to our being together in the spring. If, for many good reasons, I would prefer that it be you who once again makes the trip (if possible, both of you), I will do everything I can to see to it that our stay together is fruitful in more than one respect. In the meantime, I will try to raise the level of my efforts here yet higher. Your idea that there be a mimeographed publication for Pollock's fiftieth birthday, dedicated to him to show him that we mean it, is along with everything else a nice stimulus. But you will have to help very much with it.

To you and your dear wife, the most heartfelt wishes from both of us.

Yours truly, as ever,
Max Horkheimer

This letter of Horkheimer's to Lowenthal refers first to the book Hork-heimer wrote with Adorno, Dialectic of Enlightenment, *which was just about to appear in Holland at the Querido press.*[13]

The commentaries that follow apply to the Authoritarian Personality *(New York, 1950), and Horkheimer's commentaries on Lowenthal's book,* Prophets of Deceit.[14] *At the end of the letter the possibility of reestablishing the Institute in Frankfurt is mentioned for the first time. Wilhelm Dieterle is the well-known German-born film director; Landshoff is the director of the Querido press. This letter was originally written in English.*

July 29, 1946

Dear Leo,

Thank you for your letters of July 19th and 22nd. In particular, your handwritten letter and your suggestions for the corrections have been a great comfort to me. That you wrote them despite your great fatigue is additional proof of that kind of solidarity which makes life worthwhile. Kracauer's letter arrived this morning.

The list of corrections will be mailed to Landshoff at the end of next week. I have already gone over your suggestions and will certainly adopt most of them. However, I still do not quite understand your extreme caution about discussing the relation of democracy and fascism. Why should it be so daring to point to the trend of democracy towards fascism? In my opinion, this trend is one of the most important theses—nay, presuppositions—of any critical theory of present-day society. I do not see your reasoning quite clearly. Why do you feel that this elementary conviction should not be distinctly expressed?

Neither do I think it advisable to change the book in such a way as to convey the impression that it was written after the war. Quite apart from the tremendous amount of work this would necessitate, it would, so to speak, destroy its atmosphere. Therefore, I think we should leave the present tense wherever we refer to National Socialism. However, we shall omit the date in the dedication.

Naturally, I agree with the addition to the lawn mower of one or two cases of wine for Tillich's birthday. I will leave the whole matter to you.

On next Thursday, August first, I am going to San Francisco for a few days. The official reason is Berkeley—the unofficial, the fact that I must see Alexander. My condition is not so good. Almost every night there are one or two little attacks of the kind that I experienced in New York during my stay there last fall. This makes me unable to achieve the relaxation which normally comes with sleep. I have tried two or three doctors here but they are simply impossible. The one I have had for the last period understands very much and says the right things, but he insists on my taking so many medicines that I am liable to perish from stomach disease if I go on like this. As for my mood, I am in very good spirits. It is true that I am somewhat concerned about two circumstances which might disturb my concentration on work during the next two or three months. The first is my decision to abstain from new trips to New York, which will lead up to the disintegration of our relationships with the scientific department and the ugly phenomena connected with this process. Second, we will have to resolve the conflict with regard to Helen. There are various reasons for this which are better not put down in a letter. The one thing I want you to know is that so far we have not invited her to our home a single time, either with a large gathering or alone with Lix. There have been several discussions with Lix which did not lack in clarity, but, despite his good intentions, they will finally prove to be of no avail.

The basic facts of the Adult Study are as follows. The attitude of Flowerman has given Sanford and his gang the idea that they can monopolize the Study. In order to be able to do so they have artificially created a constant state of conflict so that they can say that there was never any real cooperation, either with Adorno, with Pollock, or with Horkheimer. He will try by devious methods to bring about a situation in which we say we do not want the book, using completely irrational complaints and grievances, delaying the writing or delivering an impossible manuscript. He does all this because he plans to break up the unit into technical articles and monographs which he and his fine associates can use to serve their respective academic ambitions. Since they have undertaken the formal obligation to work on the book until it is finished, even after the payments stop, a continuous state of war is the best method for them. I shall probably let Flowerman know that the only way to prevent that would be to ask Teddie to stay in Berkeley for three or four months full time and to give him all authority. This, however, could only be made possible by reverting to the old mode of payment through Teddie. I hope he has not yet forwarded the whole amount. Flowerman's ambivalence, which in this case has been furthered by his falling in love with Brunswick, has been most detrimental to the Committee. If he does not take a very definite stand with our side there is not even the hope of repairing the damage. I have not heard from him since his telephone call in the Stern affair and he has not written to me since my departure. I would have taken drastic action before this if I had not tried instead to concentrate on my own work. What is your opinion: do you think it would be of any use to have a very confidential, but frank, discussion with him? His attitude is completely irrational and almost criminal. However, if you want to talk to him on this level, please ask me about it beforehand, by wire or telephone if necessary.

I have read the notes on the agitator (Pages 108–270) with great interest. My impression is the same as the one I expressed with regard to the previous notes. Congratulations!

In the following I am not mentioning the various specific positive reactions I had in reading many passages. I restrict myself to some of the critical suggestions which might or might not be of any use. Some of them will certainly be based on misunderstandings because notes cannot be as distinct as a finished text. I am certain that most of what I am going to say would have been covered by you without my speaking.

One observation I made when I read the Phelps and Thomas concerns the problems of over-exploration. The discussion of so many details must lead to certain repetitions and overlapping. This would not be bad if it were not that often one cannot tell clearly on which level of interpretation a specific device is explained. Relatively superficial and uncertain remarks are followed by essential theoretical elements and vice versa. This will be overcome when you put the whole work on the fundament of a philosophical and psychological concept. There should also be a short chapter on methodology.

Another general observation refers to your use of such words as productive and constructive; also, your using religion as more or less direct antithesis to agitation. Although I am convinced that your final formulations will avoid any danger of conformism, I consider this point rather important. At various places you mention that there is some truth in the accusations of the agitator and you relativise the antagonism between agitation on the one hand and liberalism and religion on the other. However, it must be made very clear that religion had its own agitators as far back as the Crusades and liberalism was the ideology for the realities of child labor and colonial atrocities. [. . .]

There are many more remarks I would like to make but the most important must simply wait until we can speak to each other. There is one thing which should not be omitted here: the agitators will probably be unleashed upon the people at a moment of economic depression. Therefore, it seems necessary to me to bring in the economic motive much more clearly than the notes indicate so far. We speak of the audience and the masses but masses are different. The audience of the agitator in time of war or prosperity is not the same as the audience in the period which immediately procedes a totalitarian uprising. The former is constituted largely of old women, cranks, asocial elements, etc. while the latter audiences which play a role in a fascist situation are much more rational. I remind you of the fact, so often observed by both of us, that the fascists in pre-fascist Germany were better informed about economic and diplomatic matters than the average non-fascist. I do not want to over-emphasize this point because your central theme is the psychology of agitation and I know very well that the process of agitation tends to level the differences and to bring out the paranoid elements in each audience. However, we should not expose ourselves to the justified accusation that we ignore the role played by outright economic factors. There is also direct economic reasoning.

Here is one more practical problem which has come up that I would like to mention. The Dieterles are going to Europe for about six weeks in order to make a report to the Selznick Studios on new screen talent. If they go to Germany they will visit Frankfurt, where William may take up relations with the university as a member of our Advisory Board. He would ask the president of the university for information about the situation there. There is the slight possibility that we might reopen a small branch of the Institute at Frankfurt. This would naturally be a tremendous thing for Frankfurt and the relations of that university with America. I have told the Dieterles everything that they should know and you do not have to add any substantial information when they call you in New York. It is my conviction that there will be no time for them to pursue our interests. Therefore, it might be best if you avoid going into details. However, you should stress the importance of the former Institute in the German academic world before Hitler.

I told Teddie about your wish concerning documents on the Berkeley projects.

Enclosed please find a copy of my letter to Flowerman. Massing wrote me that Stern's assignment has been discontinued from September first after a discussion with Slawson. Do you not think it impossible behavior on Flowerman's part not to have written me at all? Never mind, I am thinking about more important things. I am looking forward to the time when you and I will discuss them together.

Most cordially yours,
Max

P.S. Maidon asks you the great favor not to put Special Delivery on letters which may arrive here on Sundays. During the last months we have been awakened indirectly by the postman, directly by Cookie, on many Sunday mornings between 8 and 9 o'clock. This, of course, certainly does not refer to very important messages. Shall I do the same thing for you?

Apart from that, Maidon sends you and Golde her love.

M.

The first paragraph of the letter refers to the first draft of the manuscript that appeared in 1947 as Eclipse of Reason *(German: Max Horkheimer,* Kritik der instrumentellen Vernunft, *Frankfurt/M, 1967). The mention of "Fragmente" is a reference to what was later published as* Dialectic of Enlightenment, *which, at the time the letter was written, existed only in hectographed form. Samuel Flowerman replaced Max Horkheimer as director of the scientific division of the American Jewish Committee. By Labor Study is meant once again the Institute's investigation of the spread of anti-Semitism among American workers. The study was published only in part. Lowenthal's contribution was published as "Vorurteilsbilder. Antisemitismus unter amerikanischen Arbeitern," in his* Schriften, Bd. 3, *Frankfurt/M, 1982, S. 175ff. Salomon is Gottfried Salomon-Delatour, a sociologist in Frankfurt who was Lowenthal's dissertation director. This letter was written originally in English*

New York, N.Y.

August 2, 1946

[Dear Horkheimer!]

I have given your letter of July 29 an enthusiastic reception. So far I had only time to glance over your notes but I have realized already how much they mean for the book. Of course, I endorse fully your comments on missing economic notes. One has to be careful not to forget to say the obvious, just because it is obvious. I am quite certain that in the end we will have to worry more about the necessity of using a certain reserve than about forgetting to think of the character of this society. Your notes will be studied minutely during the coming days.

I have to say a word about the process of production. The notes are the result of common conversations between Guterman and me. As far as the ideas are concerned, I have contributed considerably more than he, but without him I could not have done so well. He deserves gratitude and credit for the work almost as much as I do. He took notes all the time while I spoke and he also took notes about his additions and later on he dictated them. I found just by my superficially going over your notes that some of the things to which you take exception are his formulations but also some of the points which you term excellent have to be credited to him. It is good team work. I do not know yet how to recompensate him adequately. I might write to you about this some other day because I have a vague idea.

I am glad that you found my notes on the *Fragmente* useful. There are apparently two points on which I have expressed myself not quite clearly.

I do not think that you should eliminate every reference to the dialectic between liberal society and fascism. I am nearly insulted that you thought I would suggest such a horrible thing. I only took exception to two or three places where an American institution is stylistically treated in such a way that the reader has to interpret: aha, he means that American fascism is unavoidable and almost on the threshold. I think you find these places in my notes from Centerville as well as in my letter from 1944.

With respect to the tenses I do not agree with you. Certainly you should not only not hide but stress the fact that this book was written during the war and finished long before it has ended. But since it is not a book which is published posthumously, it seems to me a little bit too precious and could be interpreted as vanity to be so pedantic in conserving the original text. I am always tempted a little bit to smile when I read these sentences on the Nazis as if they were still in power. In any case I have not a comfortable feeling. Why not mention in the preface that for the reader's sake you have changed the tense to the past. By the way you may have noticed that I was selective in my suggestions. Wherever I deemed it possible to leave the sentence in the present tense, I did not suggest to change it.

Flowerman called me up this morning. All these weeks he was traveling around and is leaving town again tomorrow for two weeks vacation. He makes a rather disturbed impression on me. For his vacation he has selected a cabin in a New York State park, where he will move alone with his books and groceries. He has invited me to visit him there if I feel lonesome. He did not mention you or Berkeley and only spoke about the books and Mr. Stern. About the books we will have a meeting in the second half of August. He is, of course, very eager and worried because the Institute's contributions are the only tangible assets of more than conventional value on which he can count. About Stern he remarked that in a meeting with Slawson Stern betrayed so outspokenly that his first loyalty belongs to Soviet Russia that he wrote himself his own farewell ticket. As always I used this opportunity again to emphasize that I consider Stern's appointment by Flowerman as his greatest mistake in personnel matters and that Stern was slated for quite another job which did not materialize and that therefore he never should have been appointed.

Some progress has been made concerning the Labor Study. Massing and I individually as well as together, had several meetings with Lazarsfeld, who himself will do the main editing job. The fine editing in English will be done by a first-rate editor, Mrs. Siepman, the wife of Professor Siepman, whom Teddie knows. Lazarsfeld will do the job himself because he is only permitted to do home work at present and because he wants to earn some money directly, which he will use to pay for part of his debts he has with us. Since they were completely broke and had debts for taxes to the State of New York and for Lotte's tuition at the Abraham Lincoln school, I had arranged several weeks ago for a loan repayable from September on and for which Lazarsfeld had given us checks in order to secure proper installment payments. Part of these debts will be waived in the form of credits for Lazarsfeld's editing job. I hope you will okay my decisions post factum. [. . .]

I am very worried about the report on your state of health. I hope that Alexander still sticks to the diagnosis of rejuvenation. Please send me a wire after you are back from San Francisco telling me the truth about your objective and subjective condition.

Maidon is absolutely right. When I had mailed the last specimen Friday a week ago, I felt like a guilty man. Somehow I had mixed up in my memory that an early wire won't wake you up with the fact that the letter carrier still can. I shall gladly comply with Maidon's wish. Next Tuesday I intend to start preliminary dictation of the book text. Guterman will go to Provincetown in two weeks and work on Rhetorics. I can only repeat that I feel utterly incompetent in every respect for the job I have to do.

A personal letter? You are very right about it.

[Leo]

I forgot to thank you for the wonderful collection of Edgar Allan Poe.

The book mentioned in the opening paragraphs is Horkheimer's Eclipse of Reason *(In German,* Kritik der instrumentellen Vernunft*). This letter was originally written in English.*

New York, N.Y.

May 22, 1947

[Dear Horkheimer!]

When I stepped out of the elevator at the sixth floor of the Oxford University Press building, a very happy surprise expected me. You remember that there is a showcase next to the entrance door where the Press exhibits their newest publications. There was nothing else in the case but your book. Fourteen copies of it, and an extremely funny astronomical symbolism, showing a sun in its various ecliptical stages.

Miss Nicholson told me that they are very proud and happy with the book because they think it is one of the very few serious publications that have come out in this country for a number of years. I asked her about reviews and she told me that the publicity director is closely following up this matter. So far, a very long and nice review has appeared in the *N.Y. Herald Tribune* of May 18 of which I will get you a copy, and a short mentioning in the Newark-New Jersey News. The Press has sold about 250 copies before publication which they consider a very handsome success. The way in which Miss N. spoke of you, your book and her stay in your house, was extremely charming.

She was extremely unhappy about the financial problem and did not know what to say. According to her you must have misunderstood her. It would have been far beyond her power to promise you anything about technical help in the way of typing. The Press has never paid for editorial help of any kind, because it assumes that this is its own job anyway, and as far as the author is concerned, he has to take care of that if he finds it necessary.

I told her that we would, of course, accept any proposal from her side and that we are much more interested in continuing our pleasant relations than in pressing a matter about which misunderstandings have arisen.

She will bring up the matter in a business meeting next week and then let me know what the Press has decided. You cannot imagine how unhappy she was, since she felt so miserable about hurting you in any way. She indicated that if the requested payments would have to be made (which will not occur) the book would actually be in the red and this would not be very fortunate since the Press considers you now as its author.

I enclose a memorandum to Flowerman which contains an outline of my book as well as a statement on its purposes which Flowerman is supposed to pass on with the two new chapters to Dr. Slawson.

Lazarsfeld is extremely indignant about Slawson's request to meet me in connection with the completion of the book and will probably call him tomorrow, telling him that such delays are absolutely natural in the course of scientific work and that he and his colleagues have ascertained in the meantime the high scientific value of my study as it stands now.

May I kindly ask you to write Miss Nicholson that she sends me ten copies of your book at the special reduction of the author. There are always friends of the Institute who would like to get a cheaper copy and there might be a case or two where I may think it right to give a copy away.

[Leo]

This letter refers to a proposal by David Riesman to undertake a content analysis of fan mail from radio and film audiences.

February 23, 1948

Dear Max!

The following might well interest you. David Riesman, one of the most influential professors at Chicago, is currently a visiting professor at Yale. As such, he is directing a big project on the problem of apathy in present-day culture. In particular, the relation of Americans to politics and to the entire sphere of public activities altogether is supposed to be investigated. Riesman recently had the very good idea that it has always been naively believed in interpretations of public opinion polls that the people who took positions were the politically vital ones, while those who say "I don't know" were apathetic. Perhaps, thinks Riesman, it's the other way around. With the thought that, for example, the positive answers in the sphere of democratic ideology are given by conformist fellow-travelers who could also be different if the official cultural atmosphere changed, he comes very close to your own ideas. The project is to be conducted under the auspices of the Yale Committee on National Policy and is to be financed by the Carnegie Corporation. Riesman's assistant is the pleasant Nathan Glazer, whom you originally engaged for the committee and who has received a six-month leave from *Commentary* to go to Yale.

Riesman has written to me and also visited. He inquired whether I would be prepared to contribute to an anthology he would like to publish concerning the whole topic of apathy. He proposed that I do a study of fan mail. It's really very easy to assume that much of what is denied the person today in the sphere of action, or appears to be denied, lives itself out vicariously in fan mail. In a certain way, such a work would be related methodologically and in terms of content to the study of American biography. It was because of you, incidentally, that Riesman turned to me.

Generating material is not simple. The experts in this area, like Lazarsfeld and Herta Herzog have predicted that I couldn't get, for example, radio fan mail. The prediction was false. I met the directors of the research division of the radio network at the congress in Urbana, Ill., where I spoke in January. And the research director of CBS, to whom I spoke last week, has already sent me a news commentator's fan mail and he's firmly promised further material—namely, letters to a daytime serial—which would be very important.

It would truly be extraordinarily interesting if I could compare radio fan mail with film fan mail. Do you think that William Dieterle could be of help to me in this? If I could get a couple of hundred letters to, for example, Jennifer Jones or Peck or Cotton, or to any other prominent stars, it would offer a unique opportunity to use material that, as far as I know, has been treated by no other social scientist. Naturally, it would be very good if these letters referred to films that have just been shown or have been shown recently, but older material would be of some value as well.

It goes without saying that every guarantee would be given that the material would be handled confidentially. Citations from the letters would not be traceable to the writer, nor would it be necessary to name the film star. The sponsorship from Yale and Carnegie let it be recognized that the undertaking is a serious and exclusively scientific one.

If you think that we could approach Dieterle about this—who, God knows, has enough to do—I would be very obliged to you should you want to do that for me. I would, of course, be most grateful to him.

I haven't yet made a final agreement with Riesman, because I wanted to wait a bit first to see how successful I am in generating the material. Your answer to this letter will be one of the determining factors. Please let me know as soon as possible.

The most cordial greetings to you and Maidon,

[Leo]

This letter is directed to Horkheimer, who had already returned to Germany. Lowenthal expresses his refusal to give up his position at the State Department. The "Voice Project" is a study Lowenthal arranged for the Institute after it returned to the Federal Republic. It concerned the impact of the radio programs of Voice of America. Some of its results were included in the study directed by Friedrich Pollock, Gruppenexperiment *(Frankfurt/M, 1955). The Glock referred to in reference to the "Voice Project" is Charles Y. Glock, at the time research director of the Bureau of Applied Social Research, Columbia University.*

New York

February 24, 1951

[Dear Max!]

It distresses me that I've not written for so long. I accept your letters of January 22nd and February 5th, and your telegram of February 19th, as admonitions. I'm happy that you received my birthday greetings in the spirit in which I sent them. The book on the history of medicine, which I hope you've received in the meantime, is a present from me.

Meanwhile, I've gotten an impressive report about you, your work and the other friends of Herta, Lazarsfeld, and Neumann. I'm already looking forward to this evening, when Herta has promised to tell me in detail about the group study. She is just as excited about that as about your lecture and your many conversations. To my great satisfaction, in her short, provisional report of an hour she used the word "genius."

I don't need to tell you how painful it is for me that you apparently couldn't completely approve of my decision, in our mutual interest, to remain for now in the position where I am. How strongly I feel in such moments the necessity of the spoken instead of the written word, and the atmosphere of inexpressible understandings that never fail us when we are together. In present circumstances—first among which is the absence of your concurrence—I am suffering more than I can say. The gift of the Nietzsche quotation is generous and makes me ashamed. As far as I can tell from introspection, it is not the feeling of so-called success that causes me to ask you to accept my decision, as you offered yourself. [. . .]

As for the Voice Project, I'm pleased that you managed to get it underway despite your many other burdens. The financial story is simply horrible. The bureaucracy, which becomes more puzzling to me the more contact I have with it, simply takes the position that a contractor must finance his own work and money is to be paid only when the work is finished. Glock promised to write you about how one can attempt anyway to receive payments in the course of the next while. Unfortunately, he can't do a thing because the office has to struggle not only with the cumbersome governmental bureaucracy but with the much more cumbersome Columbia bureaucracy. In a series of smaller contracts that I've arranged, there was absolutely nothing for the contractors to do but use the government contracts to get a loan from the bank. The sociological roots of all these things are clear as day. [. . .]

[Leo]

Notes

8. *(Republished in: Max Horkheimer,* Notizen, *1950–1969 und Dämmerung. Notizen in Deutschland, Frankfurt/M, 1974).*
9. *(English in Leo Lowenthal,* Literature and Mass Culture, *Transaction Books, 1984, pp. 167ff).*
10. *Reprinted in English in Leo lowenthal,* Literature and the Image of Man, *Transaction Books, 1985, pp. 157ff.*
11. *Republished in Max Horkheimer,* Gesellschaft im Übergang. Aufsätze, Vorträge und Reden 1942–1970, *Frankfurt/M, 1972.*
12. *In Paul F. Lazarsfeld, Frank Stanton, eds.* Radio Research, *New York, 1944; In German, "Der Triumph der Massenidole," in* Schriften, *Bd. 1, Frankfurt/M, 1980, S. 258ff.*
13. *Amsterdam, 1947; republished Frankfurt/M, 1968 and elsewhere.*
14. *Published in 1949; In German, "Falsche Propheten. Studien zur faschistischen Agitation," in* Schriften, *Bd. 3, Frankfurt/M, 1982, S. 11ff.*

PART IV

Conversations

15

Scholarly Biography: A Conversation with Helmut Dubiel, 1979

Dubiel: In the early 1920s you wrote many articles—in part politically oriented, in part oriented toward the history of ideas—that could be summed up under the bibliographical rubric "Judaica." In Jewish newspapers and community bulletins you published articles on Lassalle and Marx, on Tolstoy and the German spirit, and on the Jewish philosophy of religion of Hermann Cohen. Some of these writings on the history of ideas were systematically collected in a long omnibus article, "Judaism and the German Spirit." All these articles, if taken together, recall a thematically similar short article by Walter Benjamin on the role of the Jews in the recent German history of ideas. Could you tell me what you consider to be the uniting link of these essays?

Lowenthal: My intellectual and political interest in Jewish affairs developed very strongly in my student days by contact with the philosophy of Hermann Cohen and under the influence of his student Walter Kinkel, by contact with the Zionist student movement in Heidelberg, and by the great influence of the charismatic Rabbi Nobel. I believed that Jewish philosophy of religion, especially that of Maimonides, contains a progressive rationalism with strong secular tendencies, which, though garbed in religious symbolism, also connote the idea of a paradise on earth. At the time I was intent on capturing in this secularly oriented redemptive thinking the utopian element that Marx, Heine, and also Freud at least inherently display. It is probably not by chance that I often gave lectures in Jewish communities and synagogues, in part to earn some money as a struggling young scholar, in part out of conviction about the Jewish element in the utopian aspect in socialism. However much I once tried to convince Martin Jay that there were no Jewish motifs among us at the Institute, now, years later and after mature consideration, I must admit to a certain influence of Jewish tradition, which was codeterminative.

Dubiel: I found among your papers the draft of a project with the title "Judaism and Jewishness in Recent German Philosophy." I read this short manuscript, as well as a few letters from Franz Rosenzweig and Martin Buber, who reacted very positively to this idea. Was it the intent of this project to gather together in one volume your scattered works in this field as a sort of German-Jewish intellectual history?

Lowenthal: Do you have a particular year in mind?

Dubiel: Yes, 1925.

Lowenthal: That was just one year before I became associated with the Institute of Social Research. This project was an attempt to find a basis for an intellectual, perhaps even an academic, existence. At that time I was not thinking of a professorship; it had only been two years since I had received my doctorate. With Buber's and Rosenzweig's help I tried to obtain a grant for this project from the Moses Mendelssohn Foundation, which was a kind of Jewish Ford Foundation. I don't remember anymore why it failed. Maybe it wasn't judged favorably; maybe Leo Strauss didn't like it—he was very influential in the foundation at that time. In any case, my association with the Institute of Social Research began soon thereafter. I would have liked to have worked on a philosophically and politically oriented study on the interrelations of Jewish and non-Jewish philosophy and Jewish and non-Jewish intellectual life. That also was connected with my earlier essay "The Demonic" and my dissertation on Franz von Baader. Even though nothing came of it, the moral impulses that motivated the project remained alive in me.

Dubiel: Leo, I would like a few more comments from you on those articles of yours that have a purely political orientation, especially those you wrote in the *Jüdisches Wochenblatt,* published by Ernst Simon. Judging by their titles, the articles are often primarily about current affairs—for example, "The Situation of the Jews in Poland" or "The Concession Law in Poland." But I'm especially interested in the essay "The Lessons of China," which contains a very sharp critique of the Jewish settlement policy in Palestine. As a reminder, I want to read you a few sentences from your article of June 25, 1925:

> China's revolution must be a lesson for Palestine. If, especially in earlier years, one looked at Zionism's ideological products, it would be easy to remark ironically on what bloody laughter it would cause in the world if, for instance, a remnant of Celts scattered on a remote island were to travel to France today and claim its territory as a national property belonging to them by historical right. Zionism's dangerous vice, its ethnocentric naïveté in historical matters, found in Jewish history a fertile field. . . . The Arab question was therefore approached in about the same way the Zentralverein Deutscher Staatsbürger Jüdischen Glaubens conceives of its relation to anti-Semites, i.e., how shall we deal with this unsavory, numerically overwhelming element? In other words, one could say that Zionism's borrowings from the arsenal of European diplomatic weapons were ill advised, that is to say, Zionism took out a larger loan that it had originally intended: for it engaged in European colonial policy against the Arabs. . . .
>
> And on looking around with open eyes, one is keenly aware that Arab youths today are studying at European universities and working to prepare for the hour that has now struck in China. Here, too, a national majority is screaming for justice. Here, too, a tremendous "danger" is approaching. It will require the concerted moral energy of the entire Zionist generation living today, indeed the entire world Jewish community, to demonstrate a willingness to change not merely its tactics, but its mentality as well. I am not so politically naïve as to make a favorable prognosis without hesitation.

Lowenthal: You know that in my student years in Heidelberg I was a member of the Zionist student organization. But I had joined because I believed most strongly in Judaism's messianic mission, its utopian political task. I had hoped that Eretz Israel would be the model for a just society. However, my experience with Zionism followed a path very similar to my later experience with the Communist world movement and the Communist Party. I experienced great disappointment; I felt that the Zionist movement was suffering more and more from what my friend Ernst Simon at that time so convincingly called the "intoxication with normality." Ideologically, I was not so blinded as to refuse a critical analysis of the settlement policy of the Jewish organizations in Palestine. As I saw it, the Jewish land purchases were an alliance of big Arab landowners and Jewish money at the expense of the Arab peasants and farmworkers. I instinctively foresaw that this could lead to bad conflicts, if not catastrophes. My comparison related to the occupation of China by the European powers and the establishment of extraterritorial zones. I believed that a lesson should be learned from the Boxer uprising, that a population had to be listened to and could not simply be raped. This article, which I signed "Hereticus," resulted in my abandoning the Zionist movement and also, quite concretely, the newspaper. This does not mean, I would like to repeat, that I had given up my relation to Jewish motifs or my support of Israel.

Dubiel: As I was going through your papers from the 1920s I found, in addition to the manuscript of your dissertation, many other manuscripts testifying to your philosophical activity. One feels in all your writings not only that you studied philosophy but also that philosophical orientations are present in all your scientific works, even though you did not write a philosophical treatise in the strict sense, apart from your dissertation. In the 1920s you wrote about the political philosophy of the Enlightenment. I also found a manuscript on Thomas More and Campanella, and one entitled "Power and Law in Rousseau's Philosophy of State and in German Idealist Philosophy." Then I found a longer manuscript on Helvétius's philosophy, a manuscript that was projected to be your inaugural dissertation but could not be completed because of your emigration. First, comment a bit on the works just named.

Lowenthal: You have traced something decisive in my intellectual life. You know that here in the United States one often has to present one's professional calling card. Someone asks, "What do you do?" and then I say, "I'm really a philosopher." My relation to philosophy began very early through my father's influence, especially through his recommendation that I read Schopenhauer, and it continued throughout my intellectual youth. There is no semester in which I did not register for a few classes and seminars in philosophy. As a very young man I went to Giessen just to study neo-Kantian philosophy. Hermann Cohen was very reactionary and nationalistic, but it must not be forgotten that one of his greatest students was Paul Natorp, who at that time was a socialist. Walter Kinkel was himself a socialist. Natorp and Kinkel have shown that Kantian ethics and socialist consciousness are compatible. The interest in Enlightenment philosophy you were just speaking of came about mainly through my Marxist orientation. You know that Marx was indebted to the Enlightenment; he criticized the Enlightenment philosophers only because, although they postulated the right goals of society theoretically, they did not state practically how these goals can be translated into revolutionary praxis. This subject has always interested me; therefore, I studied the left wing of Enlightenment philosophy very intensively: Holbach, Helvétius, La Mettrie, Diderot. You see here in my library the first editions of Holbach, LaMettrie, and Helvétius, which were dearly paid for with my scanty savings. In the mid-1920s there were no good German books about the French Enlightenment in existence. There were hardly any modern translations—for example, no translation of the introduction to the *Encyclopédie*, no translation of Helvétius, hardly any of Diderot. If you look at my bibliography in the Helvétian manuscript, you'll see how scanty the secondary literature was. It was also politically interesting that in Germany the mostly trivial German Enlightenment philosophers, such as Wolff, were praised to the sky, but the French Enlightenment was almost totally ignored. After all, Helvétius was one of the sharpest critics of German class society.

Thus the philosophical motifs in me always remained alive. Look at my later literary studies. When I write about Corneille, I also write about Descartes. When I write about Molière, I also write about Gassendi, and when I write about popular culture, I also write about Pascal and Montaigne. For me, philosophy is still the queen of the sciences, and, like most who think as I do, I mourn the present situation in which philosophy is undergoing a decline. If metaphysics is still being taught in the universities here, then it is mostly by arrogant, old, boring "nuts," while fashionable interest is inclined toward linguistic analysis, which in most (although not all) cases is a technically oriented methodology of the sciences and shares with authentic philosophy only the name.

Dubiel: In the years 1928 and 1931 you wrote a few works that were not published, I believe, until 1971, under the title *Erzählkunst und Gesellschaft* [Narrative Art and Society]. These essays show Lowenthal as he would later be known. Indeed, these writings comprise a first and very self-confident realization of a program for a materialistically oriented study of literary history. The volume contains something like an ideologically critical reconstruction of bourgeois class consciousness in terms of its most prominent literary representatives.

Lowenthal: Yes, with the exception of the first essay in that volume, on the social situation of literature, which first appeared in 1932 in the *Zeitschrift für Sozialforschung,* the other essays originated from a compendious lecture series I had developed in the League for Popular lectures. I lectured on all areas of European literature, although my main interest was German literature, because as a good Marxist I acted according to the principle of beginning with criticism at home, and at that time Germany was causing me to lose a lot of sleep. In its methodology this work is characterized by an as yet—how should I put it?—unmediated Marxism. Maybe I am doing myself an injustice by this judgment, for in these works I also apply the psychological mechanism of mediation, particularly by taking into account the socially codetermined private reactions of the literary personae. Most of what I wrote or began writing in Germany before my emigration expresses the attempt to track down the decline and disintegration of bourgeois consciousness and to delineate it in a critique of ideology. My special interest concerned the documents of literature and the documentations of literary influence. And if you take a look at the subtitles added fifty years later to these sections, they express this theoretical intention: for example, for the chapter on Goethe I choose the title "Bourgeois Resignation"; for Gottfried Keller, "Bourgeois

Regression''; and so forth. These studies are part of a larger project to describe and analyze the specific course of German bourgeois consciousness and why there was no bourgeois revolution in Germany. As I said, these essays were motivated by political critique. As far as I can remember I stopped working on this material in 1930, because I was then too burdened with Institute business, especially with the founding of the *Zeitschrift für Sozialforschung*.

Dubiel: On reading these old works I had the impression of a specific continuity and discontinuity, similarity and dissimilarity, with the essays that appeared a few years later in the *Zeitschrift*. As regards your early work, I would speak of a methodological indifference. But the studies that appeared in the *Zeitschrift* can be summed up under the intention of a study of literary history based on the materialistic and social-psychological study of the history of literature. I like the freshness of those early works and the unself-consciousness with which cultural processes were related to the substructure. I always asked myself, how does he do that, what methodological authorities does he refer to? Do these works comprise a sort of *Nullpunkt* [moment of absolute beginning], or in what theoretical, or more precisely, literary-critical, tradition does he really stand? You yourself name Georg Brandes in connection with these questions, and of course Franz Mehring; you also name contemporary Russian literary studies—very heterogeneous points of reference in time and content. So, in brief, I had the impression that you were just rolling up your sleeves and beginning to write.

Lowenthal: Precisely, Helmut, a fresh dilettantism, if you wish, though originating in a political attitude and on the basis of a more or less solid knowledge of literature, but still in the sense of a fresh impressionistic discourse—I let myself be carried by my own enthusiasm. That was the case to some extent with the work on Baader and the works on Enlightenment philosophy. Although at that time I did not yet know Walter Benjamin's wonderful statement that history is always written by the victors, I was always interested in writing the history of the losers. Baader was such a loser—a lone figure of German Restoration philosophy.

In this book we have been talking about, *Erzählkunst und Gesellschaft*, I speak of the literature of the Young Germany [Junges Deutschland] movement in light of the history of the revolution that didn't take place. The essay on Mörike traces the state of melancholy of the great German poets, who did not get from their public anything near the resonance that would have been matter-of-course in France or England. There was no public in Germany such as Victor Hugo had in France or Shelley and Byron had in England. And last but not least, I wrote on Friedrich Spielhagen, who, though he was no great artist, was a very conscious, independent, and radical analyst of bourgeois society. I was intrigued with dealing a blow to the widespread reception of Gottfried Keller's and C. F. Meyer's so-called greatness and with honoring the lost and neglected streams of German literature.

Dubiel: Thus documenting again and again the thesis that there was no genuine bourgeois consciousness in Germany, or in sociological terms, that there was no significant and influential carrier group of a liberal worldview.

Lowenthal: And consequently no carrier group of a political liberalism, either, or any historical chance of an alliance between socialists and enlightened liberals, who could have prevented the disaster in Germany. That is again the theme of my works on fashions in biographical subjects.

Dubiel: Leo, I'd like to come now to the essays you wrote in the *Zeitschrift:* first the essay "On the Social Situation of Literature," which appeared in 1932, then the 1933 essay on Conrad Ferdinand Meyer, then the 1934 study on Dostoevsky, the 1936 essay on Ibsen entitled "The Individual in Individualistic Society," and the famous 1938 essay on Knut Hamsun. The 1932 essay does, to a considerable extent, contain a methodological program in which literary history is conceived as the critique of ideology. Compared to those earlier works in *Erzählkunst und Gesellschaft,* one might say that the articles in the *Zeitschrift,* under the influence of Max Horkheimer's ideas on the critique of ideology, have a sharpened methodological consciousness. Would you agree with that?

Lowenthal: Yes, one can certainly say that. You know how these things originated historically. The first volume, no, the very first number of the *Zeitschrift,* was supposed to contain a sort of program, a position adopted by all the major collaborators of the *Zeitschrift* concerning what united them—namely, the materialistic conception of history—focused on and applied to the fields they understood best. Horkheimer wrote about philosophy, Adorno about music, Pollock about the economy, Fromm about psychology, and I about literature. I challenged established literary scholarship, its idealistic arrogance, its distinctively political reactionary function. At the same time I tried to develop a kind of program for a set of studies I considered important. When the next essays appeared—you have just named them, the one on Conrad Ferdinand Meyer and the other on the Dostoevsky reception (this was, so to speak, a pioneer work)—they also fit into the analysis of the decline of the bourgeoisie: C. F. Meyer's heroes and their exemplary attempts to magnify themselves as symbols of the superior, sovereign, and leading class; and the enthusiastic reception of Dostoevsky, who was the most widely read author after Goethe, or at least the most published novelist in Germany, as a reflection of what Fromm called the anal and sadomasochistic character of the petit bourgeoisie, if not of the broad strata of the middle classes in general.

Dubiel: Does your work on Ibsen also fit into the framework of the critique of the disintegrating bourgeois consciousness?

Lowenthal: Yes! I was not naïve about Ibsen's patriarchal character. The essence of Ibsen's drama, his method, as it were, consists of taking bourgeois consciousness completely seriously on the level at which it articulates itself and then showing how hollow, fallacious, and in every sense untenable it is. Death, deception, bankruptcy, and the smashing of all interhuman relations among friends, between husband and wife, between parents and children, are the price that must be paid for the bourgeois system of competition. His decisive statement is that the bourgeois principle of competition penetrates into the intimacy of human relations and destroys them and—very important in Ibsen—that those who are furthest removed from the competitive struggle and at the same time most deprived of rights in a society based on the principle of competition, namely women, are the bearers and heralds of a better system. This then belongs to the context of my theory of marginality, which we should speak about when we come to *Literature and the Image of Man.*

Dubiel: Yes, let us now speak about your Hamsun study. This study to some extent goes beyond the methodological program of a critique of ideology. I have frequently found it listed under the rubric "Theory of Fascism" and not as an inherently literary-sociological work, which it claims to be. To my disgrace I must admit that in my late puberty I was a great, almost rapturous admirer of Hamsun. . . .

Lowenthal: A pardonable offense! You weren't the only one!

Dubiel: Your essay had an enormous prognostic quality. For Hamsun's sympathy with the Nazis became manifest—as far as I remember—only in 1940, when the German troops invaded Norway.

Lowenthal: Yes, precisely. This prognosis of mine did not go uncontested in our circle. Marcuse and Walter Benjamin both defended Knut Hamsun. But I insisted that the subtitle of this essay, "On the Prehistory of Authoritarian Ideology," was not accidental. I tried to document my thesis not only with what Hamsun had produced in manifest political statements, but also by an immanent analysis of his characters and his principles of literary construction. It was an immanent critique, an experiment carried out in the spirit of Adorno's beautiful statement: "Art does not come to society, but society comes to art: society should originate in the work of art and not the other way around." In the Hamsun essay, and even in the Ibsen essay, one of my methodological convictions is developed—namely, that the private is unmasked as the socially mediated. Works of art can give us information about the social dimension of the private sphere of men, how society is present in the love relationship of two people, in friendship, and in an individual's return to nature. Hence, literature is treated as the documentation of social representation in the psyche of the individual. In later works I once formulated this to the effect that literature provides us the best source of data for information on a society's pattern of socialization.

Dubiel: May I rephrase this in order to appropriate it? So literary sociology is meant not in the sense of a sociology of literature, its production and circulation; rather, it means understanding literature as the material, along with other cultural documentation, in which social and cultural structures can be identified. Such a kind of literary study uses literature as the medium and material for an analysis of society.

It was also then, the second half of the 1930s, that those discussions about the relation between aesthetics and politics appeared in the *Zeitschrift*. I am referring to Benjamin's essay "On Art in the Era of Its Technical Reproducibility" and Adorno's essay criticizing it, "The Fetish-Character in Music and the Regression of Hearing." Also, if I'm not mistaken, Herbert Marcuse's essay on "Affirmative Culture" appeared in the same volume as your Hamsun essay. All these essays, even if they are not as explicitly interrelated as is often underscored in contemporary literature, really constitute the three sides of a problem triangle. This could be designated as, first, the relation of art and science; second, the relation of art and mass culture; and third, the relation of art and politics. I want to describe quickly, in very crude simplification, three possible approaches to this problem and then hear from you how you classify yourself in this scheme.

Marcuse defended the thesis, and actually maintained it until his death, that art has a dual function in bourgeois society, an ideological one and a utopian one. Art is ideologically functional in the sense that it constitutes the realm of all collective imaginations and desires, whose political realization is denied in society. All unrealized possibilities of action in bourgeois society are repressed in their political-practical frame of action and banished to the realm of art. The great classical bourgeois of works of art represent at the same time the bourgeoisie's utopian consciousness. Marcuse, at least in his writings of the 1930s—and this distinguished him then from Benjamin and especially from Adorno—was not interested in the way the aesthetic consciousness of bourgeois society could be transposed into politics directly and without consideration of the evolutionary difference between culture and politics. I am alluding to the fascist propagation of mass art, indeed to the aesthetization of political life and war that Benjamin noted about fascism in general. Thus, fascism represents the false abolition of the relation between art and politics. Benjamin—this is his most famous thesis—ultimately interpreted the development of the relation of esoteric art to a mass culture made technically possible with political optimism. In crude terms, by smashing the uniqueness and almost cultic aura of works of art through new techniques of reproduction, new historical chances for the politicization of art are released. All the same, no one saw more clearly than Benjamin himself the danger posed by the political instrumentalization of mass art in fascism. Adorno, who formulated exactly the opposite thesis, thinks of mass art as the degeneration of art only in the framework of a repressive ideological exercise of domination, and consequently he attaches political intentions only to that art and those forms of art that refuse to serve mass culture. The utopian functions of art noted by Marcuse in the late-bourgeois epoch, that is, under the conditions of a mass culture, can be realized only through extremely esoteric art.

I came across this problem in an unexpected way when I read your book *Literature, Popular Culture, and Society*. I hadn't known that the phenomenon of mass culture is not at all a phenomenon that first emerged in late-bourgeois society. In fact, you show that mass culture, and also the political problem of the relation of the esoteric and exoteric, goes back far into the eighteenth century. The whole problem we are speaking of is not necessarily typical only of mass societies. The three authors I was speaking of apparently assume that the whole problem first arose when the means of reproduction were technically revolutionized. Now, Leo, can a point be given in the history of bourgeois society, and particularly in aesthetics, when autonomous art was forced to define its relation to mass culture? Or is it just a matter of the gradual evolution of an intrinsic, ever-present tension?

Lowenthal: I would say this is another leap from quantity to quality. But I first want to respond to what you said before. I naturally find it very hard to take as clear a stand as you demand. Of course I agree with much of what Adorno, Benjamin, and Marcuse said, although I never wrote about it systematically except in the foreword to the book you just mentioned. So first of all on the Benjamin thesis, to the extent that we perceive his position accurately: he really seems to say that the dissemination of works of art made possible by mechanical and electronic means of reproduction can also have a positive political effect. I consider this wrong. It runs counter to all our political experiences. But it is possible that we have misunderstood him. If you read this Benjamin essay closely, he himself moves very quickly away from the positive aspects of the technical revolution and describes the aesthetization of politics as it had become manifest in fascism. He definitely saw this more clearly than others. But he also said that in Communism art is equally politicized.

Art is really the message of resistance, of the socially unredeemed. Art is in fact the great reservoir of creative protest against social misery; it allows the prospect of social happiness to shine dimly through. I myself indeed tried to show that even in works of art that in their ideological coloring, with regard to author and target group, are very conformist and conservative—such as Lope de Vega in Spain, Corneille and Racine in France, also Goethe in many respects—the protest shines through in many a passage. The most important thing about bourgeois art is that it depicts the individual as threatened by bourgeois society. The best works of art are, in my opinion, those that do not stand in a conformist framework: Cervantes, most of Shakespeare, Racine, and later Ibsen, not to mention Romanticism. It is precisely the marginal minor characters in such great works that often become decisive bearers of utopian protest. I therefore have essentially tried, as Adorno says, to proceed "micrologically" and to analyze intimate, private, personal situations and modes of behavior in order to uncover in them just those unredeemed utopian elements that await social happiness. For I really believe that Walter Benjamin's thesis that history is always written by the visitors is refuted in works of art. The work of art gives voice to the losers in history, who, it is hoped, will someday be the victors. A secular philosophy of redemption is visible in this theoretical nexus of aesthetics and politics. In mass culture, on the contrary, nothing is ever redeemed, everything always stays the same because it ought to remain the way it is. In Hamsun, for example, even the minor characters are scoundrels; there is absolutely no redemptive phenomenon, no assertion anywhere that things could and should be different. And that was a touchstone for me to use in distinguishing between what is and what is not genuine art.

But now to the other part of your question, the relation of art and mass culture. As long as art has existed as an institution, there has also been its opposite, in Greek antiquity as well as the Middle Ages—for example, the entertainments in the church square after the religious service presented by jugglers and performers to entertain the masses. But the essential thing is the development of this relation of high and low art, which can be observed in the sixteenth and seventeenth centuries, when in many countries of Europe the predominantly agricultural mode of production was complemented by the urban forms of production of manufacturing and industry. In short, with the beginning of bourgeois forms of life and thought, an ambiguous philosophy about the role of art also begins to develop—or perhaps one should say the role of leisure, of which art seemed to be an essential part. In my book I expressed this symbolically through the counterposition of the philosophies of Pascal and Montaigne. Montaigne suggests that man needs relaxation and distraction under the pressure of modern life, whereas Pascal says that if you seek distraction you lose your life's meaning. This motif of Montaigne's, that the greater burden of life in the bourgeois age is eased through distraction, namely, distraction through art, occurs again and again in literature—for example, in Schiller in the speech of the "weary citizen"; and Goethe, too, in his "Prologue at the Theater," speaks of how "the men arrive bored, the women to show their beautiful fashions."

Dubiel: But the joke in this linkage of art and leisure against mass culture is probably that this function of distraction must not be detached from the ethical function of art, isn't it?

Lowenthal: Quite right, exactly. Art is here a kind of mental hygiene, an ethically important leisure occupation. In the eighteenth century in England, where bourgeois forms of life and ideology developed the fastest and strongest, there was clearly a great movement among the intellectuals to elevate the citizens' taste. Many of these authors, like Richardson and Oliver Goldsmith, are quite schizophrenic on this point; they are uncertain whether what they produce as literature is art or not, written for the market or for art's sake. Goldsmith says that the time of literary patrons is over and that the market is now the patron. Marjorie Fiske and I studied the literary scene in eighteenth-century England. There already existed literary genres that have become quite popular today, such as, for example, books on love, on how to win friends, on how to obtain a big dowry, popular and popularized versions of Homer and other items of classical literature, a whole world of journals and libraries with literature for entertainment. In short, all these phenomena of an ultimately market-oriented mass culture were already taking shape at that time.

Dubiel: Can you give a reasonably accurate dating of the origin of this contrast between art and mass culture?

Lowenthal: Certainly! That begins with the *Spectator* and the *Tatler,* Addison and Steele's journals, and it reaches its peak in Romanticism and also in German classicism. Wordsworth and Coleridge then first declared war on melodrama and shallow entertainment-literature. They decried the fact that now everything is written from the standpoint of quick comprehension and enjoyment so that one wouldn't have to exert oneself.

Dubiel: But the development of this relation of high and low art, of esoteric art and mass culture, can be derived not only from the perspective of the development of mass art itself, but especially also from just the opposite perspective. For the phenomenon of an autonomous art following only its own laws is a relatively late product of bourgeois consciousness. So, if it is true that an esoteric art conscious of its own laws arose only relatively late, then that must affect their relation to so-called low art. I mean that in the period we were talking about, the seventeenth and eighteenth centuries, the difference between high and low art must have been much more indefinite than in the late nineteenth century.

Lowenthal: Yes, much more gradual, of course. In any case, the concept of mass art is rather complex. When we speak of masses we mean of course only certain bourgeois strata in a few urban cultural centers, although Ian Watt maintains the interesting thesis that the reading strata in eighteenth-century England included not only the well-to-do housewives but also their personal maids. But aside from that, of course, there can be absolutely no question of reading in petit-bourgeois circles and the proletarian masses, for they were completely overworked and did not even have the money to buy themselves candles for reading. There is a marked change, however, in the course of the nineteenth century as literary and reading material rapidly increased. We enter the era of a big culture industry that is made possible because printing techniques become cheaper. More and more books, booklets, magazines, and newspapers became available in large quantities before radio and cinema were introduced.

On art and culture industry all of us generally held the same position, although there once was a period in the development of Marcuse's thinking in which he put greater value on partisan literature and spontaneous political art. He later abandoned this view and came around again to a firm belief in the utopian character and independence of the great work of art. Adorno's position that art has been pressed more and more into defensive positions is in my view perfectly justified. The greater the dangers and seductions become for an artist, who after all is also a member of the bourgeois-capitalist world, to earn money through circulation figures, film rights, and so on, the more difficult it becomes to preserve the integrity of artistic consciousness. The artists and writers of the nineteenth century worried about this constantly. I mean, it is trivial, but in such a situation the technique of esoteric communication becomes the weapon for the integrity of the artist; I am thinking of Kafka, Joyce, and Proust, who are "inaccessible" in a certain respect, but precisely this "inaccessibility" is their goal. The same thing applies to abstract painting. But bourgeois society has a big stomach; we have always underestimated how much it can assimilate and digest.

Dubiel: If we examine the objects of your literary analysis, it is always a matter of paradigms of the bourgeois consciousness that didn't come about in Germany. That is really relevant only in the framework of the critique of ideology. In positive paradigms, for example in Ibsen, it is only the depiction of immanent bourgeois self-critique. What we have just formulated in positive terms about the political purpose of esoteric art is, in your case—in contrast, for example, to Adorno—not positively stated in individual studies. You have never written about avant-garde literature. Sometimes I wonder, when you make such an emphatic distinction between the cognitive and the symptomatic significance of art, whether that can still be maintained for avant-garde literature.

Lowenthal: Yes, I plead guilty. Adorno urged me repeatedly to write about contemporary literature. I didn't do it. Perhaps I am more a literary historian in the conventional sense. At any rate, to this day I refuse to make binding "sociological" statements about modern literature. I have two reasons for that. The first is that modern literature has not yet passed through the sieve of history and it is more difficult to distinguish what, in the Lukácsian sense, will one day be typologically significant for a knowledge of social contexts. The other reason is that, for me, sociology of literature is supplementary to a purely aesthetic contemplation. If, for example, I want to examine changes in the relationship of genders or of generations, I do not need literature, which, after all, provides only indirect access. I can study these phenomena empirically. They are accessible, whereas the human phenomena I have analyzed in my writings have become inaccessible; my studies are, if you wish, great obituaries on the patterns of socialization and acculturation of former centuries. I can only repeat: other sources are available to analyze our modern situation.

Dubiel: I just want to make sure I've understood you correctly. The specific nature of your social-scientific study of literature consisted of using literary historical documents as material for your sociological interpretations. To judge the representativeness and validity of this material, the sieve of history—as you so beautifully put it—is indeed indispensable. Now this type of study of contemporary and avant-garde art is impossible, not because it would be impossible to distinguish whether we are dealing with real art or not, but

because it cannot be determined to what extent these documents of modern
art really stand in a reciprocal connection to significant social tendencies. I
have sometimes been bothered by the self-assuredness with which Adorno
identified, for example in Stravinsky, certain decoded sound patterns with
political options. Adorno did not seem to have the same scruples you have
just formulated. The combination of immanent analysis of avant-garde art
and political attribution he practiced sometimes seems questionable to me.

Lowenthal: Well, I don't know. Of course I was very happy when he was so
friendly as to add a footnote on Sibelius to my essay on Hamsun, showing
that the same symptoms I discovered in Hamsun's work could also be seen
in Sibelius's. I wanted to point out one other aspect, since we happen to be
engaged in assigning grades. I always asked myself whether I'm not smart
enough to apply my analysis to modern materials. Let's take Kafka. People
say that this or that in his work reflects the alienation of the modern world,
the entanglement in the bureaucratic maze of highly industrialized civiliza-
tions, the administrated world. They say that absurd theater critically reflects
the impossibility of real communication in the modern world. And that
Thomas Mann reflects the disintegration of the bourgeoisie. So what? What
has been said? Certainly nothing about the artistic value of these products,
and from an advanced vantage point of social philosophy you're still in the
realm of banalities.

Dubiel: I'm glad that our prejudices on this point coincide.

Lowenthal: I would only apply to this literature something I have already experienced elsewhere. It is quite different when I write about Shakespeare. I
know what happens to Romeo and Juliet only from this source itself.

Dubiel: Leo, I would like to talk with you about your two biographical studies. By
that I mean first the essay on the "Biographical Fashion," which appeared
in 1955 in the first volume of *Sociologica,* the festschrift for Horkheimer,
although it was written much earlier. The English version of this essay
appeared in a festschrift for Marcuse. The other essay I am alluding to is one
with which you made a name for yourself here in the United States,
"Biographies in Popular Magazines." How did you come to write these?

Lowenthal: Well, the essay that appeared under the title "Biographical Fashion"
deals with popular biographies of German writers, such as Emil Ludwig and
Stefan Zweig. I would like to mention here two motives for writing it. The
first is interest in the genre; I wondered what kind of literary form popular
literature uses. One of the least understood problems of the sociology of
literature is precisely genre. This was first developed magnificently in Lukács's *Theory of the Novel.* Generally in the sociological analysis of literature
it is a matter of content aesthetics. My biographical works are thus a parallel
case to my Dostoevsky study. Dostoevsky was the most widely received
novelist in Germany, at least shortly before the end of World War I. And
biography was the most widespread form of nonfiction writing. And so I
asked myself why, which leads to my second motive for writing about this.
If you ask what really was the common denominator of the people at the
Institute, the answer would probably be the shared concern for the fate of
the individual. Horkheimer's "Egoism and the Freedom Movement" or
Marcuse's "Affirmative Culture," some works by Fromm, and my own
literary studies are variations on the theme of the increasing fragility of the
bourgeois individual. And here, biographies seem to me to be an especially

characteristic genre, in which individuality makes an appearance and is at the same time destroyed. The German popular biographies combine two extremes: while describing the heroes with tremendous superlatives as creators of something unique, they at the same time bring those same heroes down to the level of ordinary people. This *coincidentia oppositorum,* that they are on the one hand unique and on the other hand like everyone else, deadens our consciousness of history and politics. The repetitiveness of this literature has a lulling effect. Just as, for example, entire passages in various novels of Hamsun could be interchanged, so could various biographies. The representation of Hindenburg at that time was barely different from that of Jesus. With great glee, I compiled entire lists of superlatives and other stereotypes that were repeated over and over again. Historical data was debased to the level of commodities for mass consumption. I finished writing the essay in the 1930s. We did not publish it then out of courtesy, for a good many of the authors I analyzed were German-Jewish emigrants who were having great difficulties at the time. Some even committed suicide. I first published it only after the direct references to contemporary authors had lost their sting.

Dubiel: Let us now get to the second work on biography, "Biographies in Popular Magazines." The extraordinary positive reception of this essay by American social scientists somehow illustrates its genesis. Wasn't this essay the result of a suggestion by Paul Lazarsfeld?

Lowenthal: Lazarsfeld knew of the unpublished essay on biographies we were just talking about. He asked me whether I would be interested in doing that sort of thing in the framework of American literature. This coincided with my experience at the time, that every single issue of the *Saturday Evening Post* and *Collier's,* extraordinarily popular consumer magazines then, always contained biographies. I looked at all the issues from 1901 to 1940 from the methodological viewpoint of their "symptomatic" significance and reflected on the extent to which these market products might be indicators of social processes. I found that in the first twenty years of this century the heroes of these biographies were taken from the field of production: successful merchants, professionals, inventors, and entrepreneurs. In brief, it soon became clear to me that these biographies served as political-educational stimuli. Their motto was "It can be done"—in short, the unbroken Horatio Alger myth. These heroes were models, and to follow them meant to join the competition of the free enterprise system. Not everyone could be a general, but every dishwasher had a chance to amass the bank account of a millionaire.

That situation changed radically at the end of the thirties. The so-called heroes were suddenly people from show business: movie actors, radio stars, famous impresarios, singers, in other words, people from the entertainment field. A good number of sports heroes were also featured, as well as a whole group of freaks, meaning people who were carrying on some kind of business or had invented something odd or comical. In short, the heroes were no longer the heroes of production. The theme was no longer the industry of individual enterprise but a matter of characters who were supposed to entertain us. But that was only one side of it; the other side was the change in categories through which people were portrayed biographically. Their consumer habits, their hobbies, were particularly stressed. Whereas in the

first phase you had producers, about whose productive qualities statements—however banal—were made, in the later period the consumer hero,
with consumer needs and preferences, became the theme. This corresponded
exactly to two modern tendencies: first, that in the society of corporate
capitalism the rise of the entrepreneur increasingly becomes a pure fiction;
and second, that bourgeois society turns into a consumer society. People are
interested essentially only in consumption. The theory of consumption-
heroes can be harmonized with David Riesman's typology, and also with
Fromm's "market-oriented personality." Anyway, Robert Merton, one of
the most cultured and progressive American sociologists of the late forties,
praised this essay as one of the few successful examples of a synthesis of the
European theoretical stance and American empirical research. I was very
proud of this. My friend Paul Lazarsfeld, who unfortunately died a few years
ago, then said to me, in his typically empiricist-positivist way: "So far you
have shown what a bad biography is; now you ought to demonstrate what a
good biography is." Thus he failed to see the political and analytical meaning
of my study.

Dubiel: I would now like to discuss the *Prophets of Deceit*. This study appeared
here in America in the year 1949, as a single volume in the series *Studies in
Prejudice*. In 1970 *Prophets of Deceit* was reissued in the United States with
a very now-oriented introduction by Herbert Marcuse. I will first try to
characterize this book, and if this description stimulates or annoys you, feel
free to react to it. It is a reconstruction of the typology of fascist agitators,
collated from speeches and articles by American agitators of the interwar
period. Do you agree with my characterizations that in this book you
essentially limited yourself to grasping typologically and collecting the usual
topoi, figures of argumentation, and rhetorical figures of agitators?

Lowenthal: Yes, we tried to collect the rhetorical stimuli on the basis of speeches,
pamphlets, journals, and similar materials. I would characterize the technique of agitation basically as turning psychoanalysis on its head. Moreover,
I would say this of mass culture in general. It makes people neurotic and
psychotic and finally completely dependent on so-called leaders. I tried to
translate the manifest stimuli of these agitators into what they actually mean.
My purpose was to unmask the aggressive and destructive impulses hidden
behind that rhetoric. The American edition has as an introduction a kind of
ideal-typical montage of an agitator's speech. This montage, incidentally,
was constructed by Irving Howe, one of the best-known intellectuals of this
country, following our detailed instructions. At the end of the book we added
a speech that decodes the introductory one, to show what the agitator really
means: kill the Jews, destroy the democratic institutions, follow me and no
one else, and so forth.

Dubiel: An essay from this time that impressed me very much, despite its small
size, appeared—as far as I remember—in January 1947 in *Commentary*. Its
title was "Terror's Atomization of Man." In it you write about the disintegra-
tive tendencies of man under the terroristic conditions of concentration camp
internment. As far as I know, this essay goes back to a lecture you gave at
Columbia University during the war.

Lowenthal: Yes, that was in 1944 as part of a whole series of lectures at Columbia
University on National Socialism by Pollock, Marcuse, Otto Kirchheimer,
and myself. This essay, which stemmed from that lecture—I don't find it

easy to talk about—is an analysis of the first terrible reports about what was going on in the concentration camps. I got hold of this material even before the end of the war. I then tried to describe how, under the conditions of totalitarian terror, the victimized individual completely disintegrates, how he almost takes on the features of the murderer, how under such conditions any sense of solidarity with other people ceases to exist so that humans seem to regress to an animal phase. I was much inspired by Bruno Bettelheim's important article on behavior under extreme conditions. Apparently my lecture was very effective. The audience consisted mainly of Columbia University students and professors, that is, people of good will who were very shaken by what they heard. One of the best-known professors, Robert Lynd, author of the famous study *Middletown,* told me that I absolutely had to publish my lecture manuscript. At his suggestion it was then sent to the *American Journal of Sociology* in Chicago for publication. The editor at that time was a teacher of a whole generation of sociologists in America. He sent the manuscript back to me with the statement that unfortunately it could not be published because the empirical data base was too slight. I then wrote back to him and sarcastically excused myself that I was not in the concentration camp myself and so could not have gathered my data right on the spot. I often since had to shake my head at this political and historical naïveté not untypical of American social scientists. I then sent the piece to Elliot Cohen, the editor and founder of *Commentary,* and that is where it was published.

Dubiel: Leo, can you again give us some information on the *Studies in Prejudice* series in general? The institutional framework in which these studies were made was the research department of the American Jewish Committee. Did this integration of many members of your former group with another research team really mean a substantive break with your theoretical past?

Lowenthal: No, the task of this research department consisted basically in applying to the area of anti-Semitism all the decisive theoretical and empirical insights we had developed in the Institute over the decades. It was also similar to the format at the Institute and on the journal in that essentially the work was done by members of the group, but other intellectually friendly scholars could be called upon to collaborate. We had already worked with Marie Jahoda before; then Bruno Bettelheim, with whom we had also had contact, joined, and Morris Janowitz in Chicago, and the psychoanalyst Nathan Ackermann. We wanted—quite in line with Critical Theory—to accomplish scientifically meaningful work in a manner that would allow its application to political praxis. Horkheimer's dream, which was never fulfilled, was that each of these books in the series *Studies in Prejudice* should be rewritten in the form of small booklets in popular format for distribution in a given situation of anti-Semitic political outbreaks or the like here in America— namely, to teachers, students, politicians, that is, to so-called multiplicators. That was sort of the idea of a political-educational mass inoculation program, a "fire brigade," as the Americans say. Unfortunately, it never materialized.

Dubiel: That's interesting, I didn't know that. I do remember the introduction to *The Authoritarian Personaltiy,* in which the idea of a preventive democratic mass-education is formulated, but I considered that to be just a rhetorical ornament.

Lowenthal: No, that was meant quite seriously. You're talking about a foreword by Max Horkheimer not only to *The Authoritarian Personality* but to all the volumes of *Studies in Prejudice.* We meant that quite seriously.

Dubiel: Were these various volumes of *Studies in Prejudice* conceived in relation to each other only in their original conception, or also in the actual execution of the research—be it methodologically, or by the exchange of materials, or in drawing up the analytical framework? Did you, for example, try to coordinate your work with that for *The Authoritarian Personality*?

Lowenthal: Now, these are all very different questions. On the whole it was a research strategy about which Horkheimer consulted a few leading people in the American Jewish Committee and us. *The Authoritarian Personality* is really a direct continuation of our interests, which started with the *Studies on Authority and the Family*. In California Horkheimer met Nevitt Sanford, the founder and first president of the Wright Institute and a good friend of mine. Sanford took a great interest in our problems and subsequently brought us together with two of his colleagues, Else Frenkel-Brunswick and Daniel Levinson. I participated in the preliminary discussions for *The Authoritarian Personality,* and at Horkheimer's request came to California to discuss with Sanford the general organization of the entire research project.

Dubiel: *Prophets of Deceit* became quite well known in its time. You once showed me the folder with the reviews of this book. It got a lot of attention, not only in scientific circles but also among the nonscientific general public. Might one say that *Prophets of Deceit* is better known in the United States than *The Authoritarian Personality,* or is that a false compliment?

Lowenthal: I must reject that compliment in all modesty and with indignation. The most important book was *The Authoritarian Personality,* which still has strong influence today. Compared with that, *Prophets of Deceit* had a relatively modest influence; one might even say that it stood in the shadow of *The Authoritarian Personality.* But I don't want to understate my book's influence. It did have an influence, especially among students and instructors in the field of mass communications research.

Dubiel: Now we come to the 1950s. The appearance of *Studies in Prejudice* coincides with the beginning of your work with the Voice of America; we spoke about your various activities there on another occasion. I suppose it would be accurate to describe the nature of your work basically as research organization, as a result of which you produced only a few scholarly products during that period. Do you agree that we now skip that time?

Lowenthal: Yes, let's speak of the time after that, when I have a much better conscience about my output. That was 1955 to 1956, when I was working in Stanford at the Center for Advanced Studies. My ever-faithful friend Paul Lazarsfeld, who had been instrumental in getting me invited to the Center, said to me then: "In this research year you have the alternative of either embarking on what the Americans call 'having a good time,' and at the end of the year you can become a dog-catcher in Palo Alto; or you can write a few books and subsequently become a professor." Lazarsfeld's advice really proved to be sound. Since I was not very interested in catching dogs, I sat down to write. In that year I wrote the book *Literature and the Image of Man.* The German title, *Das Menschenbild in der Literatur,* originated in part from the revision and systematization of older essays that had already appeared in the *Zeitschrift.* The Shakespeare chapter in the book was completely new, as was the one on the French drama. The chapter on Goethe already existed in a rough version but had not yet been published. In addition

I wrote the longer study with Marjorie Fiske on the relation of art and mass culture in England during the eighteenth century. Immediately afterward, in the fall of 1956, I was appointed professor at the University of California in Berkeley.

16

"We Never Expected Such Fame"
A Conversation with Mathias Greffrath, 1979

Greffrath: You come from a generation whose school and early university years coincided with the First World War, and, perhaps, something of the sorrow that runs through Critical Theory can be attributed to the experience of a world perishing in the war. When I take a look at this theory today, ten years after the time we studied it so intensely, I have the impression that there is much more [Georg] Simmel and much more [Max] Weber to be found in the thought of the "Frankfurt School" than Marx. In any case, more than we thought as we were adopting the theories. What role did irrationalists, vitalistic philosophers like Simmel play in your university years? Is it not the case that more of their thought found its way into Critical Theory than is to be suggested by its explicit statements?

Lowenthal: I would like to answer your question by referring a bit to the dialectic in which my friends and I found ourselves. We belong approximately, not exactly, to the same generation—born around 1900, some a little later, some a little earlier. And the orientation which we shared as students and young Ph.D.s was probably quite naive-optimistic, theoretically, but optimistic. And had you asked one of us the question which you are asking now, we would most likely have pounced upon you and said: "But those are our mortal enemies. They're all part of this whole irrationalism—not only Simmel but, above all, [Henri] Bergson, not to mention more banal instances. It's basically one of the forerunners of reaction"—and, though we didn't yet know this at the time, would later become a forerunner of fascism. "As heirs to Marx, we stand in the tradition of the Enlightenment and hold with Marxist theory that the Enlightenment posed the right questions, but did not understand the mechanisms of their solution." In a certain sense we were revolutionary in our position, even if we were not very active politically. Incidentally, we not only strongly opposed vitalism, but Max Weber's sociological impulses and theorems seemed to us anathema as well. Not because they were irrational—they were, in fact, exactly the opposite—but because his analysis and prognosis of increasing rationalism had at the same time an element of sorrow and pessimism and, one may say so in retrospect, of desperation, which we did not share at that time. The process of decades of development—also the shock of what became of the Russian Revolution, which many of us saw very naively at first as positive—had the effect of making true Hegelians of us. We gradually came to understand (perhaps by way of a mediation over Nietzsche) the legitimate themes in fact contained in vitalism, and our confidence in the utopian increasingly diminished. What struck us more powerfully, on the other hand, was probably a glimpse of that which [Walter] Benjamin expressed, that it is necessary for one to hope, for the sake of the hopeless, but that, fundamentally, there was something desperate in this hope. And what we all probably learned from vitalistic philosophy, each in his own way and formulation, is that, ultimately, the problems of human life, including the social problems, cannot be resolved completely, even if they might be resolvable in some foreseeable technical or psychological way. I mean, we usually expressed this in a somewhat sentimental fashion, by saying that death remains.

I think that today each of us would probably say (in any case, I would) that we neither betrayed nor gave up the critique in any way. Critical Theory remains in fact the announcement and characterization of an infamous world. But, as concerns the question of a solution in the sense of social or economic action on the political plane, here we have become relatively skeptical.

As you know, for a large part of my life I concerned myself with questions of art, especially literature. And I have always sought to maintain, except for completely naive statements from the early Frankfurt years, that it is precisely art which gives notice of the insoluble and yet must be retained as hope for a solution. And the worst that one can do to art, as radical thinkers or philosophers, or however you want to characterize us, is to press it, so to speak, directly into the service of social or political tasks. That is art of the worst sort. My friend Herbert Marcuse takes the same position, and in a text on Marxist aesthetics which has now appeared[1] he emphasizes that the unmediated transfer of artistic matters onto political action implies a genuine betrayal of both radical politics and art.

So I would say that this whole exclusivity of a materialistic conception of history—back then very satisfactory, if, of course, in the context of our convictions, and not to be dismissed today—that this exclusivity which rejects everything that appears to be irrational is no longer possible.

That is also one of those big misunderstandings under which Horkheimer and Adorno certainly suffered in their last years; to what extent that influenced Juergen Habermas, I don't know. For the younger generation, which really knew us more as a kind of myth and not so precisely as a reality, it is very difficult to understand how we apparently became extraordinarily conservative and don't simply take as positive everything that seems to be left or radical or dissenting. Or that we don't simply go through the last century or two and, with a kind of judicial wave of the hand, condemn everything that looks like conservatism. On the contrary. It strikes me, as an old man, almost like some sort of omen: I wrote my dissertation on Franz von Baader, the most conservative philosopher one can imagine around the turn of the nineteenth century. And, still today, I am most deeply moved by the truly critical elements in conservative theory, which, at bottom, sees through and criticizes that which is bad in liberalism, including a naive and vain enlightenment psychology.

Greffrath: As a young student, you were an ardent Zionist. You were associated

with the circle around the Freies Jüdisches Lehrhaus [Free Jewish Lehr-
haus], as was your colleague at the Frankfurt Institute, Erich Fromm. Was
that merely a rebellion against your secularized Jewish home life that at
times in your biography drove you back to orthodoxy? Or was this approach
to the Jewish movement, in which, of course, socialist ideas played a very
strong role, a kind of socialism on your part that had not yet come into its
own? And which experiences from the Jewish tradition and from Jewish
mysticism were, so to speak, appropriate to 1922–1923, promised a solution
for historical problems arising at the time?

Lowenthal: I think that what was extraordinarily characteristic of the time after the
First World War was, let me say, a kind of readiness to take up everything
that was different. That was, first of all, of course, the socialist, if not
actually communist motif. But that coupled itself at the same time with a
rejection of everything that seemed bourgeois, including the bourgeois organization of science and bourgeois philosophy. Everything that was different
and seemed to point out a new way was absorbed by some of us in a fashion,
one can only say today, that was naive-syncretic.

So, to speak of myself: My first publication was an essay, "The Demonic.
Outline of a Negative Philosophy of Religion." It was a terribly ambitious
thing, and earned me a great deal of criticism at the time from Siegfried
Kracauer and Franz Rosenzweig, but also excited praise from Ernst Bloch
(an "old" man—he was ten years older than I), whom I then met in
Heidelberg. "The Demonic" is a mix of Marxist theory, phenomenology,
psychoanalysis, and religious-mystic-Jewish themes. It all seemed to go very
well together.

Zionism, at least as concerns me, played a role to the extent that I believed
for a time to see in the Zionist movement a redemptive movement, which
pointed out a new path socially, philosophically, and religious-existentially
as well. I was also very strongly impressed by Rabbi Nobel and his circle.
He was largely responsible for founding the Jewish Lehrhaus in the mid-
twenties. With Ernst Simon I founded a Jewish newspaper, the *Jüdisches
Wochenblatt [Jewish Weekly]*. But I left it when—I almost want to say, in a
presentiment of history—when I saw that the Zionist settlement policy would
lead unavoidably to a horrible conflict with the Arabs, that an alliance was
being made with the rich Arab landowners to drive out the poor Arabs. With
a very pointed article, which I titled "The Lessons of China. By Hereticus,"
I left and never again identified myself with the Zionist movement. It is true
that I spoke in the Jewish Lehrhaus, also in imitation and truly in memoriam
of the charismatic Rabbi Nobel. For a while, I also kept a religious-orthodox
household. But only for a short time, probably largely out of rebellion against
my parents. My parents' home symbolized, so to speak, everything I didn't
want—bad liberalism, bad enlightenment, and two-sided morality. And,
somehow, as a young person I tried naively to reconcile all this by leading a
religious life. But I didn't keep it up for very long.

I do believe that a Jewish element, if you want to call it that, was alive in
most of us, consciously or unconsciously, in the sense of "it is yet to come,"
that is, of hope, of the unspeakable, which cannot be named but only sensed,
which can only be negatively determined. And that I want to acknowledge
even today, for it does unite, in a certain way, the hope, now seriously
compromised, for a life of dignity for every person with the thought that that

will probably not happen and that a tragic element is bound irrevocably to our life.

But a tragic element can also be tied to the life of human beings while they themselves live with greater dignity. So I don't want to fall into a cynical nihilism and say: it all has to stop, the radical and change. Of course that should not stop. But I almost want to say, if I may indulge my fantasy, that if we did have on earth a truly human society, we would perhaps only then discover how difficult to be a human being it is.

Greffrath: As the young Marx already said, then would human problems really exist . . .

Lowenthal: But he forgot that later! I mean, that was not exactly the real tenor, at least as Marxist theory developed and was continued, that then it would be genuinely known what human problems are. Rather the tenor was actually that then human problems would be essentially solved. Marx never concerned himself greatly with the relation of man to nature or man to animal or man to death—about that he didn't think at all.

Greffrath: While it was precisely these thoughts which became ever more prominent over the years in the thinking of Critical Theory.

Lowenthal: That is very important and I would like to emphasize it strongly. Not so much Fritz Pollock, but [Max] Horkheimer, [Theodor] Adorno, and myself emphasized extraordinarily strongly in our respective areas how Marx also remained a bourgeois thinker insofar as nature appeared to him to be a completely ready object of exploitation, without that meaning that something thereby happens to human beings. We learned to criticize this in our way, philosophically, aesthetically, and psychologically, and we disavowed this position. This theme of reconciliation with nature, which you can call utopian, ultimately forced its way into the foreground.

Greffrath: Therefore already very early—the disseration about Franz von Baader, rehabilitation of the mystical—the kernel of a conservative orientation, if one can translate theory into orientation, in the sense that you just named. An orientation that is in danger of becoming a historical agnosticism, as someone in your circle once said, that can lead to privatism if it does not tie itself to a historical movement . . .

Lowenthal: Yes. I mean, we don't want to exaggerate it. Today I regard it as a portent of my future development. I probably wasn't so conscious of it at the time. Although, I have to say, Baader did coin the concept—Marcuse, of course, couldn't have known this—of "one-dimensional thinking." That is a Baaderist concept, that the whole secularized Hegelian philosophy is one-dimensional and fully neglects the multi-dimensional, the truly humane and religious. Back then that very much impressed me. And what impressed me further was that Baader became a spokesman for the proletariat in his critique of liberal society. The word "proletarian" does appear in his work, and you find it in Bonald and De Maistre as well—a very strong sympathy for proletarian society. Of course, it is represented and conceived there as an alliance between the church and the nation's lower classes against the secularized bourgeoisie. But, *quand même,* this way of not submitting to what seems to be the going trend and to have compassion for those who bear the burdens is in fact a very significant motif in conservative philosophy. Of course, I didn't remain there. I went along completely different paths. But I'm nevertheless not ashamed of it.

Greffrath: And, however, a motif, precisely when one thinks of Horkheimer's last years, which became increasingly prevalent considering the postulated impossibility of genuine practice . . .

Lowenthal: In my opinion, he went somewhat too far. He really became very extensively an advocate of Catholicism and the Catholic hierarchy and, I think, flirted a bit too much for my taste with the institutions of religion instead of religion itself. So I'm not entirely happy with the very last of Max Horkheimer's things, assuming that the press reported them correctly. I didn't see him anymore then. But I don't want to offend the reputation of this important man, who basically created the entire Institute. What is decisive is this: in his thinking he was always very conscious of the Jewish heritage, of this delving conceptually into the human problems which arise once human problems appear to be solved. I certainly don't want to take that from him.

   You mustn't see these things with the "Frankfurt School", with all of us, so monolithically. Over and over again there are tendencies in which the one's thinking is a little more utopian, while the other's remains somewhat skeptical, and yet another's becomes optimistic again. It was, after all, a long dialogue. And the dialogue involved other people as well. Starting in Frankfurt, we had conversations over decades, which continued in America, with Paul Tillich, with Adolph Loewe, and with other intellectuals of the time who came to the United States. There are so many gradations that it would be difficult to be altogether definite about it.

Greffrath: What was your position on the "positivization of Critical Theory," that is, on the attempts to transform the abstract "it should be," as Erich Fromm tried to do in ethics, or as Marcuse likewise attempted, at any rate at times, into a materialist anthropology, and thus not to leave it with the utopian hope or with the "however" beyond hopelessness, but to lend it a foundation *in re?*

Lowenthal: I don't think it's any longer possible—not for a long time now—to mention Marcuse and Fromm in the same breath. As you know they carried on a polemic against each other. You know that the Institute's narrower group separated itself from Fromm relatively early on, roughly 1940, 1941. The theoretical background of this estrangement can be seen essentially in the positivity that slipped into Erich Fromm's thinking, which we couldn't go along with. I can suggest to you the lines of separation nearly in the manner of textual criticism. If you take his well-known book, *Escape From Freedom*: the first half of this book was written in the way all of our things were done, as a kind of collective achievement. It was naturally Fromm's theory, his achievement, but it was discussed thoroughly by all of us. The second half, the positive half, so to speak, is solely Fromm's responsibility. The Frommian position is a kind of, I almost want to say, sentimental synthesis of critical observations about the bad society and recipes for moral reconstruction.

   With Marcuse it is completely different. In Marcusian positivity, not entirely uninfluenced by Wilhelm Reich and not uninfluenced by his friend-enemy relations—though there was more of the friend—with Norman O. Brown, there is serious reasoning about the necessity not only of changing society but of changing human beings and human nature. So this thought—that no socialist society, no society of free people, can exist without a change in the structure of human drives themselves and a change in the principles of life, life functions, and people's ways of interacting seamlessly with their understanding of the necessity of changing the world—this is in itself a fine and profound thought. And, in itself, this serious Marcusian speculation actually does have something of, if you will, sorrow.

Greffrath: I would like to return to history. You came to the Institute in 1926. But then, for the next four years, you still worked primarily in the Prussian civil service and for the Volksbühne [People's Theater].

Lowenthal: I was introduced to Horkheimer by Kracauer, one of my oldest friends. I had already known Teddie Adorno since his last years in school. And we got along well with each other immediately. At that time, [Carl] Gruenberg was officially the director of the Institute, but, in fact, Horkheimer and Pollock were the leaders. I was then invited to join the Institute. But they didn't have a large budget for new members. So I was there quarter- or half-time. I had an office in the Institute and began to write my historical and sociological works on literature; and I was involved in the development of internal Institute activities and the seminars. It had been agreed that I would join the Institute full-time once Horkheimer became director, which was reasonably certain. But, in the meantime, I simply remained a highschool teacher. I already had a family, and had to have a secure position.

I was always interested in popular lectures, actually since my last years as a student. I gave mostly literary-sociological lectures about everything possible (in all of world literature nothing was safe from my reach) and got involved in the theater movement through the influence of an older friend, a cultural activist in Frankfurt. I was then an artistic advisor for the Volksbühne in Frankfurt, and had for a time a certain amount of influence over program direction and selection among Frankfurt's public and private theaters, and I wrote many program notes for plays. That was most closely tied to my literary interests; it was, in itself, absolutely no contradiction at all. And then, starting in 1930, I worked full-time at the Institute. We had two major tasks there. The first was the founding of the Institute journal, for which I was managing editor, and the other was our preparation for emigration, which we pursued energetically since 1931, as you know.

Greffrath: One more question on your work for the Volksbühne. In this context, did you become acquainted with what Benjamin termed the "bad positivism" in educational policies for the workers?

Lowenthal: Of course. That was naturally one of the biggest problems. This frivolous know-it-allness—it wasn't only workers in the Volksbühne, there were also many white collar workers and "elevated bourgeois"—that I tried to combat through lectures, through program notes. But that was like an ant battling an elephant. I suffered a great deal from all this. What I tried to do was to navigate a bit—inside the Volksbühne too—against the educational philistines, mostly groups of Social Democrats. We founded a film community and showed avant-garde films with introductions. How much good it did, I don't know, but I was very conscious of all this. And especially, on occasional trips to Berlin to negotiate with the central authorities of the Volksbühne movement, the educational positivism of the Social Democrats of the time became extraordinarily clear. But that didn't make up a large part of my work. Through the atmosphere at the Institute I came into contact, like everyone else, with interesting people like Piscator and Brecht and

Eisler, and so on. The rest played a very minor role. It was, so to speak, a small occupation on the side.

Greffrath: It is, however, apparent in your writings, apropos the avant-garde, that you limited yourself in the literary material you treated sociologically essentially to the nineteenth century, plainly out of a kind of love-hate for the works popular among young people, among the gymnasium pupils of 1915, 1916 . . .

Lowenthal: Yes, that is true. But perhaps it is also a generational difference between us. Fifty years ago, popular wasn't what popular has meanwhile become. There does exist a small distinction. But I think I have to resist a little here. Not everything that I contributed to the sociology of literature is to be found in the books I wrote. Rather, a great deal of it was contained in lecture activities, seminars, etc. And what always appeared to me essential in the sociology of literature is to use literature to gain knowledge of human and social contexts for which no other sources are available. To study the socialization process of modern people or to research here and now the social conditioning of feelings, values, orientations, experiences of nature, or love in the present I don't need literature. There, after all, I can study the people directly. But for the past, great literature is the only reliable source, in my opinion. The writing of history reports nothing of this; diaries and letters are full of rationalizations. Only the great work of art represents in a certain way typically the relation of people to one another, to nature, to their feelings, to society.

And that is why I referred, essentially for didactic reasons, to past documents. It wasn't all German literature either.

Presently I intend to take another look at the whole of avant-garde literature, including Strindberg, Wedekind, and Artaud to see whether it was in fact so unambiguously avant-garde, or, just as with some other things we read afresh today, whether there were not motifs involved which were not strong enough to protect us against the atmosphere of fascism. So a new look at the so-called avant-garde is very important to me just now. Whether I can still manage to do it, I don't know.

Greffrath: A new look in the sense (as is suggested in Marcuse's last work) of a return to the "great bourgeois" art, after which there comes nothing more of note?

Lowenthal: You will perhaps have seen, if you have read the little book, that Marcuse and I think very similarly about this. But maybe we are somewhat old-fashioned in that our examples, as in my publications as well, break off more or less with Ibsen.

Greffrath: Somewhat later, then, than [Georg] Lukács . . .

Lowenthal: I am certain that art has been pushed into a defensive position. And it is really sad to think that the great paintings and sculptures of modern abstract art have, on the one hand, become a big business, and, on the other, stand there ununderstood and have no effect. That truly is a great tragedy. How much, indeed, the art, the great literary art of the seventeenth, eighteenth, and nineteenth centuries, really accomplished; whether it changed people—that is very much yet to be decided. For, ultimately, those are our ancestors and forefathers, and what, after all, has become of our society? And we experience that now as we sit here. It is also such an afterglow, such a sort of romantic afterglow, of which we dream and which, at bottom, we want to transcend. Like Adorno always said: as a kind of message in a bottle, to keep the emancipatory, the imaginative alive. But the extent to which it really fulfilled this role, I don't know.

Greffrath: In the text you mentioned, Marcuse suggests a much more critical attitude toward non-objective art, that is, art in which sense—if one can say that—is replaced by the treatment of material as material. This process exists in literature as in music and painting. Isn't the recourse to literature of past centuries now a solution for lack of better, because nothing new, beyond art that has freed itself of sense, yet appears on the horizon?

Lowenthal: Yes. I don't want to use that as a alibi. It is very important to me now to take another look at these things, especially expressionist art, to see whether it's not much more multi-layered than we actually assumed.

Greffrath: You spoke of great art as reliable source material for past epochs. You draw a distinction between great art and trivial art. With one, one inquires after the truth; with the other after the effect. Are they to be distinguished so purely?

Lowenthal: No. They are not to be distinguished purely; but they are to be distinguished. There exist certain literary, weighty art works, which are unambiguously art works. There exist also things which are nothing other than trivial literature, trivial art, made for the market. Of course, there are always intermediate phenomena; but a lion is an animal and a rose is a flower. And so is it ultimately with Shakespeare, on one side, and detective novels, on the other. History also expresses its judgment. One doesn't need to be so hypersensitive; history expressed its judgment on this. Euripides or Dante, Shakespeare or Hölderlin are representatives of great art. You know, when one is overly cautious here, nothing comes of it.

Greffrath: For me, it has nothing to do with leveling the criteria of quality. It concerns more the questions, whether fundamentally, in less differentiated form, simply in trivial form, similar motifs—utopian motifs: happiness, sorrow, death—are not common material for great as for trivial art. And whether this distinction is not one between truth and untruth, but one between classes.

Lowenthal: But, yes, there is a big distinction. For trivial literature in general handles all of these things that you just touched upon as if they were accessible to solution. The happy ending is inseparable from trivial literature, while the tragic ending or the open question is inseparable from great art. That the same words are indeed used does not mean that the same things are meant and intended.

Greffrath: I don't want to argue about this, but one could maintain further that the "insipid" reconciliation in a Harlequin romance finds it correlate among the upper classes in aesthetic form as a kind of reconciliation.

Lowenthal: That is true. But it is something else. Now you are speaking of the effect, not the work. That the effect in fact offers the cheap consolation that everything was finally solved in the idea, because it is so expressed in the art work—that is fully correct. We have to say it critically in relation to classical literature and object to it. What the art work itself expresses critically requires interpretation through our critical dialectic.

Greffrath: Concerning emigration. You just said that you began preparing for emigration early, at the very same time as the founding of the journal . . .

Lowenthal: In 1930, we began conducting surveys on the psychological and ideological behavior and modes of thinking among the progressive blue- and white-collar workers in Rheinland and Westfalen. As I always say ironically, we invented American methods, so to speak, because we didn't know them. On the one hand, we asked completely open questions: what the people think, how they vote, for example. But then we asked psychological projection questions: "Who are the great figures in history? Who should be master of the household?" Everything that was later identified in connection with authoritarian personality traits. This study was conducted in Rheinland and in Westfalen, and Otto Suhr, who was secretary of the labor union there, helped us very much. As we received the results—that was probably the beginning of 1931—our hearts leapt to our throats. For, on the ideological surface, these good Social Democrats and left-of-center voters were all very liberal and republican. But on a deeper, psychological level, the majority were completely authoritarian, with admiration for Bismarck and strict upbringing of children and "the woman's place is in the home"—whatever. So it was really terrible, what all was revealed. Instead of proceeding with the study, we thought, for God's sake, what is going to happen in Germany? For, if that is the psychological make-up of the most progressive circles of the German population, is where, after all, resistance to the apparently unstoppable advance of National Socialism would have to be centered, then there would be no stopping it. And then, I think it was September 14, 1930, as 107 Nazi representatives were elected for the first time, we said to ourselves: it is not possible to remain in Germany. Then we founded the branch office in Geneva, as, so to speak, a place to start. We transferred our money, gave the library to the London School of Economics, and traveled often to Geneva; we began investigations with the International Labor Exchange and engaged Marcuse so we could send him there. We thus carried on a policy of emigration, fully consciously, a few years before anyone thought of it.

Greffrath: Was there a division at that time between the various factions of the Institute, that is, between the core members with this view, which had proved itself propitious, and, let's say, the activists, like [Kurt] Mandelbaum, [Karl] Wittfogel, and others?

Lowenthal: We didn't ask them. Wittfogel was rarely in Frankfurt anymore at the time. He was usually in Berlin. I mean, that was in essence a matter of the core group: Horkheimer, Pollock, Fromm, myself, and Marcuse, who wasn't yet completely in the core group, he was just then beginning. And, of course, Adorno, who didn't want to leave at first; he hesitated for a terribly long time. This group represented the Institute, so to speak. Mandelbaum was a friend of the Institute and assistant to Friedrich Pollock and Adolph Loewe. These things were not discussed in broader circles. But we did finally help everyone leave.

Greffrath: And the decision in favor of America was reached relatively quickly?

Lowenthal: At that time, America wasn't in the discussion at all. What we imagined was that we would establish ourselves in Switzerland. We knew little of the Swiss policy of hostility toward foreigners; although we brought money with us, they didn't let us settle here. The only one who received permission to establish residency there was Max Horkheimer. The others received only temporary permits; every couple of months they had to travel to France and then reenter. Other things were pending as well. We were also invited to go to England. The Institute of Sociology had invited us, and we founded a small branch office there. Then the Ecole Normale Supérieure was friendly enough to invite us to come to Paris, and we founded a branch office there and arranged to have the journal appear again through Alcan Publishing House. That was a great cultural gesture of French solidarity, and right away Alcan brought out the third issue of the journal. France was considered, England was considered, but Switzerland seemed to be the right place. But as the Swiss policy on foreigners became unambiguously hostile, we said to ourselves (falsely) fascism is not be stopped in Europe, and Switzerland will ultimately be affected as well. We didn't think of war at that time, but of living and surviving and being able to work. And then America appeared on the horizon. The credit here belongs to Fromm, who had already been there once and spoke very warmly of it. And we had also received invitations from America, from Columbia and Chicago and other universities, to establish ourselves there as we were in Frankfurt, that is, as an institute affiliated with the university that remained, nonetheless, independent. We finally decided to accept the offer from Columbia, partly because we had the feeling that New York was much closer to Europe, and that was also very nice, although that was not the original intention. We thought we would survive in Switzerland until the criminal was done away with. But then came the fear of expanding fascism. And, in a certain way, it would have been difficult to have survived there, perhaps—I don't know.

Greffrath: The works in the first years of emigration were centered around *Studies on Authority and the Family.*

Lowenthal: Yes. And the publication of the *Journal for Social Research.* The authority theme was also the one which defined the study in Germany that saved our lives—one of the few examples, although not the only one in world history, in which social research helped the social researchers themselves.

Greffrath: Comparing *Studies on Authority and the Family* to *Studies in Prejudice,* which appeared roughly fifteen years later, *Studies in Prejudice* represents a marked shift from economically based social theory to psychology. Can that be traced to or related to the opinion expressed by a few that, in fact, it was only in America that the members of the Institute really discovered the fundamental role of anti-Semitism?

Lowenthal: For one thing, political sociology was at that time much more oriented toward politics proper, less toward the psychological mechanisms of mediation. And the other, that we became much more conscious of anti-Semitism, as a phenomenon and as a symptom of western civilization, over the course of the years in America than we had ever been before—that is without doubt completely correct. We did conduct this remarkable study, financed by the American Jewish Labor Committee, on the reaction of the American workers to Hitler. And it demonstrated very shockingly how deeply anti-Semitism is actually rooted, even in American society.

Greffrath: Is that the study that was never published?

Lowenthal: Yes. It was lost; it's just not there anymore. I have no idea where it is. In any case, it was never published—following the wishes of the sponsor, I might add. And then as the American Jewish Committee, that is, the representative of Jewish interests in America, approached Horkheimer with the request that he found a research division, it fell on fertile soil, because we had the idea that there was something very important that we had not really seen properly in its full significance. And, you know, when I think about it, it seems as if all this was never really so clear to me until I started speaking with you about it now. It is embarrassing for such "sophisticated" literary people and intellectuals, who were mostly of Jewish origin, so suddenly to have made anti-Semitism into the central problem. It smacks of parochialism—God knows, that wasn't what we had in mind. But we ultimately came to understand the enormous significance of the subject.

Greffrath: That is surprising, because you were involved with the German university, presumably one of the most anti-Semitic institutions of the Weimar period. I don't know how things were for you in the Prussian teaching profession . . .

Lowenthal: You can't say that . . .

Greffrath: Was there nothing there of what would come to be noticed?

Lowenthal: No, you can't say that. I was a senior instructor in Frankfurt, which was one of the most liberal cities. There was nothing to be heard of it. And the University of Frankfurt had many Jews after 1918. Naturally, there was anti-Semitism at the universities, partially hidden and partially concentrated in the smaller places. Thus, in Heidelberg there was no anti-Semitism to my knowledge, nor in Berlin, but very much, for example, in Erlangen or Rostock. No, you can't say that. You can't say that the universities in the Weimar Republic were a hotbed of anti-Semitism; it is simply not true. . . . So I was aware of little anti-Semitism in the German universities. . . . And, if I think of my entire biography, I suffered little from anti-Semitism. My father was a doctor and had a practice mainly among those with social insurance— we lived in an area in Frankfurt where there were few private patients. And where we lived, there was a somewhat rough street more or less around the corner—Kiesstrasse, it was called—and there sometimes someone would shout "Jew" at someone. That was really my main confrontation with anti-Semitism, and that wasn't so terrible. The school, the Goethe gymnasium, had at least 30 percent Jews, if not more, out of the better circles, so to speak. There was no anti-Semitism there. I experienced it the five or six months I served in a railroad regiment in Hanau in 1918. There I experienced personally the dull anti-Semitism of the sons of workers and farmers. But, later, at the university, it didn't exist there. You can't say that.

Greffrath: In your own contribution to *Studies in Prejudice—Prophets of Deceit,* written with Norbert Guterman—you undertook a psychoanalytical investigation of the rhetoric of radical American demagogues of the time. If you could look back on this book, with the experience of the thirty years that have passed—haven't these demagogues of the 1930s and 1940s become antiquated in world history, at least in Europe and America, because they were the last who were demagogic "ideologically"? According to the theses in your book, the success of these demagogues depended upon dammed-up, unexploited psychological energies. Is it not the case that they have meanwhile been channeled in every possible direction by the increasingly dense network of capitalist socialization, so that such a combination, which was already more difficult then for American than for European demagogues, has become much less promising of success today as a mechanism of radical right politics?

Lowenthal: Certainly. I mean, these things that I investigated then were naturally, in a certain way, marginal phenomena. But whether they were marginal phenomena, couldn't be predicted with certainty. For such men did have a whole lot of followers. One couldn't know—especially if the war had run its course a bit differently—whether a strong wave of anti-Semitism wouldn't have flowed over the United States. But they were marginal phenomena. And my position is that investigations of marginal phenomena are always especially important. Today I would still say that the mechanism of that which I termed agitation is something that in no way belongs to the past. The kind of stimuli I attempted to distingiush, those produced in a situation of *ressentiment,* which characterize the agitator, the "Leader" as the indispensible master who is always to be attended to and from whom nothing is to be learned in the sense that he would, like a good teacher, make himself superfluous, this mechanism certainly remains of extra-ordinary significance. Even if the material is old, I still believe that the mechanisms I attempted to point out, which, so to speak, make the agitator appetizing, have in no sense ceased to be effective. [For instance, just now one can find any number of "self-styled" leaders of fashionable sects and pseudo-religious movements, the ones that are frequently tinged by a phony eastern mysticism.][2] One could also say that in certain situations in a thoroughly organized capitalist society the use of agitational mechanisms can be of extreme significance and in many countries is still of great significance.

Greffrath: The reproach has often been heard that the Institute in America made of itself a kind of colony which maintained the German language and not only didn't come to terms with the American academic establishment but often worked directly against it. How would you judge such reproaches, attacks, in retrospect?

Lowenthal: If I hadn't kept my sense of humor, I could almost fly into a rage now. Why should that be something worthy of reproach? It is, on the contrary, our great claim to fame, if you will, that we, a small group driven out of Germany, settled in America where the door was generously opened to us. We received a building at Columbia University and we insisted that we continue to exist as an island of German culture in our sense, in the spirit to which we were committed. Since we could also afford it financially—there the money was a blessing—we took it to be our task to preserve and continue that which we had begun in Frankfurt. And that could essentially only be done in that we tended the German language and continued to think within the German tradition, each in his own area. I don't know why one should call that a colonial existence. That was, in the good sense, an existence in exile, also in the sense that the banished return once the "tyrant" is driven out, as was already the case in classical Greece. I didn't do it, but others did. They returned to the place they were thrown out of. That was a completely conscious step. The Americans often suggested to us reproachfully, or often asked of us: why do you do that? why don't you publish the journal in English? etc. We intentionally didn't do it, because we really thought that we were fulfilling a unique function. We didn't know what great success we would finally have after Hitler. On the contrary, we printed only a few hundred copies and many of the copies were given away. That only stopped as American entered the war and many of us went to work for the government and we could no longer publish the journal. There can be no question whatever of any emnity toward America. It is correct that we were not very integrated. We also didn't trouble ourselves a great deal about that.

Some did: Fromm left us very early; Neumann became a professor at Columbia University.

But, otherwise, all of our relationships were friendly, just not very intimate. Of course, we took a polemical position toward many things, to the extent we understood them, that were going on in American social science. But that was the same position that we had adopted toward German phenomena: namely, against positivism, against the lack of theory and the uncritical, against quantification gettting the upper hand. One always begins just there where one is. And in Germany during the Nazis, nothing was going on. What should one have confronted in Germany, aside from ideologies? And we had already done that.

No. To make a reproach of our very self-definition suggests to me a complete misunderstanding. And—what none of us could know—world history, within a narrow frame, ultimately proved us right, for that which we achieved then goes on indefinitely. Just now a book of mine has been republished in Italian; the discussions continue, and what would have come of it all had it all appeared in English?

You see, that is precisely the distinction between the Institute of Social Research and the Graduate Division of the New School for Social Research founded for emigrant professors in 1933. The latter was a teaching institution and was funded by American money; it was not easy for the professors, money was often short, and our colleagues there essentially taught. Many of them were our friends; as members of an American teaching establishment they really felt themselves, and I don't mean this as a reproach, increasingly to be Americans. I still recall a small shock I received as one of the speakers at a little party at the New School said in English, "We feel ourselves happily at home. . . ." Well, we did not feel happily at home. We felt ourselves actually, in a certain sense, to be strangers. That gradually ceased, for, as we did the studies of anti-Semitism, propaganda, and American subjects, we were no longer such strangers. But, as you can also see from the behavior of Horkheimer and Adorno (who were key figures of the Institute) they didn't feel themselves "at home" in the slightest. And they returned to Germany at the first opportunity. Our cultivation of what otherwise had no home anywhere in the world really needs no further justification. And we also provided considerable support, in a certain sense for many emigres, whom we helped materially and intellectually.

Greffrath: Do you feel "happily at home" today?

Lowenthal: But it's completely different today. Marcuse and I are, if you will, integrated members of the American educational system and the American intelligentsia, without having given up what's German for it. One can be both; the one doesn't exclude the other. But I don't feel today like an exile. I won't go back. The work that I do always interested me, and I haven't regretted it a single day. I'm very pleased with it. America offered me an extraordinarily rich experience, first in the government and later as a professor in Berkeley. Moreover, I am of the opinion—this is a true of Marcuse at least as much—that remaining in America did significantly more to spread a European-German style of critical thinking than would have been the case from Germany. There is something movingly tragic in the fact that just now, many years after the deaths of Adorno and Horkheimer, their writings are becoming known in America, and then in very esoteric form, in *Telos* and other periodicals. It has become something like a type of Talmudic expository hermeneutics. On the other hand, I'm baffled and happy that in America now there is such a strong need for "Critical Theory" and that the Frankfurt School is helping to bring a theoretical orientation, including the dialectic, to American social science.

Greffrath: You spoke of the transfer of European thinking to America, in which Marcuse, you, and many other emigres played an important role. Was there also a reverse process? Were there also theoretical experiences you had in America that you would not have had elsewhere?

Lowenthal: Absolutely! It is difficult to be so conscious of it . . . but absolutely. Above all, I would say that my horizons concerning social phenomena became much broader, simply because American social science—sociology, political science, economics—is infinitely more differentiated than that which takes place in Europe. I learned an infinite amount there. Then I learned a great deal through a much closer contact with colleagues in English literature, in other literatures, about literature itself. Then I simply learned a great deal about the modern world. I mean, the simple circumstance that I live in such a gigantic country, in, ultimately, a very cosmopolitan, if also in a certain sense provincial, world, where Japan, China, Argentina are household words—that in itself broadened my horizons immensely. And I feel myself to be much more cosmopolitan, much more a man of the world, than I ever felt myself to be in Germany or perhaps would have felt.

Greffrath: So you no longer hear the sounds of Weber's "Freischutz" every time you have a taste of venison?

Lowenthal: No! I think that the empirical horizon of experience grew enormously. I mean, I always say, on the one side, that I mustn't let my understanding be bribed by my sense of gratitude. Because the Americans saved our lives— that's no reason for me to glorify America. But on the other side, it is really completely self-evident that in the course of the decades since 1934—that is practically forty-five years already—I have gained a great deal. There's absolutely no doubt of that. I think I also have acquired a much greater sense of tolerance, pedagogical and theoretical, through life in America. Nevertheless, I have to say that if my good fortune didn't allow me to travel so often to Europe, I would, perhaps, be very unhappy, precisely because I also gain tremendously when I, like Antaeus, touch European soil. Whether it's a good Wienerschnitzel or a good glass of wine, or meetings with European intellectuals—it is really necessary.

Greffrath: But the antipathy, for example, of Adorno for America never played such an important role?

Lowenthal: God, there are many things I don't like. I also don't like many things in Germany. It is yet more embarrassing when you walk around Hamburg and see all these dreadful things like MacDonald's and Burger King and so on than when you see them in America. Naturally, I have antipathy for many things. But look, Adorno resisted it—he simply never really wanted to make a home for himself. I am finally very much an American; certainly, I am a German Jew, but also an American. And much in America is good. Above all, the tolerance is much greater. I enjoy the absence of this exaggerated distance between students and professors. Although it's naturally ideological nonsense that it's a middle class society, nevertheless individual Americans do have this certain common sense pride, something that is to be valued very positively. Sometimes, of course, it's annoying. But I would say that if there is something like a vision of an ideal society, then the American is perhaps more of a model than the European.

Greffrath: Can you substantiate that?

Lowenthal: Yes. There is an atmosphere of democractic consciousness or half-consciousness in America—which is certainly ideological in the sense that great class distinctions exist—but, nevertheless, it is an atmosphere in which the people express a relatively understanding common-sense tolerance toward one another. Sometimes it all goes wrong, I mean, we already know that. . . . We have undergone a few domestic and foreign "Vietnams" in the last twenty-five years in America! But in principle I've had the experience over and over, despite severe crises, that when "the chips are down," as we say, the common sense of a relatively understanding, rational way of life prevails. Even in politics. Despite all the horrors, we haven't yet had a catastrophe. Nixon didn't last very long, after all. And McCarthy didn't last very long. A kind of common sense does finally prevail. Good, everything is dialectical. On one side you can say: sure, we Europeans, we stick by our opinion and make no compromises and that's that, and the other one is the enemy, as always, ideologically, politically. And the Americans tend to make compromises, to say: That's your opinion; I have another opinion. You're entitled to your opinion, and so on. When I returned to Europe for the first time, I was Research Director at "Voice of America." It was 1949, and, when I came back, my colleagues asked me. "How are things in Germany?" I said, "The Germans today are like the Germans always say the Americans are: materialistic, pragmatic, focused on what's right in front of their noses, relativistic. When things go well with the Americans, they're for America; when things go well with the Russians, they're for Russia, and so on. In comparison to that, the Americans are the people of poets, thinkers, and dreamers." For the Americans are really very moralistic. Some things in foreign policy, too, are only to be understood when one has understood the moralism of the Americans. I think that the old dichotomy—here are the great idealistic, idea-oriented Europeans, especially the Germans, and there are the banal Americans—must be forgotten. And today, please, American cultural life is so differentiated. The best painters and sculptors are in New York, the leading literary periodicals are in New York or at a few universities. And, God knows, many American intellectuals mount a very strong critique of the political, cultural, and economic institutions of their country.

Greffrath: Your work at "Voice of America"—that was four years that you, as an emigre intellectual, were in the service of . . .

Lowenthal: Well, now, it was essentially, in fact, *research* work. What it had to do with was that I was charged, through accidental connections, with creating a sizable organization to study the effectiveness internationally of "Voice of America." To my great surprise, no such thing existed. An acquaintance of mine, a historian whom I met in the Office of War Information (where all of us, part-time or full, worked in government service), stayed with the government after the war and was at the time political director of "Voice of America." All their offices were in New York, and one day he asked me, "Leo, what would you say about developing an international, scientific research division for the biggest propaganda section there is in the State Department?" My hands flew to my head: "You spend the taxpayers' money and then you don't even investigate whether it's doing any good?" Then that's what I did. I mean, it was a challenge (I have a certain organizational-administrative talent) to see if I could do it. And for a while I was successful. We undertook sizable operations and had many investigations conducted through universities and private research institutes; we did some of the investigations with my own staff.

What was interesting to me was the methodology: how does one conduct research on people who are not immediately accessible? For the main task of this propaganda apparatus is, of course, in the East—that's still true today. Now I no longer have any relation to it, but there were serious problems there. The broadcasts were jammed—one didn't know how many people listened, how they were affected, whether any connection existed between the State Department's propaganda activities and emigration, flight, and so on. These things were of enormous methodological interest to us. There were many psychologists and sociologists collaborating on it. And it didn't last all that long. I thought at the time, as I accepted the position in 1949, "Well, this is how I'll spend my life now. So I'm going to become a civil servant in the foreign office." I really fooled myself, didn't I? Everything is always in flux, everything changes, different constellations arise. As the Eisenhower administration took over from the Truman administration, there was once again opposition to *research*; everything was supposed to become *intelligence* work again, and my department was destroyed. I could, of course, have stayed, but it was all terribly boring then. I didn't have anything proper to do anymore.

I mean, it's the same for me as for Marcuse,who was also in the government. Always these serious indictments: "How could you have?" Why shouldn't one be in government service? It wasn't a government of scoundrels. And, besides, what we did were scientific or administrative tasks. God knows we had no influence on American foreign policy. So I'm not ashamed of it for a moment. It was for me an extraordinarily interesting experience.

Greffrath: Did you have to restrain your critical spirit in this post? Could you do and publish what you wanted?

Lowenthal: Publish . . . ? They were government works. We did publish a few things; and I supported certain books, like *Transitional Society* by Daniel Lerner, directly. Of course we could do what we wanted. We even gave work to the Frankfurt Institute. We gave critical work to Harvard, to Columbia University—we didn't censor ourselves in the slightest. We were also not very popular. The program directors hated us. The director of the "Voice" used our results to justify his budget. The undersecretary responsible for it, however, did take a look at the critical things. We were, so to speak, a football among all these interests. That didn't bother us any further; on the contrary, sociologically it was extraordinarily interesting.

Greffrath: Was there something politically self-evident about this work, roughly in the sense of a "theory of the lesser evil?" I am thinking of [Karl] Korsch, who wrote to someone in 1948: "We cannot realize our ideals in the moment; we must decide in favor of one of the imperialists if we still want to be politically active at all." For the "Voice of America" was, of course, a voice into the East. Was that a problem for you? Or, did you, as a sociologist, simply think of the work as another intellectual challenge?

Lowenthal: For me it was in a certain way a puzzle to be solved: what kind of investigations can be conducted, and so on. For example, we did a big study of "communication habits," as we called it. The Americans were so naive as to assume that if one broadcast a radio transmission—let's say to the Arab countries or to Africa—then one could already count on having some kind of success. We demonstrated that, first, radios were largely unknown in such places, and, second, that a communications system as a whole poses an anthropological problem, that one cannot simply assume that what is listened to in America will be listened to in completely different cultures. A few scholarly books came out of that too. It was a theoretically interesting assignment. Ultimately, it was a failure, for it didn't exactly flourish and was later done away with. It was too expensive, the political constellation, as I already said, became unfriendly to research. Thank God I didn't have to suffer too long, since influential figures in the American social scientific establishment became very angry about the bad treatment I received from the State Department and the United States Information Agency—destroying such a fine research empire. People then did a great deal to help me. Soon I was invited to Stanford and the Center for Advanced Studies and then very quickly I got the teaching position at Berkeley—so the cunning of reason was, so to speak, working for me. The frustrations of government service helped me, at the advanced age of fifty-six, to become a professor in America. But you see that is, for example, something I'm always saying: in Germany, in France—take any western European country—my career would have been completely unthinkable. At forty-eight I became departmental director in the foreign office of the United States—with my accent, as a German Jew. And at nearly fifty-six, without ever having had an orthodox university career, I became a professor at Berkeley. That is something that doesn't exist in Germany, this way, not so tied to tradition, of bringing a person into a position which he hasn't slowly grown into.

Greffrath: One last question. You experienced the resurrection—in a certain sense astounding—of Critical Theory . . .

Lowenthal: It's become an industry, a culture industry . . .

Greffrath: This theory, which emerged from a unique historical constellation—you
  spoke yourself at the very beginning of the very German intellectual historical foundation, the specific historical constellation—this theory is now being
  accepted by students and younger intellectuals, by now practically all over
  the world, as a type of renewed Marxism, as a universal theory. Isn't, on the
  contrary, that which was thought then rather to be understood as the product
  of an epoch, to be precise, the epoch from 1914 to 1945? And aren't these
  young social scientists making a big mistake, if they all but close themselves
  off to contemporary experiences by applying themselves to these thoughts
  as if to the Talmud?

Lowenthal: I'm split on that. Often, I don't know for certain what the young people
  are talking about, but I'm wholeheartedly behind them. My heart is with
  them. I mean, the motives which apparently move the people to occupy
  themselves with our writings are noble ones, political, philosophical, moral
  motives. Admittedly, it often seems to be to be a kind of nostalgic entanglement, a flight from the real problems of the present into a sure thing. We
  never in our lives expected this fame. Not one of us, in my opinion, laid
  claim to an active legitimation for playing a world historical role, no one ever
  had the expectation. Certainly good things were accomplished. But why it is

suddenly spreading like a wild fire, I don't understand entirely—even if it does warm my heart.

Notes

1. Herbert Marcuse, *The Aesthetic Dimension: Toward a Critique of Marxist Aesthetics* (Boston: Beacon Press, 1978).
2. 1988 edition.

Afterword

The first section, "German Jewish Intellectual Culture," brings together a selection of articles treating the manifold relations of eminent Jewish scholars to German intellectual history. They were originally newspaper articles published by Leo Lowenthal in the late-1920s in Jewish journals. Taken together, the individual articles about Moses Mendelssohn, Salomon Maimon, Heine, Lassalle, Marx, Hermann Cohen, and Freud amount to an impressive historical documentation of the contribution of Jewish intellectuals in the Weimar Republic to German philosophy, literature, and science.

The second part of the volume brings together some of Lowenthal's more recent lectures. Even if the immediacy of the spoken word is largely lost in these written versions, the lectures' references to the respective academic and cultural-political occasions of their origins nonetheless remain. "Adorno and his Critics" is a lecture delivered to a conference organized in honor of Adorno by the University of Southern California in Los Angeles in the summer of 1978. The lecture, "Recollections of Theodor W. Adorno," concluded the Adorno Conference hosted by the University of Frankfurt and the Institute for Social Research in September 1983. "The Sociology of Literature in Retrospect," which appeared in a festschrift honoring René König on his 75th birthday, derives from a lecture Lowenthal delivered in the summer of 1981 to both the Free University in Berlin and the Max Planck Institute for the Social Sciences in Starnberg. "Goethe and False Subjectivity" is Lowenthal's keynote address delivered in the Paulskirche at the invitation of the city of Frankfurt on the 150th anniversary of Goethe's death. The lecture, "Walter Benjamin: The Integrity of the Intellectual," opened the colloquium organized by the University of Frankfurt and the Suhrkamp Verlag for Benjamin's 90th birthday in July, 1982. "Caliban's Legacy" is a contribution to a conference hosted by the Free University of Berlin in June of 1983, on the occasion of the fiftieth anniversary of the book burnings by the National Socialists.

The third part of the volume contains a selection of letters by Leo Lowenthal to Theodor W. Adorno and Max Horkheimer. These letters document the manifold intellectual, personal, and institutional relationships which existed among the collaborators at the Institute for Social Research. Beyond that, they convey an impression of the political and historical context in which Institute activities took place during the period of exile in New York.

Part IV consists of two biographical interviews with Leo Lowenthal. The one conducted by Helmut Dubiel concentrates on his intellectual biography, while the conversation with Mathias Greffrath ranges more broadly in terms of the issues discussed.

Index